MAR 0 3 2010

MIDDLETON PUBLIC LIBRARY
DATE DUE

D0064849

Carjacked

ALSO BY CATHERINE LUTZ

Homefront
Reading National Geographic (with Jane Collins)
Unnatural Emotions
and
Breaking Ranks (with Matthew Gutmann)

Carjacked

The CULTURE *of the* AUTOMOBILE *and* ITS EFFECT *on* OUR LIVES

CATHERINE LUTZ AND
ANNE LUTZ FERNANDEZ

palgrave
macmillan

First published in 2010 by PALGRAVE MACMILLAN® in the United States—a division of St. Martin's Press LLC, 175 Fifth Avenue, New York, NY 10010.

Where this book is distributed in the UK, Europe and the rest of the world, this is by Palgrave Macmillan, a division of Macmillan Publishers Limited, registered in England, company number 785998, of Houndmills, Basingstoke, Hampshire RG21 6XS.

Palgrave Macmillan is the global academic imprint of the above companies and has companies and representatives throughout the world.

Palgrave® and Macmillan® are registered trademarks in the United States, the United Kingdom, Europe and other countries.

ISBN: 978-0-230-61813-8

Library of Congress Cataloging-in-Publication Data
Lutz, Catherine, 1952–
    Carjacked : the culture of the automobile and its effect on our lives / Catherine Lutz and Anne Lutz Fernandez. — 1st ed.
        p.   cm.
    Includes bibliographical references and index.
    ISBN 0-230-61813-8
    1. Automobile—Social aspects—United States—History.   I. Fernandez, Anne Lutz.   II. Title.
HE5623.L88   2010
303.48'32—dc22

                                                                          2009037724

A catalogue record of the book is available from the British Library.

Design by Letra Libre, Inc.

First edition: January, 2010

10   9   8   7   6   5   4   3   2   1

Printed in the United States of America.

For Kristie and Gordo

Contents

Preface

It is 1968. In the way-back of a sky blue Pontiac station wagon, we lie cozily wrapped in well-worn car blankets, bouncing home. Looking out the rear window, we watch the lights of the George Washington Bridge flash overhead as our chatter dies down and we start to doze off. We took many trips like this one, growing up as two sisters in a big family of six kids—trips to visit Grandma in her New Jersey apartment, to our nearby beach, or to a summer rental at a lake in New Hampshire. These car expeditions carried us through our happiest family adventures.

It is now several decades later. Since then, between the two of us, we have owned nine cars and driven eleven others belonging to the important people in our lives—our parents, boyfriends, husbands. We have driven or ridden an estimated 600,000 miles, consuming around 30,000 gallons of gas. To do this, combined, we have spent an estimated 25,000 hours in the car—if this were a job, each of us would have been at it for 3,125 eight-hour days, or more than six years of our lives.

We have totaled one car, been rear-ended by a drunk, spun out a few times on icy highways, and bent some fenders. We have been pulled over for speeding and let off with a warning, and paid dozens of parking tickets. We have made our share of visits to the DMV and mechanics in seven states, from Idaho to North Carolina. We have driven across the Golden Gate Bridge, through the Rocky Mountains, and over the Chesapeake Bay.

In our cars, we have eaten McDonalds and spilled coffee, applied mascara in the rearview mirror, had deep conversations about life, waged petty fights, sung with Springsteen at the top of our lungs, changed clothes, thrown up, role-played job interviews, slept overnight at rest stops, taken kids to tap dance classes and baseball practice, slow-burned in traffic jams, and, like many Americans, had youthful sex in the backseats.

On a far heavier note, we have lost five beloved friends or relatives to car crashes. Two people to whom we were close were devastated by the responsibility of having killed someone with their cars. We have looked on in pain as dozens of others we know have lost an immediate family member or close friend to a crash.

A few years ago, over a Thanksgiving weekend, the two of us, one an anthropologist (Catherine), the other a businessperson (Anne), sat down and started planning in earnest a book about automobiles that we had been talking about since our cousin Kristie's shocking death in a 1998 crash. In her forties with her son still in school, she had only recently gone back to college when, driving home one night, she and her fresh start were both obliterated by a car making an illegal turn. Her death and the subsequent loss of Anne's close friend on a highway had pushed us to take a harder look at the automobiles in our own driveways. We had started to question how an everyday object, our most valued machine, had such awful, awesome power in our lives. Once we had asked how something that we relied on so much could cause so much pain, we also found ourselves wondering how something so terribly dangerous could bring us such tremendous pleasure. After all, hadn't our cars brought our family together in celebration once again that Thanksgiving? It was these contradictions, we decided, that we wanted to investigate.

At that point, as car owners and drivers and as Americans, we thought we already understood, on some level, a great deal about what the car meant to us and to our society. But we also knew there was much to explore, and we were surprised that no one, as far as we knew, had done the work to find out more about how Americans live with the car on a day-to-day basis—how it structures their lives and how they feel about it. This lack of information was in part the result, we felt, of how well and how relentlessly the car has been marketed to us. We take the car for granted as a social good, which renders it nearly invisible as the source of a range of problems.

Catherine had spent the past twenty-five years as an anthropologist, studying how everyday things we take for granted—like the words we unthinkingly use to express our love, or the images in the magazine we casually scan in the dentist's waiting room—are in fact quite exotic. After conducting classic overseas fieldwork on how people live on a coral atoll in the western Pacific, she returned to the United States to study aspects of our own cultural mores and social institutions. This has included looking at how another elephantine national phenomenon, the U.S. military, affects Americans, touching even those who have never stepped foot into a war zone or onto an army base. Anne worked for many years in senior corporate management, learning firsthand how companies grow by targeting customers and then advertising, promoting, and selling their products to them. Together, we thought, we could discover how Americans had come to love their cars, to live in their cars, and to pay for them in ways large and small.

We sought out drivers of all ages and ethnicities, in numerous zip codes, and with a broad range of experience with cars, and ultimately spoke at length with more than one hundred drivers. We found that when asked to talk about the role cars play in their lives, those drivers were eager to share memories of learning to drive, anecdotes about commuting or negotiating at the car dealership, and opinions on the price of gasoline and its role in the wars in the Middle East.[1] As the two of us anticipated, these people described delights, frustrations, and tragedies resulting from the car system. That system is a mix of industry, infrastructure, land use, governmental activity, consumer behavior, and habitual patterns of daily travel. It is the system in which we operate each day with only a dim sense of its complexity or reach.

We also traveled to glossy car dealerships and seedy used car lots, funeral homes and hospital emergency rooms, a Detroit auto factory and proving grounds, and courtrooms where people contested their speeding tickets. We spoke with people whose jobs give them special insights into cars, drivers, and the car system more generally—car salesmen, automobile brand marketers, neighborhood mechanics, car museum directors, toll booth operators, cab drivers, emergency room doctors, police, and epidemiologists who study air pollution–related diseases. We talked to paralyzed crash victims and the emotionally brutalized family members of those who were killed, and we learned from activists and government officials who work each day toward solutions to each of the myriad pieces of the problem of car dependence.

Based on these interviews and field research, as well as on advertising analysis, auto industry information, safety data from the National Highway Traffic Safety Administration, and government economic surveys, our book throws a new light onto the complex impact of the automobile on American society. We ask about the forces that shape the choices we make and the values we hold as individual car owners and drivers.

While the car's critical contribution to global warming is now widely known and the effects of volatile gas prices and U.S. car company bailouts and bankruptcies have been much in the news, we discovered that the problems Americans face because of their cars are much wider than this, and will not disappear if we somehow return to stable, low gas prices or transition to a nonpolluting fuel, or get the U.S. automakers back on their feet. Even if our cars could be filled with water from a garden hose or we could somehow magically make our fleet of gas-guzzling TrailBlazers disappear, we would still be a nation with 220 million vehicles whose costs of purchase, insurance, and repair have us bleeding financially for the car, car loan, insurance, and energy companies. We would still have workers—those who can afford to, at least—commuting hours each day from the suburbs (any predicted exodus from these communities caused by volatile gas prices would reverse in a hot minute if a cheaper alternative fuel were to appear). While the departure of the sport utility vehicle (SUV), more deadly to other motorists than passenger cars, would make our highways safer, we would likely still see around 40,000 deaths and 160,000 disabilities each year due to crashes.

Because the gas-powered fleet would take several decades to phase out, we would still be breathing its lung- and heart disease–producing fumes. We would still be getting fatter from the lack of exercise that comes with car ownership. We would still have poor households getting poorer at a rapid clip because they are carless and, because of that, jobless. We would still have a hapless customer pool for chains like Rent-A-Tire, which gives the poor the opportunity to buy tires but then repossesses them the moment the renter misses an extortionate installment payment. They would still be victimized by the car title loan outfits that, in one state alone, Tennessee, have opened almost a thousand storefronts and repossess over 17,000 vehicles a year.

While most people are distinctly uninterested in leaving their cars for the thin public transit system we now have, and while policy makers, subject to industry influence, have moved glacially to address the diverse safety, environmental, and economic problems associated with the car system, our national romance with the automobile has been seriously challenged.[2] We reached the tipping point in our car culture in 2008. That year, gas prices hit a peak, exceeding $4 per gallon; car companies began their visible slide into bankruptcy; personal car indebtedness soared; and the relationship between foreign wars and domestic energy use dominated Sunday talk show chatter. By the fall, the seriousness of the economic downturn had crystallized. While previous recessions had crimped the nation's car buying and driving, this one seemed potentially more transformative. The perfect storm of financial collapse, massive layoffs and home foreclosures, and Detroit's implosion pulled a number of foundation stones out from under the car system. With the disappearance of the home equity that people often use to buy cars and the resurgent value of saving, owning a smaller car and driving fewer miles began to seem less like a sacrifice and more like good sense, a benefit— even, perhaps, a liberation. On top of this, environmentalists and other scientists, as well as Al Gore and a band of eco-minded celebrities have broken through about the threat of global warming. The greening of American consciousness has meant that car buyers increasingly go hybrid or proudly drive a 12-year-old coupe to advertise their eco-friendly identity.

The American Dream, the desire for freedom, and belief in progress, among other widely held values, helped build the car system, but these beliefs and values have also provided the language with which people have begun to articulate their unhappiness with it and their desire for a better way.

Still, asking individual Americans to take a close look at the problems caused by the automobile can elicit a defensive gut response. Just as suggesting that a loved one sit down with a marriage counselor or a nutrition advisor can evoke fears of divorce or draconian diet restrictions, asking a driver to examine the full impact of the car on his life can prompt deep anxiety that he will be forced to give up his car. But for most of us, the choice is not between the car and no car. It is about whether it is possible to drive less and pay less for it; it is about recognizing the powerful lure of car advertising and educating ourselves about the schemes of the dealership; it is about making careful choices about where to live when we move; it is about demanding that our government create better tax and regulatory policies for the car and oil industries, higher safety and air quality standards, and, crucially, a world-class public transportation system. And it is about quite likely enjoying life more, not less, as a result. Taking a new look at the problems of our car system will reveal some surprising solutions. Taking back control of our lives from the car—making it, once again, a tool rather than a very greedy member of the family—will give us a more convenient, healthful, inexpensive, greener, and safer system than the one we live with now.

Chapter One

THE UNITED STATES OF AUTOMOBILES

Hundreds of halogen lights on the vaulted ceiling of the convention center beam down on the New York International Auto Show, making everything look good—the rich, pearlescent surfaces of the Ford Explorer and the quirky compactness of the Mini Cooper, the attractive young product specialists for Mercedes and Chrysler, the couples and teenage boys strolling among the cars. The whole place sparkles. Like Times Square moved indoors, the show blazes with giant television screens and brilliantly colored and dramatically lit backdrops for each company's display. Some cars rotate out of reach on giant turntables, others pose majestically on risers, but most are open to sit in and touch. Squadrons of buffers and polishers fly through, quickly erasing each new handprint and smudge. Brilliant chrome engines sit on pedestals, the convoluted guts of the vehicles presented with as much reverence as their sleek exteriors.

Visitors swarm around the cars, admiring the baroque intricacies of the tire rims, the lush interior surfaces and high-tech gadgets, and the sweeping, powerful lines of one car after another. They are imagining themselves as drivers. As one young man said to us, "What do I like about this car?! I like the way I look in it!"

This is not just a convention of gearheads, but a wide-ranging sample of America's two hundred million drivers: a pregnant woman and her husband shopping to replace their two-door coupe with a vehicle that will more easily accommodate an infant seat; a band of retired buddies who note they share a pragmatic approach to cars, replacing them only after "driving them into the ground"; and couples just browsing for their next car, although this is still some years off. The gearheads are not of a single type, either: one fifty-year-old has come, he says, to appreciate the new cars with the reverence for industrial design that his mechanic father passed down to him. Another man proudly announces that he owns five cars and drives 60,000 miles a year. And a woman wanders through with her twenty-something boyfriend, offering with a bit of admiration that he subscribes to three different car magazines.

And then there are the people walking through the auto show who don't own a car and can't afford one. Many of the slim-walleted teenage boys swarming around the cars fantasize a future in which they occupy the driver's seat. The Mercedes-Benz product specialist doesn't mind these young adult nonbuyers at all: "Though they might not even have drivers' licenses yet, it's the car that they have a poster of over their desk when they're doing their homework, and hopefully ten or fifteen years from now when they have a good job and they're ready to go out and buy a car, they'll buy a Mercedes . . . and they might not start out with that extreme, beautiful convertible, but we have entry-level. You can get a C-class sedan for twenty-nine-nine, or they can buy a certified pre-owned for a lower price . . . but it gets them into the brand, and they get started on it, and that's it. They can't go back to driving a lesser car."

One African American man came from the Bronx by subway, bringing his two young boys on a sort of motivational tour. He did this, he said, joking paternally, "So when they become some kind of superstar, they know what kind of car they are going to buy me!" For this man and many others, the cars on display are the big carrots available to those who work hard or win the lottery, and each, from the lowly Kia Rio to the regal BMW M-class, represents a rung on the ladder of success.

In our affair with the car, the auto show is just one afternoon of romance. As a result of the whole, long love story, and the corporate and government planners who helped write it, we have become a nation whose transportation and residential system is fundamentally based on the private car, not on public transit.

THE UNITED STATES OF AUTOMOBILES

In 2003, the number of vehicles in the national fleet surpassed the number of Americans with a driver's license for the first time. Today, a total of 244 million cars, trucks, SUVs, and motorcycles ply the roads.[1] Nine out of ten U.S. households own a car, and most now own more than one. This statistic may not surprise, since so many of the families we know own more than one car, yet the multivehicle household is a relatively new phenomenon. Over the last several decades, middle-class Americans have come to call it a necessity for each driver in the family to have his or her own car. Teens now often get one soon after their first license, though the steepest growth in the number of cars per family came as women began entering the paid workforce in larger numbers back in the 1960s. At the beginning of that decade, just 20 percent of households owned a second car; now over 65 percent do.[2] More and more families also happily buy a third or even fourth vehicle as a recreational or weekend car or as a collectible.[3]

We don't just have more cars, of course, but more *car*. Our vehicles are much bigger and more powerful than ever before. American manufacturers have put their vehicles on a course of steroids over the last decade or two, almost doubling their fleets' horsepower.[4] Sales of the largest pickup trucks were two and a half times higher in 2006 than they were in 1992, and while such sales declined with the recession, the outsize Ford F–150 remained the fastest-selling vehicle into 2008. And the giant SUVs sold 25 times more vehicles in the first decade of the 00s than they did in the 1980s, with the aid of what has been called the "Hummer tax deduction," which allowed business owners to write off up to $100,000 of their SUV costs. Advances in fuel efficiency technologies have been offset by increases in horsepower, with the result that average gas mileage has remained basically flat: the

Model T got an astounding 28.5 miles per gallon, and in 2004, the national average was down to 24.7 mpg.[5]

At the same time that cars have gotten larger, oddly, it would seem, the number of people in them has declined. Solitude is the default condition for drivers, with the average occupancy rate per car in 2006 at 1.6 people.[6]

When people are asked why they like their cars, their first answer tends to be the convenience they provide. However, most Americans see the car as much more than their most important tool for getting around. In a 1975 survey, 71 percent said that a car was essential for them to live "the good life," a higher percentage than any element of American life other than home ownership, a happy marriage, and having children. But by 1991, the figure had risen to 75 percent, making cars more important to us than children, who were bumped to a sad fourth place. While some argue that this simply reflects an ever-rising consumer ethos, it also shows that the car is the king of all commodities we desire.[7] The car has parked itself at the very heart of our notions of happiness.

While some take a simply pragmatic approach to the auto, others buy and maintain cars that they may not need or may not be able to afford, such as the man we spoke with who was trying to hold onto his $40,000 truck despite being underemployed and behind on his child support payments. And people sometimes keep a car even if it causes great daily exertion. For example, one New York City resident described growing up in Brooklyn with a rarely used minivan. There, street parking is tight and parking regulations require a continuous effort to park and repark the car: "You have to move the car constantly to keep up with the alternate-side-of-the-street parking rules. And so my mom would just be circling around all of the blocks near our house trying to find a spot. And she and my dad always had to make a really concerted effort to tell each other where the car was, because it wasn't always in the same place. And there were a couple of times where they forgot to tell each other and they would be walking around the blocks by our house with the car alarm button."

Across the country, there is evidence that convenience is not necessarily at the root of our love of the automobile. Many people drive to work even when public transportation or carpooling is less of a hassle and cheaper. In Pittsburgh, Pennsylvania, for example, thousands of office workers drive downtown every day even though they pay four times more to park in a garage than they would spend to take a city bus that would drop them off at the same corner. In one office building in Providence, Rhode Island, many employees drive to work rather than carpool or walk, even though the available parking comes with a two-hour limit, requiring them to leave the building two or three times a day, sometimes slogging through rain, sleet, or snow, to circle the area looking for another spot. The car's handiness can be more perception than truth.

Our potent desire to drive and the government policy preference for cars over other modes of transportation are reflected in the relative size of the U.S. mass transit fleet, which comprises just 129,000 vehicles nationwide.[8] For every eight public dollars spent on transportation, only one goes to public transit; the other seven dollars go to car-related needs.[9] And on any given day, recessions aside, an average of 150,000 Americans pour in to new and used car dealerships to buy a vehicle.[10] As a result of the improvements in car quality and the rising cost of new cars, Americans drive their cars longer and are more and more likely to buy them used, but they keep on buying them. Though it may slow the purchase rate, even a slumping economy doesn't stop the buying frenzy: when the recession began, in 2007, Americans simply stopped buying SUVs with such fervor and started buying more used cars.

Once they've bought those cars, people take for granted that they rarely find themselves more than a mile from a gas station—or two or three for that matter—as 120,000 stations dot the land. Once centered on car repairs and gas sales, these stations are now usually mini-marts, selling food and lottery tickets along with windshield washer fluid, and reflecting the centrality of the car to shopping and the time crunch American families find themselves in. With remarkable near invisibility, the gas arrives at those stations via hundreds of thousands of miles of pipeline, and a vast fleet of tanker trucks ply the roads daily to make delivery.[11]

And drivers get to those gas stations by using *the* construction project of the twentieth century: the massive pouring of concrete and erection of steel that became our four million miles of roads and streets and 600,000 bridges[12] (compared to just 200,000 miles of major railroads[13]). Drivers can belly up to their destinations in one of 105 million parking spaces in the United States. Together, these paved surfaces match the square mileage of the state of Georgia.[14] While people imagine that road system thick in some places and thin in others, our beloved automobile has demanded access virtually everywhere, including the diminishing wilderness areas of the West. There is no spot in the lower 48 of the United States more than 22 miles from the nearest road, outside of some unbuildable swampland in southern Louisiana. While the most road-remote location is in the southeastern corner of Yellowstone National Park,[15] even such national parks and national forests are crisscrossed with miles and miles of roads and play host to traffic jams in the summer.

We traverse our dense spiderweb of roads to a startling degree, with the amount of driving we do having skyrocketed over the past quarter century. Even with the decline in driving prompted by the gas price spike of 2007 and 2008, the Department of Transportation estimate of the number of vehicle miles traveled in 2008 is 2.98 *trillion*—almost double the number of miles driven in 1983.[16] And this is not just more cars and people on the road: from 1990 until 2007, the total number of miles driven in the United States grew at twice the rate of population growth. The combination of increased mileage and worsening traffic congestion has each of us on the road for an ever greater portion of our waking hours—on average, we spend 18½ hours per week in our cars.[17] Much of this travel is discretionary, as we will see later.

We don't just enjoy cars by buying and driving them. We also enjoy them when we go to the movies or stay parked in front of our television sets. Putting the pedal to the metal has joined football, baseball, swimming, and skating as a revered spectator sport. NASCAR racing has become the second most popular sport in the United States (after the National Football League) as measured by TV ratings. It now claims 75 million fans, its auto races accounting for 17 of the 20 largest attendance sports events in 2002. Revenue flows in accordingly, with $3 billion in NASCAR-licensed goods sold yearly and with Fortune 500 companies sponsoring racing more than any other sport.[18] Car fun transcends the track: a plethora of car clubs, car shows, auto museums, Internet car forums, car magazines, and a cable TV channel called Speed, which is devoted exclusively to cars, all reinforce our idea of the car as big entertainment.

Then there are the Hollywood movies that provide the important stories we tell ourselves about who we are as a society and what is important to us. While computers might play an important supporting role as the miraculous tools of spies *(Mission: Impossible)*, heroes *(Bourne Identity)*, and ne'er-do-wells *(Live Free or Die Hard)*, there is no artifact more central to more American movies than the automobile. Unlike other tools of modern daily living such as the microwave or cell phone, the car is not just a prop, but is often the central element for character development and dramatic intrigue, and remains central to Hollywood's archetypal plots. Few movies set in contemporary America made in the past few decades are without a car chase or car crash, a car interior rocking with teen high jinks or family conflict, or characters who find themselves physically lost or spiritually found on road trips.[19] Such movies are sold not only as tales for boys and men; cars are the settings, plots, and even characters in chick flicks and kids' films as well.

Some movies draw in audiences by being virtually one long car stunt, crash, or race scene *(The French Connection, The Blues Brothers, The Fast and the Furious)*. Others anthropomorphize or flat out celebrate the car *(Transformers, Cars, Herbie: Fully Loaded, Christine)*: when *American Graffiti*'s high school buddies get together for a last night before heading off to college, they cruise the neighborhood, hit the drive-ins, and drag-race, with one character proposing to his wheels, "I'll love and protect this car until death do us part." Few dare to run against the grain of car celebration and consumption. In *Reality Bites*, Winona Ryder's philosophical teenage character, Lelaina, rejects her parents' materialist lifestyle, putting cars at the top of the list in her graduation speech: "And they wonder why those of us in our twenties refuse to work an 80-hour week. Just so we can afford to buy their BMWs?" In short order, though, Lelaina's parents gift her with a BMW, and she finances her post-graduation malaise with "daddy's little gas card."[20]

Whether we are driving them or watching them, the number of hours we spend immersed in car culture means that cars are everywhere—not just on the road—and we seem to welcome their pervasiveness. Yet, paradoxically, this close embrace has hidden many of the car's more harmful effects.

ENGINE OF THE ECONOMY AND FUEL
FOR CONGRESSIONAL CAMPAIGNS

After the car's invention at the turn of the last century, the industries that emerged to provide automobility to the public became the most important sector of the U.S. economy. This became painfully obvious in late 2008 when several car companies were threatened with bankruptcy. The industry includes not only auto manufacturing but also the auto parts, gas, oil, tire, and road-building industries, repair shops, insurance companies, and the large segment of the advertising industry and media centered on selling cars. Although Wal-Mart ranked #1 in the 2007 Fortune 500, the next six largest corporations in the United States were all automobile and oil companies. Auto manufacturing represents 4 percent of the GDP, and a much larger proportion of the nation's productive output when all car-related industries are included.

By one auto industry research organization's estimate, one in ten working people have livelihoods related to the car.[21] In 2004, that included a total of 1.3 million people directly paid by the auto manufacturers. Layoffs have shrunk the number of employees at Detroit's Big Three in recent years as those firms have stumbled, but foreign automakers have picked up some of the slack, and there are still millions of employees in the auto supply and other industry-related companies and in the used car industry.[22] According to the monthly industry journal *Parking Professionals,* more than one million Americans are employed directly in some aspect of the "parking profession," administering access and fines, handing out tickets, moving cars and taking payment in garages, and manufacturing parking meters, building garages, and paving lots.

At the beginning of the twenty-first century, and several decades into the Information Age, the computer has not replaced the automobile as the centerpiece and engine of the U.S. economy. As recently as 2002, sales of General Motors vehicles were seven times the dollar value of sales of Microsoft products.[23] Even with the economic crisis of 2008 and 2009, the United States and the world continued to buy cars by the millions, as well as the various ancillary services and parts that go with them.

This economic power of the car and all its secondary industries has translated into formidable political power. The car and oil industries have regularly supplied decision makers to the highest levels of government—just recently two U.S. presidents (the Bushes), one vice president (Dick Cheney), one defense secretary (Robert McNamara), a presidential chief of staff (Andrew H. Card), and a raft of presidential candidates (including Nelson Rockefeller and Mitt Romney).[24] And auto manufacturers, car dealers, and United Auto Workers grease the wheels with political action committee (PAC) funds, soft money, and individual contributions ($15 million going to members of Congress in 2006). This money has historically gotten results: of the top 15 Senate recipients of industry largesse, not one voted for a 2005 bill raising fuel economy standards for cars.[25] It took American automakers being brought to their knees by the recession to create the conditions under which the Obama administration could propose new emissions and mileage standards. While the automakers professed satisfaction with the new rules, which would require the attainment of a national standard of 35.5 miles per gallon by 2016, this close to 40 percent improvement from current standards was only possible because the industry was momentarily disempowered.[26]

And while the Detroit bailout bill ran into some trouble in Congress, opposition was largely orchestrated by the representatives from the mainly southern states in which the Japanese automakers have built manufacturing plants. The auto industry's economic centrality and remaining political clout ensured that the bailouts would go through in any case.

As a consequence of industry influence, the American affair with the car has long been well funded by government. General Motors lobbied powerfully for the Federal-Aid Highway Act, passed in 1956, which put down 41,000 miles of interstate across the country. Federal and state budgets continue to draw on massive public support for adding new lanes and highways as roads have become congested. Add the large network of lobbyists, including the American Automobile Association (AAA), pursuing more government spending on roads, and you have the radical expansion of the car system that has been ongoing since the 1950s.[27] The alternatives to the car system, including the vigorous electric trolley networks, which were so popular in the early twentieth century that they made up the fifth-largest industry in the United States, died with the assistance of General Motors. Together with Firestone, Standard Oil, and Phillips Petroleum, GM eliminated their competition, buying and then ripping up entire street car systems in 45 cities between 1936 and 1950.[28] The car system we have today is, in a thousand ways, a creature of the year-in-and-year-out decisions of these corporations and of government, including especially the choice to invest what is a comparatively very small amount in public transportation.

As the various stimulus bills made their way through Congress in 2009 with the urgent prompt of the economic crisis, it was hardly surprising, then, that the government targeted much of the money to "shovel-ready" projects, which were most often roads and bridges—infrastructure for the car system. This is an example of what Naomi Klein has called "disaster capitalism," the phenomenon in which companies garner their most massive profits in extreme or crisis conditions such as wars, earthquakes, tsunamis, hurricanes, and housing price collapses.[29] While most people saw the crisis of 2008 as comeuppance for the car industry (and it certainly was unpleasant for the tens of thousands of laid-off auto workers), it in fact helped the car industry—both directly through bailout money and indirectly (and more importantly) through massive new road and road repair subsidies that will help sustain the car system far into the future.

At all levels of government, from federal to local, dollars have long been profusely spent building and policing roads. Large chunks of the federal budget in normal times go toward sustaining a car-centered America, with subsidies for the industries that build cars, extract and ship and refine oil, and move goods by truck. Over the last ten years, the federal government alone spent an average of over $30 billion a year on transportation, the great majority of which was to build and repair roads and bridges used primarily by cars and trucks, and to improve air quality degraded by their exhaust.[30] Some portion of these expenditures is paid with car and gasoline taxes and parking fines, with the rest coming from more general tax funds levied on the public at large.

Our car system is not simply expansive and powerful, it is also dangerous, polluting, expensive, and inefficient, and leaves us with an America more socially unequal than it would otherwise be. The car and gas industries and their infrastructure would not have become so large or entrenched and these problems so little discussed or understood, though, had those industries not created their own receptive public. Decades of relentless advertising and corporate lobbying have helped fashion and disseminate a pervasive set of beliefs—a full-blown car ideology. That car ideology, like many elements of culture, is invisible to us because it is what we see *with* rather than *what* we see. Like a set of chrome-tinted contact lenses, the frames of thought with which we have been raised structure and limit our most basic perceptions: of how to get around, what to spend money on, what kinds of risks are acceptable, where to live. As anthropologists like to say, humans are to culture as fish are to water. That is, culture is what we swim in, but we are the last creatures to truly understand it because it is everywhere.

The car ideology that we take for granted consists of a set of myths and draws nourishment from preexisting American values that have led us to embrace the system, or at least to consider it as unavoidable as the weather or as ignorable as background noise. This way of thinking and seeing leads us to treat as normal what would otherwise seem untoward at best or bizarre at worst—like putting our beloved children in the thing most likely to kill them, or spending hundreds of thousands on autos during our working years when we do not have adequate college funds for our children or retirement caches for ourselves. Our dreams of cars and our real lives with cars are constructed with the help of a series of powerful myths and values that warrant a closer look.

Chapter Two

DREAM CAR

MYTH-MAKING, AMERICAN VALUES, AND THE AUTOMOBILE

D ark and so handsome it's practically cruel, the celluloid play-boy billionaire (also a military industrialist and technologi-cal wizard) grips the wheel of a sun-glistening silver sports car as it explodes across the landscape. He is soon plunged into deadly in-trigue, determined to save the world from a maniacal Afghan warlord who has gotten ahold of cutting-edge weapons produced by the billionaire's own company. In his futuristic workshop, against the inspirational backdrop of his collection of insanely expensive supercars, the industrialist invents and then clads himself in a flying suit of high-tech armor in the radiant red of one of those vehicles: he virtually becomes an airborne car, with the explo-sive power and speed to win the day. This man and his formidable sports car are Tony Stark (aka Robert Downey Jr.) and his Audi R8, the hero and sidekick of 2008's box office blockbuster *Iron Man*.

Movies and commercials are our nation's mythmakers, spinning out compelling versions of the stories we tell ourselves about what we love and what we fear, what we aspire to, and what we seek to protect. These fantastical images are so elevating, so engrossing, and so much damn *fun*. As they entertain us, though, they distract us from their purpose: to create a return on the investment of the billions of dollars spent making them. When these images surround the car, as they so often do, the reality of the vehicle parked in our driveway, or the one we wish to see parked in our driveway, becomes wrapped in myth.

The fact that these myths exist does not mean the pleasures of the car aren't real. They are much more basic, of course, than those enjoyed by Tony Stark. These simpler pleasures were clearly visible to Sommai, a computer technician now in his late 30s, when he first immigrated from rural Laos in 1976. Riding from the Indianapolis airport "was kind of like a dream. The car was taking you somewhere without you doing any work. I knew I was going from one place to another, but it wasn't noisy and no one was running, out of breath. Everyone was very relaxed and I was like, wow, what a neat way to transport people!"

Lifelong experience with the car does not dim some of its delights. Under the happiest open road conditions, the majority of people say they enjoy being behind the wheel, and they like or even love their cars (though you are statistically more likely to be so smitten if you are male, a luxury car owner, and live in the western United States).[1] Driving gives people a sense of cognitive skill and physical mastery, and it is rare to find someone who does not claim, like Dustin Hoffman in *Rain Man,* that he or she is "an excellent driver."[2] When people expound on what they like about cars, they also focus on the convenience of just hopping in and driving away, or the sense of power they have behind the wheel. They like that the car provides a cozy conversation pit to share with their spouses, buddies, or children, or alternatively, they like the solitude it provides, the chance to crank up their tunes and belt them out. This particular pleasure expands with each new electronic device optioned onto late-model cars: some are now virtual concert arenas, with satellite radio providing hundreds of commercial-free stations, as well as cinemas or multiplexes, with screens for watching TV and videos.

Many of us enjoy buying, owning, and driving our cars, not just because they allow for mobility, mastery, and are toys to play with, but, at a deeper level, because we hope the car will help us live out our values, many of which we share and can identify as particularly American, distinctive and adapted to the national ways of life. These include the idea of freedom; a vision of the ideal man, woman, and family; an abiding faith in progress; and the belief that individuality is superior to collectivism and conformity. Finally, our love of cars is entwined with the very American Dream of opportunity and success itself.[3] Each of these values provides a pillar of the temple of car mythology that we must first understand in order to see how these myths have shielded our view of what the car system really looks like. Uncovering these myths allows us to rethink our relationship with the car and genuinely pursue or even rethink our core values.

RIDING OUT OF A CUBICLE
INTO THE ASPHALT FRONTIER

Of the many values Americans identify as their own, freedom may top the list, and there are few more potent and tangible symbols of freedom than the car. This is the freedom, not simply of the open road—Walt Whitman was able to celebrate that long before the car existed—but independence from reliance on the schedules and desires of others, whether a family member holding the car keys or a train conductor wielding a timetable. The car is experienced as the ultimate tool of self-reliance—which Ralph Waldo Emerson promoted well before the automotive age as well, of course. But in a world where transportation is centered on a road built for cars, you must be a driver to achieve the valued status of a truly independent person. Unlicensed and carless adults know this better than most; they cope with the anxiety or guilt of relying on others for rides or the shame of seeming somehow immature, inadequate, or incompetent.

Cars tap into the notion, as old as the nation, of a frontier ripe to be explored and expanded by the intrepid traveler on an epic journey. Since the Model T, Americans have used or at least aspired to use the car to get away and explore less peopled places. Many explicitly identify the car's offer of freedom with a long historical tradition. Said one man in his fifties, "I think that you can almost analogize that to the Wild West. I sort of think of it as the modern equivalent of the wagon going to the West, again to get away, to explore new things, to have, you know, ultimate mobility." When a mundane trip to the supermarket tacitly evokes this grand American tradition, why wouldn't we see a visit to the car dealership as a prelude to adventure, and a patriotic one to boot?

Car advertising has long exploited this ideal. Vehicles are poised at the edge of a vast wilderness or zip along winding, empty roads in the middle of a beautiful nowhere. In a 2006 Ford Escape ad, a gleaming red SUV poses alone in a majestic forest, as streams of sunlight pierce the surrounding trees and cast an ethereal glow. "The great outdoors," the ad copy entices, "is now within reach." A two-page spread for the Chevrolet Silverado HD shows the truck in close-up against a tree-lined backdrop of rugged landscape, which is in turn reflected in the truck's giant chrome front bumper. This truck is not just part of the Western frontier—the Western frontier is part of the truck. "Why buy the middle of the road when you can buy the middle of nowhere?" asks a 2007 Subaru Outback ad set on a craggy mountainside. In virtually all of these ads, other vehicles and humans themselves are nowhere in sight. In some, even the road disappears, leaving no obvious way for the car to have reached its remote destination; it is as if it has sprung from nature itself.

Model names invite the driver to see him or herself as an explorer in nature. There is not an automaker without countless such names: Ford's Expedition, Explorer, and Escape; the Jeep Compass and Liberty; Land Rover's Range Rover; the Lincoln Navigator; the Isuzu Ascender; the Mercury Mountaineer and Mariner; Chevrolet TrailBlazer and Avalanche; Mitsubishi Outlander and Endeavor; the Nissan Pathfinder, Quest, and Xterra; the Toyota Highlander; the Saturn Sky and Vue; the Subaru Outback; and the Honda Ridgeline and Odyssey. Still other vehicle names tap specifically into the frontier spirit of the American West—the Canyon and Sierra, Mustang and Ranger, the Sequoia and Tundra, the Forester and the Baja, the Silverado, Wrangler and Grand Cherokee—or you can take your pick of wild locales in the Santa Fe, Tahoe, Rainier, Tucson, Reno, Yukon,

Durango, Dakota, Tacoma, Sedona, or Montana. Or you can cover all the bases with the Frontier.[4]

The brand language was not always so environmental. In the 1950s, car names more often pointed to elegant European destinations such as the Riviera, Monte Carlo, or Seville, swift powerful animals such as the Mustang and Impala, or were aristocratic-sounding, like the Regal, Imperial, and Invicta. Automotive naming and commercials have headed into the wilderness, perhaps as wishful compensation, as sprawl, population growth, and car infrastructure itself have made driving ever less often a pioneer experience—unless one counts the increasingly unregulated highway as a kind of Wild West.

But in all of these model names and when Americans discuss the car, there is an intense association with the idea of emancipation and the fantasy that another life is possible down the road, just over the horizon, or in some faraway exotic locale. In a kind of "Dilbert's revenge," the car represents an escape from the metal cage of a cubicle or from the banality of modern life as a whole.

The notion becomes a nationalist one as well, a dream of being truly and happily American when driving. During the long Cold War, freedom was held up as the key difference between the United States and the Soviet Union. The daily repetition of this message implicitly linked the car even more firmly than it had been to American national identity. Chevy ads have been especially explicit about equating the freedom and strength their cars provide with Americanism itself, a connection that was only strengthened as Japanese car sales surged in the United States in the 1970s, and one that has ironically survived the nation's inexorable shift away from buying American. The war in Iraq, in many eyes a war for the black gold we put in our cars, was defended by the Bush administration with the rationale that the United States was expanding freedom's reach. Then, as the gasoline-powered car hit a costly crisis point, public discussion centered on another kind of liberation—from foreign oil dependence.

The car cannot endow liberty, many feel, without an accompanying release from government regulation. Helmet and seatbelt laws were fiercely resisted when they were introduced, as have been any regulatory restraints in the size, expense, or fuel economy of the car one chooses to buy or in the number of highway lanes built. The sale of radar detectors is widespread and accepted. On the other hand, over the century that cars have been in existence, and despite their sometimes fierce antigovernment streak, most Americans take for granted that they are required to have a state-issued license to drive. Or that, outside major cities, most come face to face with the police only when driving the roads. Still, ambivalence remains about government interference in our driving lives, even if stricter regulation—of cell phone use or car roof strength, for example—would make us all much safer. As some of the more recently instituted safety laws have been slowly taken up across the states, the compromise often reached is that these laws can only be enforced when another law has been broken. So-called secondary seat belt laws, for example, mean police can only ticket people for not wearing their belt if they have already been stopped for something else, such as running a red light.

Movies and marketing help nourish this resistance to car regulation. In the popular comedy *Superbad,* two policemen befriend a teenager who is using the alias "McLovin" and take him on a boozing and cruising adventure through the suburbs. They complete the undermining of their own authority as traffic regulators by shooting up and destroying their squad car. The vehicular stars of car ads zoom around mountain roads at high speed, their freedom from limits depicted as breathtakingly powerful. And when Detroit takes the media out to company proving grounds to unveil their new models, the journalists relish their envied job of getting behind the wheel and careening around curves on vast expanses of unregulated asphalt.

Americans expect and enjoy the freedom to speed, as evidenced by the small minority of cars on any unblocked U.S. highway driving at or below the speed limit. Most drivers have a rule of thumb about how many miles per hour over the speed limit (often from 5 to 15 or more) is normal, good, or acceptable. Meanwhile, the automakers have engineered their cars to be able to reach speeds as high as 110 to 160 miles per hour.[5] None but a handful of drivers will ever attempt these speeds, so the capability is practically useless except in exciting the imagination of car buyers. A few enthusiasts, of course, unfortunately do indulge the fantasy, endangering themselves and others.

While for some, the pleasure of speeding is in the transgression itself, others distinguish between the legal codes as written and the tacit rules of the road. Many believe that these road rules require that you "keep up with the flow of traffic" and feel therefore that speeding is both ethical and virtually required on most highways when traffic is moving freely. And many subscribe to the commonly held belief that speed laws are "nothing about safety and everything about generating revenue from tickets."

Some people see speeding as a skill an accomplished driver should use to avoid crashes. This is the view of one man in his forties who, running late, drove to be interviewed about car culture at slightly above his usual high speed. An alarm on his speedometer pings at 90 mph, and he had bumped it, he said, nine or ten times on the way to the appointment. But his driving skills, which include intense attention to other, presumably less safe drivers, keep him out of trouble, he believes. When he passes other cars, he said, "I'm thinking if I pass a Honda Civic, it's a mid-90s version, it can brake at approximately this rate and turn at approximately this rate. It looks like it has standard wheels on it and it doesn't have one of those big funny exhaust things on the back so it's probably a normal driver, not one of these racers who is going to want to engage me in my BMW. I'm watching all the other drivers. Are they distracted? Do they have other people in the car? I'm factoring all those things into it as I'm driving. I'm a very, very active driver. Even when I'm on the phone."

The lure of freedom calls loudest to the teens approaching their first driver's license, their young lifetimes having been immersed in tens of thousands of hours of exposure to its siren song in car ads, video games, and TV and Hollywood car adventures. Even in the ordinary chaos of a typical urban Department of Motor Vehicles, they are hard not to notice. At the Norwalk, Connecticut, branch, the adults stand resignedly in line or sit slumped in the crowded rows of plastic chairs, but these supplicants are different. Eagerly clutching their paperwork, they fidget and shuffle and then break into a sweat as they reach the all-business bureaucrats to answer their questions. They queue up in front of the "New Licenses/ Testing" sign, anxious about the written, eye, and road tests they will be surprised are so cursory. As the names of those who pass are called, they bolt up to get the little laminated objects of their long desire. Stopping for a moment, they examine it and then turn and walk, beaming, back to their families. They have been waiting for their sixteenth birthday as though their fourteenth had been a prison sentence and fifteenth a denial of parole. They have been waiting, according to fourteen-year-old Brendan, who just watched his older sister get her license, for something bigger. Asked what it would mean to get his driver's license, Brendan felt his one-word utterance—"freedom"—required no elaboration.

Getting a driver's license is a central rite of passage in this country, one that stands above all for freedom from the family and the family's schedule. As one teen said of her recent big day, "It was kind of the most grown-up moment I'd ever had. I'm sure it feels the same way to turn 21. You're like, 'Wow, I'm a grown-up. I'm independent.' . . . It's like, you go through puberty, and then you go through cars!" A young man from Colorado remembered the day he got both his license and the gift of a car from his parents: "We went out to dinner and I drove my car to dinner. All four other members of the family got in the car and went and I'm like, 'Yo, I'll just *follow* you guys,'" he said, laughing, "and I like put on my John Mayer and my Dave Matthews that I was so into when I was 16 and I remember driving and being like, 'I'm the shit now!'"

Teens exploit this newfound freedom and control to go where they want, when they want, finally in charge of the radio. Most also use it at some point early on to experiment with sex, drugs, and/or alcohol. Despite this, parents, too, tend to celebrate when their teens get a first license, reveling in their own liberation from the hundred miles per week they may have been driving as they chauffeur their kids to school or activities or their ability to get help running the household through the time crunch that faces many, especially working class, families.[6] Whatever their misgivings and fears for their children's safety, as one mother said of her daughter's new license: "It could make my life a lot easier. I spend every day between the hours of two and five, or six, seven, eight, nine, ten at night—I am driving her places. I pick her up at school and several afternoons a week she goes to this theater in the neighboring town and I drive her there. And then frequently I have to drive her somewhere else and then back. I thought," she said, laughing, "that her getting her license would be a big feeling of independence for her *and* for me."

The ideal of freedom that taps into our American identity as pioneers, libertarians, and rebels is a powerful one, and we continue to assume that the car is allowing us to live out those roles. These days, however, the car is not so much freedom's tool as its obstacle, as that mother of the newly licensed teen, relieved of her daily driving grind, makes plain. It is the reverse of freedom when we are trapped in ubiquitous traffic jams instead of pursuing the activities we love, wrapped in the chains of car loan indebtedness, and stuck in the quagmire of a foreign policy tethered to the supply of oil. The myth of car freedom causes us to ignore these costs and ask our government to spend more of our tax dollars on more roads and lanes, despite research that shows that those new lanes will become as congested as before within just a few years. We don't see, as Lewis Mumford once quipped, that this transportation strategy is like dealing with obesity by buying a bigger belt.

DAD'S JEWELRY, MOM'S TAXI, AND DETROIT FAMILY VALUES

How much we invest in the cars we buy and how often and for what purposes we drive are entwined with our sense of what kind of man, woman, even what kind of parent we want to be. The myth is that buying and using our cars can make us manlier or more feminine or a better mom or dad. So when some young men learn everything they can about engines and brands, they are demonstrating that they know what only men tend to know. And when some women devote hours to driving their kids to school each morning and to activities each afternoon, they are demonstrating that they will spare no effort to care for their children. Of course, some women know a lot about cars and, likewise, some men are happy to be the family chauffeur. Our ideas about gender and gender roles, though, can add additional layers of pleasure, or at least compensation, to driving. Wherever diverse beliefs about gender may stand in the wake of the feminist movement, men and women continue to drive cars differently, to different destinations, and to enjoy them differently.

While women are now the main decision makers in a bit more than half of all car buys,[7] and they drive in patterns and amounts that are converging with those of men,[8] the car remains a more important part of men's lives than women's. Men drive more miles and are responsible for almost all professional and home car repairs, and women still represent a tiny, single-digit percent of car salespeople.[9] When the great majority of heterosexual couples get into a car together, the man remains more likely to sit behind the wheel, whether or not he is sitting next to a feminist or he is one himself. In their first few years of driving, girls are often under tighter regulation than boys, and many families maintain a division of labor in which the garage and its contents are man's work, and the rest of the house is mainly the woman's domain.[10]

Many people continue to see the car as a man's tool and take pleasure in being, or being attached to, a man who loves cars. Like a man who watches football rather than tennis, and drinks scotch rather than chardonnay, he is considered a man's man if he understands and takes control of a car, especially a powerful one. When people tell stories of the car-obsessed—the person who, beginning in high school, began to put all of his energies into a car and knows *everything* about the automotive world; the person who got the nickname Mustang Joe or goes by gearhead437 @aol.com—they are usually talking about men. And when women talk about cars with some authority, they can feel the need to joke, as did the Minnesotan who said she prefers the Volkswagen "because it has more under the hood . . . Oh, boy, I sound like a guy now!" And then there is the culturally celebrated road movie, which usually has an all-male cast. *Thelma and Louise* is the memorable anomaly.

Young men who are learning to drive and be a man at the same time feel more than just the sense of freedom that their sisters also experience. "I feel," said one 21-year-old from San Diego of his first years at the wheel, "like I'm a *badass*. You know what I mean? Like I had the back window down, I had 'My Newfound Glory' like blasting out the stereo. I definitely felt more like an adult, I would say, and more like a man in a way," he added, laughing, "rather than having to ask my mommy for a ride to the bagel store or whatever!"

Shedding mom and getting the girl are both linked by young men to the momentous occasion of getting their license. One 22-year-old described his happy memories of first dating in a car: "I loved it. I loved picking up a girl and going on a date. I had a girlfriend for a while at the end of high school. I remember driving around and holding her hand and she has her hand on my shoulder. I'm sure this is like all sort of sexist, but my romantic feelings about the car derive from socially ingrained ideas about the man in the driving seat and the woman fawning over him while he's doing nothing other than driving, right?" Chuckling, he said, "It's sort of like, 'I'm so powerful and manly.' I'm aware of that, but, still, it doesn't cheapen the experience!"

Our beliefs about the machismo fueled by horsepower suggest that megamilers, sports car drivers, and SUV owners have better sex lives than men who walk to work, ride a bike, or drive a compact car. While myths of masculinity and the car may suggest that the boy with the biggest, flashiest wheels gets the girl, they deflect our attention from the fact that women own their own cars and that a couple without excessive car payments may have more money to spend on a date. These myths also enable us to accept certain potentially fatal car behaviors, like speeding, as the adult equivalent of "boys will be boys."

The image of cars and speed as a manly combination can be quite dangerous. While both women and men can be attracted to the car's power-through-velocity, speeders tend to be male. For example, in a new Rhode Island program for drivers charged with serious moving violations such as DUI and speeding, most of those sent are male. In the program, the drivers make a mandatory visit to the emergency room to see up close the effects of crashes. The men often swagger in, boasting to each other about how they got there. Despite safety efforts in driver's education and such occasional public health measures as this hospital initiative, more men than women, at all ages, die in car crashes. The differences are most striking in the teen years: in 2005, 2,575 boys and 892 girls died at the wheel.[11]

Jokes and arguments about "men drivers" and "women drivers" still percolate through American conversations. Whether we believe that gender differences in driving skills and habits are intrinsic or learned, there's little doubt those beliefs still have a hold.[12] The legendary "woman driver" lives on in tales like those told by one Michigan man who explained that it's because of his wife's poor driving and ignorance about cars that he doesn't "like sharing" a vehicle with her. With mock exasperation, he mimicked her attitude to the little nicks and scratches her stubborn incompetence creates: "'What are you going to do about it?' That's what Mama says." At the same time, mothers and wives are often described as "more safety conscious," "safety obsessed," "nervous," or "neurotic." Fathers by contrast tend to be portrayed as "relaxed" and "cool." When fathers or male partners come in for criticism, it is often for being "lead footed." Some people reject such flat gender pictures, as did one young man, poking fun at the idea that "the faster you drive, the more daring you are, the braver you are. That's the way some people see it. 'Live fast, die young'—sort of a John Wayne, James Dean thing. It's not the way I see it. No. For me, it's 'live medium speed, die old!'"

The importance of driving skill to men's status and power is especially clear in cases where that proficiency is baldly missing. One young woman talked about her dad's many crashes and their effect on her: "I had a lot of moments in the car with my father in which I realized that he didn't deserve the authority that he had. Once when he was about to back up and I could see that there was a car behind him and I was like, 'Dad, what are you doing, there's a car behind us,' and he said, 'No, there's not, what are you talking about?' and he backed up and smashed up the other car. And there was another time that he had had a few beers and he got into the car and I was like, 'Dad, aren't you not supposed to do that?', and we were trying to take a shortcut and he said, 'I don't know why this road is blocked up,' and there were cops there and they made him get out of the car and they were like, 'Sir, have you been drinking?'"

Speed is a form of power that draws people, and especially men, to the car: they flat-out love the heavily marketed idea that they can be the master of a forceful, rapidly accelerating vehicle. "Performance" is the industry's code word for speed. Car salespeople report that many of their male buyers concentrate on horsepower and acceleration. As one saleswoman put it, they "get really excited about the horsepower and the torque. When they look at the engines, and how fast they go zero to sixty and what's involved, it blows them away." While the steeply rising cost of putting gas in such vehicles is reversing the long trend to larger and more powerful cars, as Henry Ford's great grandson said, without blushing, of the passing of the V–8 era: "We all grew up when the coolest guy on the block had the most cubic inches under the hood. That feeling dies hard."[13]

The reality is that even more than allowing them to impress women, cars seem to enable men to display their manhood to other men. One car enthusiast, a New York City entrepreneur in his thirties named Keith, took out an *Automobile* magazine as he relaxed on a plane trip and jokingly told his seatmate that he calls his classic BMW 308 coupe "The Magical Mechanical Masculinity Enhancer"; his wife calls it, more bluntly, "The Penis." Getting serious, he echoed many men when he said that he had inherited his love of cars from his father: "I remember Dad's GTO parked in the driveway of our freshly built suburban home. There it was on the glistening asphalt." In turn, his own young son, Dakota, has been bequeathed his father's love of cars. Keith marveled at how Dakota knows just when he is about to shift gears and signals this with a matching noise. He then shifts and "it's like Dakota's driving." Keith would never trade in his "race-prepared" BMW for a more practical family vehicle, in part, he says, because he is convinced that people do judge others by the cars they own; for this reason, he would never own a minivan. That they are now considered the quintessential "mom's car" made it an apt illustration of his point.

Many understand that cars are a form of male display, often flaunted for the benefit of other men. Said one man in his fifties, "They're sort of like men's jewelry. So, you know, a woman will buy pieces of metal and hang it all over her body to kind of individualize herself, and men don't wear jewelry generally, so they will pick a car that will have an individualistic aspect to it, you know, that they will kind of self-identify with, and that's their way of kind of expressing their aesthetic sensibility." One insightful 16-year-old boy argued that, for the most part, cars were "a guy thing," functioning for boys the way clothes do for girls, as a means of self-expression. Boys had interests in different makes and models of cars the way girls had loyalties to different clothing labels and styles.[14]

Mothers and fathers both say they like driving because it gives them the chance to express care and love for their children by getting them to school, to sports, and to other activities. But women are still children's primary caretakers, and so they are the predominant chauffeurs as well. Women take twice as many trips as men to drive loved ones somewhere.[15] Some of those trips are essential, such as driving an elderly father to a doctor's appointment, and others are optional. One suburban woman spoke for many when she explained that she drives her son to school because she "hate[s] the idea of him getting wet" at the bus stop or having to walk home. Many parents spend more hours caring for their children by driving them to school, activities, and to friends' homes than by cooking or any other domestic task. In this way, cars are now families' main child-rearing tool. That means that the car system cannot be understood or changed without talking about how we raise our children and the larger landscape in which we do so. Randi, for example, left her career as a lawyer to teach, in part to spend more time with her son as he grew up. In a group of women sharing their summer travel plans, she explained with a blend of resignation and pride that her summer trips would consist of driving her son to and from camp and sports activities. She received a round of knowing nods and indulgent smiles.

The myth that good parenting means ferrying one's children in the car prevents our seeing the alternatives. For example, a child could be taught responsibility by being expected to bike to the sports field. This kind of car use is also fostered by the idea that the world is too dangerous to allow children to exert their independence by taking public transportation, but this obscures the fact that a child is far more likely to be killed in the family car than harmed riding a bus. Parents also tend to see the car as the space for the only quality time they can find with their children, ignoring other, healthier choices, such as signing the child up for one less activity or working one less hour and using that time to play a game or take a walk together in the woods. The bumper sticker that brags "Mom's taxi" might raise the questions of whether parenting is becoming more a service than a teaching profession, and whether we are being misserved by the myth of the car as the vehicle of family values.

PIMPING OUR RIDES, PIMPING OURSELVES

Twenty-something Cecily enthusiastically argued that "a car, for me, has always been my outward sort of expression on the highway—it's *me*, basically." Her first car, which she drove in high school, was a used Volvo station wagon she perceived as having a "crunchy" hippie image that she did not share. She got around this by plastering the car with bumper stickers, turning it into something that said she had a quirky sense of humor. Her current car, a new Scion xB, is one that can be elaborately customized, but she didn't do so in order to avoid being seen as someone who "tricks out" or customizes their cars to seem like individualists. Nevertheless, she views Scions as having a countercultural image, and sees people who drive them as, like herself, a little "weird." She also likes her green Scion because she thinks it resembles a small Land Rover, which she perceives as a high-status vehicle. Cecily thinks her customizable (but uncustomized) Scion, in all its contradictions, expresses who she is: a little bit rebellious, a little bit high-class. She also likes that people are intrigued by her car, because she explains, "I'd like people to be curious about me."

"Insist on yourself; never imitate," urged Emerson in his 1841 essay "Self-Reliance." This sentiment could easily appear today as a car advertising tagline, given how strongly America has since embraced the idea of itself as a land of individuals and the car as an expression of self. When Henry Ford introduced the Model T in 1908, opening the car door to the middle class, he was not interested in producing a variety of models and he insisted that every car that rolled off his assembly line be painted basic black.[16] Consumer choices were limited and personal tastes were not to be indulged. Today, the American consumer has hundreds of models from dozens of makers to choose from. Once buyers select a make and model they can individualize their cars further by choosing options, accessories, and colors. Buyers are searching for the cars that fit not just their transport needs, but, they feel, their truest selves.

The auto industry has encouraged the consumer's idea that the car should be an expression of who he or she uniquely is, as competing makers segment the market, trying to carve out certain demographic groups for their different brands. Volkswagen's 2005 "Beetle People" campaign was typical of this effort. In quirky and colorful magazine ads and on the brand's web site, actual Beetle owners were profiled, described as unique people who smile often, talk to their plants, daydream, tip well, and are "a Force of Good. Kind of like the car." Marketing messages like this have helped convince us that some cars are macho or feminine, some black, some white, still others gay.

In a 2004 survey conducted for Mercedes by the Roper polling firm, 46 percent of Americans agreed with the notion that their car reflected their personality.[17] And some people who believe that their car does not echo who they are said it was only because they couldn't afford to buy the car they really wanted—the one that would indeed communicate their identity. One thirty-something woman from Long Island explained that her Volkswagen Passat mirrored her "informal" personality. She also thought the way she took care of the car said something about her; it is always neat, but she doesn't always have regular maintenance checks on schedule. In fact, she said, the car made her feel "like a grown-up," but at the same time she admitted that her father still changes her oil for her. The Passat, a car with an image that is adult but still youthful, seemed to this woman to be just the right fit. In fact, a recent Volkswagen ad echoed her view in its tag line: "It's all grown up. Sort of."

One BMW owner in his thirties goes even further in his identification, as some car enthusiasts do. "What I have with my car is definitely a relationship. It's definitely a part of me, part of my personality. When my car is in the shop, I feel an emptiness inside, as pathetic as that sounds." Like this owner, many may feel embarrassed to admit how intensely they relate to their cars, but decades of research has demonstrated that material possessions in every society—and especially in consumption-based societies—do help form a sense of self. Studies have, in fact, shown that this holds truer for automobiles than for other products, which is a problem given cars' budget-busting price tags.[18]

Many Americans, especially those hundreds of thousands who customize their cars, collect them, or treat them as a kind of canvas in the art car movement, are happy to talk about how their cars are a form of self-expression. Many of these folks mock the mainstream idea that just buying a mass-marketed car can somehow make a person special—special like they are, because they mess around with them. Car customizing, referred to as pimping or tricking out a vehicle (or, in earlier decades, "souping up"), has been going on for decades, allowing people to adjust their mass-produced vehicle's appearance, package of accessories, or performance to their personal taste. Noted automobile journalist David E. Davis Jr., who has been doing such alterations himself since the 1950s, explained: "I see cars as a means of self-expression—canvases for the eighth-grade automotive fantasies that never went away."[19] And customizing, although growing in popularity, is still largely a male preoccupation, with the terms of art used to describe different customizing processes, including "nosing," "decking," and "frenching" sounding more than a touch sexual.

At one of many venues for car customizers to put their work on display, the Right Coast Association's Eastern States Nationals in Berlin, Connecticut, Debbie and Paul Hoffman described their enthusiasm for cars. They fell in love under the hood of a Corvette they worked on together in their teens, and their children, now adults, have customized cars of their own. For the Hoffmans, car customizing is not just a family pastime but a social performance: "People don't know us, but they know our vehicle. We have a '46 Chevy street rod, we have a custom-built wing on it, and we have a dog that runs alongside of it. People ask us, where's your car? Where's the dog? It's a way to get to know people." Paul says that the people he meets through his hobby are what sustains his interest in it, and many participants at the car fair see each other as "friendly types."

This roving band of long-term and often nostalgic hobbyists have been joined in the last few years by a large new younger crowd of customizers pumped up by the hit TV show *Pimp My Ride*. Younger car customizers, also known as "tuner guys," tend to prefer altering imports to restoring classic American cars. They get together at events like Hot Import Nights, a roaming and hyperkinetic, nightclub-like evening of sexy cars, hip-hop music, and busty young models that is a world apart from the tame nostalgia of relaxed afternoon hot rod events like the Eastern States Nationals. There, attendees can buy products to make their wheels unique, such as specialty paints with names like Teal Tease™ or Red Hot Meltdown™ with iridescent or crystallizing undercoats. The vendor of these particular paints points out that the car customizers "might have the same model and year, but they all want to separate themselves. They don't want to be the same."

Young or old, customizer or simply customer, Americans want their cars to say who they are to others. The car is as or more important to

Americans' individual and collective identity, as personal and as socially communicative, as dress, tattoos, or hairstyling—those things that an-thropologist Terence Turner tellingly called our "social skin."[20] Missing from this merger of the car with the value of individuality, however, is the recognition of how much the desire to conform—the wish to do and have what others do and have—is involved in our passionate relationship with the automobile. Car marketers, as we will see, know better than most of us how unoriginal and predictable our "individuality" seems to be. They happily recognize, for example, that the Prius owner is someone who was convinced by car advertising to broadcast that he is an environmentalist, not by driving less, or recycling more, but, ironically, by buying a car. The mystique of car individualism makes it hard for us to see that expressing our identity and values by buying a certain car gets in the way—finan-cially, timewise, and otherwise—of expressing them in ways that are more positively consequential.

BRIDGING THE GAP TO THE AMERICAN DREAM

Jens is a 55-year-old man from Massachusetts, a successful businessman and immigrant several decades removed from his native Sweden, who has joined other buyers of very high-end luxury cars in taking the identifying numbers and letters off his trunk. "I don't like to advertise brands," he told us. "You know, why should I buy something and then be a commercial for them? On the one hand, people who are in the know, I figure, who are the people I really care about, people who understand automobiles, will know . . . so it's kind of like being in sort of an insider crowd. So I care about what people who are in the know and who are the aficionados see, and they often will drive by and see my M5, which is the race car engine version of the BMW 5 Series . . . and will give me the thumbs up." Jens's status reference group is such a small, exclusive one that they will know, without having it spelled out for them, how rare and expensive his car is, a clear signal that he is one of them: a member of the elite.

Jens's car, like millions of others, came coated with the showroom shine of the American Dream. The dream tells us that success is waiting for anyone who tries, because in this country opportunity is there for the grabbing, and it tells us that one's effort will be rewarded and indexed by many things, but first and foremost by a nice house and a nice car. The Dream also suggests that each generation can expect to have more wealth and material comforts than the one before it. The automotive expression of this expectation is that we will eventually own a car nicer than our parents'. The car we end up owning, then, is a symbol of our success and the greatness of the country that rewarded our hard work. For this reason, when someone announces that they have bought a new car, the traditional, almost involuntary response is "Congratulations!"

Many feel that America promises its citizens a fair shake and equality of opportunity and access. From this point of view, the car looks less like a measure of material success and more like the great equalizer. We are all subject to the same rules of the road. The rich man in his shiny new sports car pays the same price for speeding as the poor one in his rusting ancient sedan. Regardless of social class, we all stand on the same line at the DMV waiting, waiting, waiting to register our car or renew our license. Behind the wheel, a 110-pound disabled person harnesses the same horsepower and has the same maneuverability as a 230-pound bodybuilder. In fact, the automobile has provided physical and social mobility for some groups once left behind in their homes, including women, residents of rural areas, and the disabled. It is an important means by which people can advance themselves.

Search the archives of any good-size American newspaper and you will find stories that celebrate the idea of the car as a great social equalizer for the disabled. The handicapped get to work, start businesses, and help others who are disabled in cars outfitted with special adaptors. An armless man in North Carolina, for example, was the subject of a local feature highlighting a special steering device in the van he used for his landscaping business. The article was illustrated with a photo of him, on the way to a job, filling up the tank by using his feet.

More potent, though, than the feel-good idea of the car as equalizer is the feel-better notion of the car as distinguisher, enabling its owner to telegraph his or her success and stand out from the masses. Having *any* car confers the status, most basically, of being a grown-up and of being at least out of the basement of the U.S. class system, as many nondrivers note with chagrin. Said one man in his early thirties, recently back from some harrowing and exhilarating times in Afghanistan and with little reason to be unsure of his own maturity, who was carless by choice: "To be picked up by people, whether by dates or by friends, to be always that person, is an awkward thing. People are like, why would you not have a car? Is it because you can't afford it?"

Beyond the hurdle of carlessness, each brand and model that a person buys suggests a level of income and success. The status system of cars in America was once quite simple—as a person moved up the income scale, he moved, as GM intended, from the Chevy to the Buick to the Cadillac. With greater model diversity and the niche marketing of those models to a complex set of demographics that began most vigorously in the 1970s, the automobile became more than a marker of class.[21] And in an environment where credit is sold so aggressively, the car today is less a reliable sign of hard work done and money earned than of hard work yet to be done and money yet to be earned. (Now the more appropriate comment to a new car buyer might be "Congratulations on your debt!") Despite these fudging factors, class remains legible in one's car, a fact that provides some of the sweetest pleasures to those who drive more expensive and late-model cars.

Even the way some talk about how they drive sounds a lot like how they think about getting ahead. Said one man: "I have a life philosophy. If you do what the herd does, you get what the herd gets." So when he sees packs of cars moving together, he said, he zooms up to them, gets through and barrels away as fast as possible. Another man in his twenties said, "If you're a fast driver, that's a good thing; if you rhetorically analyze these things, it's a good thing." As long as you're not reckless, he said, it means "you're breaking from the pack. This is how I feel society would conceive of it. I consider it reckless when someone's passing me very, very quickly. I find it negligent. I don't like weaving in and out. It would definitely be gracefully passing, but not quickly or not aggressively." The kind of car you drive and how you drive it has come to reflect a philosophy or etiquette of ambition.

Many in America celebrate the idea that opportunity and accumulation go hand in hand. They are sure that competition allows the best to rise to the top. These widespread beliefs have allowed carmakers to mar-

ket, and Hollywood and TV to represent, the biggest and more expensive
cars as the domain of the high achiever and self-restraint or self-limitation
as something for "losers."[22] So people speak of having "earned" or as "de-
serving" a new and expensive car, and those in high-status occupations can
see the car as representative of their having "made it." A Porsche dealer regularly sells his cars to people like the St. Louis man who stopped into the
showroom the day after the drug testing company he started was acquired
by another company for a significant sum. That the car has mainly cooled
its heels in his garage in the several years since makes it an even purer em-
blem of his success. His wife found this largely symbolic purchase perfectly
sensible, in part because her father had given her a car when she graduated
from pharmacy school.

Support for the idea that the car is both signpost and route to the
American Dream is shaky, however. The car system in fact blocks the poor
from making their way up the ladder of success because an automobile is
often needed to get the job that is, in turn, needed to get the car. For those
who do own a car, the Dream may have been more than a dream when
workdays and commutes were shorter and people were more able to enjoy
their success over the barbeque in their backyard. It may have been truer
in the days when more people paid for their cars with cash, and a new car
was a meaningful sign of hard work rewarded (rather than of possible indebtedness). And it may have been more real when it was less over-
stretched. In recent years, however, the American Dream of a car in the
driveway expanded to the dream of three cars in the driveway, and many
are now downwardly mobile because they took on the expense of a car or
a fleet that is milking them dry. Unlike the man who can afford the luxury of leaving his Porsche in the garage with the goal of keeping it in mint
condition, a multitude of SUV and truck owners now face the embarrass-
ing prospect of not being able to drive their guzzlers or make their
monthly payments. While gas prices push family budgets over the brink,
the total cost of their vehicles brought them unknowingly to the edge. The
car sitting unused in or disappearing from the driveway becomes proof to
their neighbors that they have been living behind the credit card facade of
the American Dream.

TECHNOTOYS AND TECHNOFIXES

Americans need no more proof of the fact, beauty, and power of progress than the latest cars on the lot. Each new model year brings technical innovations: in the 1950s, it was power windows; in the 1980s, antilock brakes; and in the 2000s, voice-activated cell phones and GPS navigation. The car is, in fact, a sacred site for the practice of what some have identified as the most widespread American faith after Christianity—Progress.[23] This is a faith in which the future suggests improvement, not fear: the newest is the best, and better yet is just ahead. While this value has historical roots older than the car, it dovetails with car marketing efforts: it is these "signs of the future" that draw people to showrooms wanting that new something their old cars don't have.[24] From the perspective of carmakers, the ideal consumer is one who is unhappy with what he has within a year. The car is seen as the very model of technological development, with American consumers eagerly awaiting each new innovation in driving performance, design, comfort, and safety and, until quite recently, trading in their older cars earlier and earlier to get them.

From high art and culture to low, this faith in technological progress has had its agnostics. Writers who imagine post-societal collapse render the result by focusing on highways emptied of cars (Cormac McCarthy's *The Road)* or highways so clogged with cars that drivers eventually abandon them and begin to make a new community with each other next to the road (Julio Cortázar's *La Autopista del Sur* [The Southern Thruway]). Moviemakers' apocalyptic images linger darkly as deer graze on grass pushing its way through unused roads *(I Am Legend),* or on the ruins of bridges and roads submerged in the rising waters of a cooked planet *(Waterworld, The Day After Tomorrow).* These visions and a few other images of Frankenstein-like vehicle technologies notwithstanding, the car itself is only rarely portrayed as betraying the people who use it.

Where the public critique often goes is not to the car or the car industry but to the government for failing to fund enough automotive science. One engineering student who had travelled to an auto show to see the new fuel cell car technologies argued: "We need a Manhattan Project–type thing, when you build a whole town with 70,000 people and you put billions of dollars into the project, but what are we doing? We are spending money in Iraq, a trillion-dollar war. We could have been way ahead, we could've had the fuel cell for every citizen in this country."

While many Americans see the car companies as having done all they can do, some fault corporations for failing to engineer a safer or greener car. So Frank, a 50-year-old Indiana plumber who keeps a pristine Corvette in his garage and regularly reads car and popular science magazines, argues that the car companies could have engineered a high-mileage, powerful car if they had wanted to: "The fact is that carmakers have always had the ability to get very high gas mileage out of a car, and they can do it through many, many systems now. They have the technology to keep the mileage up there all the time, but they don't care about that. They care about how many cars they sell. Bigger and better was 'in' in the early 90s. But who needs a truck with a V10 Viper engine in it from Dodge that gets 4 miles to the gallon?" Frank believes the technical solutions are there, but that nothing will happen "until you cut the legs off the oil companies, until you take that power away. They still lobby, they still run government, you know what I mean? So we'll have a better car when the battery guy gets big or the solar guy gets big, to where *he's* lobbying, and *he's* cutting the legs off of fossil fuel."

Yet millennial America has mostly maintained its faith in the idea that the car is evolving and progressing. There is widespread confidence that America's engineering genius will find a solution to the problems— pollution, traffic, crashes—that the car itself has created. The faith is framed this way because progress is seen primarily as a scientific and technical matter. Frank and his ilk aside, many people see solving car-related problems as an engineering issue alone, not a cultural or political challenge, requiring behavioral changes or social innovations. They are the many, many "irrational futurists," in the words of one iconoclastic GM executive, people who assume that science will solve, and the market will commercialize, technical solutions to the problems of pollution, congestion, or highway fatalities.[25] After years of market fundamentalism—or the belief that the market is the mechanism that, if left alone, will produce the best outcome for the most people—as the credo of government and media, people generally assume the market will make happen the things that need to happen.

Many, especially the young, are convinced that global warming, in part caused by auto emissions, will be reversed by the invention of a non-polluting fuel or superlight materials for car manufacture. A recent survey of American attitudes toward innovation found that one-third of adolescents think that by just 2015, the gasoline-powered engine will be obsolete, a reflection of their overwhelming belief that new technologies are on the cusp of solving critical global energy and environmental problems.[26]

People also commonly believe that car crash fatalities will be eliminated by the creation of an automobile safe enough to walk away from after a 70-mile-an-hour collision. In this vision of the future, highways will have car-interactive sensors that help keep traffic flowing smoothly, engineering away the tendency to rubberneck or overrespond to congestion ahead. And people read with hope the stories about the engineers at MIT's Media Lab who have designed the stackable, sharable electric City Car, which can slide sideways into small parking spaces, and the blast of reports about the possibility of oil being replaced by biofuels—even though those stories were soon followed by the disturbing news that producing and transporting biofuels creates more global warming and higher food prices.[27] Politicians draw on these hopes when pushing programs that suggest we can be free from the problems caused by cars, as with the Bush administration's 2002 proposal to invest $1.2 billion in research on a hydrogen-powered "freedomCAR." The ideals of progress and freedom converge to recommit Americans to the car as the centerpiece of the nation's transportation system.

So what's wrong with being optimistic about progress for the car? Most importantly, it obscures the fact that we could be living the future now: less polluting and safer cars have been available for decades. Looking to the future lets us overlook dozens of partial zero- and ultra-low-emissions vehicles already on the market, which we ignore in favor of cars of greater size, horsepower, or cachet. For years GM dangled the future prospect of its electric car, the Volt, in front of consumers as a just-out-of-reach innovation with no set launch date, when it had already launched and withdrawn an electric car from the market, the EV1. Although the test was successful, the EV1 was pulled off the market in 2003 and recalled from buyers because, according to GM's web site, "its timing wasn't quite right."

EV1 owners like Bob Rice sure thought the timing was right. Rice, president of the New England Chapter of the Electric Auto Association, like the other owners, loved his electric car. Rice reminds people that electric cars are hardly futuristic—they actually predated gas-powered ones—with this bumper sticker: "Electric cars: the first and last cars." Americans can see an EV1 in an auto museum and a Volt at an auto show but, as this book goes to press, we can't buy one. Oddly, the electric car took the reverse route—from a reality to a concept car.

The reason why we do not have a much safer, nonpolluting car right now is not because our scientists and engineers have failed us but because our politicians and corporations have. The politics of faith in the future of the car run across the shades of green, from the profit-conscious to the eco-aware, but the faith—especially its tenet that science leads social progress—obscures the real obstacles to a new kind of car system. The car and oil companies will not lose their power for years to come, and, as they morph into transportation and energy companies, they are positioning themselves to control and profit from whatever comes next, and on their timetable, not the public's. And unless the government provides significant incentives, then meaningful automotive technofixes, when they come, will be available at first only for the wealthy. High up-front costs (as for solar panels now, for example), if they are borne by the consumer, will allow the rich to buy the safest and most nonpolluting cars while the rest of us wait for the slow trickle-down of used cars. Ten or twenty years from now, many of us could be in a car that does not use gas, but our image of the way there needs re-visioning.

Freedom and family, individualism and identity, success and progress: these core American ideals have enabled a layered host of myths to form around the car. These myths reinforce our positive emotions about and intense desire for the car, prompting us to focus on its real and imagined

benefits. At the same time, the huge scope and scale of the car system—
our hundreds of millions of cars and all the asphalt, politics, and cultural
ideas that support them—lead to a sense that what we currently have is,
at worst, inevitable and immutable, and at best, just needs a technofix.
The system has its serious drawbacks, but these we tend to ignore, misled
by its myths, or to accept, daunted by its power. When faced with evidence of the car system's many problems, Americans tend to retire to an
appeal to pragmatism—the car is convenient, our country has been built
on roads, we have no real alternatives yet—that smacks of resignation and
lack of imagination. The irony is that the car, this paramount symbol of
freedom and independence, can make us feel trapped and impotent. By
exploring the downsides of the car system, as the following chapters do,
by setting aside our myth-nourished resistances and asking new questions
about what needs to change, we can restore our sense of freedom.

Chapter Three

THE PITCH

HOW THEY SELL

Suburbanites Jeff and Elizabeth were looking for their next car. Like many consumers, they had researched their purchase by trawling the Internet and studying car and consumer magazines. They also had reviewed their past experiences with different brands and carefully considered their needs. Finally, they attended an auto show where they could check out several new car models they had been reading about. Elizabeth sat in the driver's seat of the Honda subcompact called the Fit. She examined the dashboard, petted the upholstery, and pivoted around to check out the back seats. The Fit was one of the smallest cars on display at the show, but Jeff and Elizabeth were seriously considering it for their "around town" car, even though they have two dogs that would often travel in it. Elizabeth concluded that there would be plenty of room in the Fit's small rear seats for both dogs to travel comfortably. Many American consumers have justified the purchases of large cars and SUVs for less defensible reasons than owning multiple dogs, but Jeff and Elizabeth seemed very rational in their purchase process. As Elizabeth put it, "It's a lot of money. It's a big purchase. We think it deserves a lot of research."

She was right. Cars are in the category of what marketers call "high-consideration products," that is, those usually expensive products that consumers spend more time thinking about before purchase. When asked what they look for in a car, most buyers will tick off a carefully considered mental checklist that is quite pragmatic, often including reliability, handling, safety, cargo space, and cost. Yet, if buyers followed through on that practical checklist, we would all be driving the handful of least-expensive, highly reliable models out there. We might all be in the base model Toyota Camry. And we aren't.

"The buyers are liars," one retired auto executive stated bluntly, repeating an industry adage. "They'll tell you this is what I want, and that's what they want . . . they *think*. But that's not what they're going to buy." Many of us have, consciously or unconsciously, accepted the notion that the car is a personal statement and as a result have lost our practicality in how we buy and own them.

The professionals who help car companies craft their products' images understand this well. Some of these pros work inside the auto companies, others at the many marketing, public relations, and advertising firms they hire. Modem Media, an advertising agency focused on interactive marketing, helps companies advertise and market their products and services on the Web. Modem's Customer Insights and Research Group was run by Kevin Hill, who described car marketing as a unique challenge because the product appeals to both emotion and reason. On the one hand, he said, selling cars is like selling perfume or this year's fashions; how the product makes you feel is more important than what it actually does. "But at the same time," he continued, "it is a very rational purchase. So then it resembles banking and appliances. . . . You've got to appeal to both sides of that. Who you are talking to drives the lead message." Some buyers are more receptive to emotional appeals, others to rational or tangible ones.

Image and message became more critical when the real differences between cars became harder to see. Hill noted that in the past, the auto companies offered fewer, but more differentiated models. But in the 1970s and 1980s, car companies began building multiple vehicles on a shared platform or chassis. People started to recognize, he said, that certain Buicks, for example, were basically the same cars as certain Oldsmobiles, with a different brand badge slapped onto them.

Hill pointed out that consumers have gained power as the Internet allowed them to obtain a great deal of information about cars, information over which automakers and dealers once had more control. This would imply that emotional appeals might be less effective than in the past. Hill admitted, however, that for most people, the car is an object of desire or viewed as a "treat," and so buying one is in the end very unlike the process of buying a washing machine. We become attracted to a class of car or a brand because of the "soft" or emotional appeal of its marketed image; then we use the hard information available to us not to evaluate or test our decision to buy that brand but to rationalize it.

Men are particularly prone to rationalizing their car purchases. Generally, as compared to women, men read more about cars, gathering extensive data about the new models. They tend to appear highly knowledgeable about what is available from the various makers. Ironically, much of this research goes to waste. One experienced auto salesperson found that men are more likely to show off what they already know about a car than to ask the salesperson the kinds of questions they should in order to make a careful decision. She claimed, "Women process it, I think, before they make the decision about cars; it's a much longer process. I think men make the decision of what they just respond to from a very primal place." Men will justify an emotional decision, she believed, through the thought process that "if I like the way it looks, I like the horsepower, I'll make it work. Even though I can't afford it, or I don't have the miles per gallon, or the car seat doesn't fit."

Marketing executive Wendy Wahl explained to us that all good advertising taps into the desires of the target customer with the purpose of activating this kind of emotional override. Advertisers seek to discover the emotional hot buttons for their client's target customer. What they have to do, she said, is "home in on that one key insight that drives the advertising. What is the one thing that is burning in the consumers' hearts? Is it a fear of something? Is it a passion about something? Is it something they're secretive about and don't want people to know? You can turn that into an ad and reach people on a different level."

One method by which automakers tap into these secret wishes and fears is by employing people like Sheryl Connelly, whose title at Ford Motor Company is Global Consumer Trends and Futuring Manager. Connelly analyzes sweeping societal trends and brings them to the marketing people, who use the information when they craft their messages for consumers of the various Ford brands. Under the theory that fear can be a more powerful motivator than desire, one of a handful of key trends Connelly has been staying on top of for Ford is the nation's profound concern over safety and security issues. She explained that Americans believe that crime is rising even though it is not, and that this is because media sensationalism gives people "a sense of [crime's] omnipresence." Deep worry has also been created, she said, by "new threats" like terrorism. Based on her analysis, Connelly reported to Ford marketing executives that "people are taking a lot of action" (including making particular purchases) based on this worry because a rising "mistrust in business and government has made people feel it is incumbent on the individual to take care of themselves."

This understanding allows Ford the opportunity to tap into our fears for ourselves, our families, and our property, especially as they have discovered that, in the words of one Ford executive, feeling safe inside and outside of your car is "very fluid." So while we might think we are buying a GPS system to make it easier to get around, on some level, we may be spending more for it because it makes us feel in control in a dangerous world. And while a car alarm may be a smart choice in a city with a high rate of car thefts, a military-grade vehicle like a Hummer is an irrational purchase that may be propelled by a well of anxiety about being a citizen in a nation fighting two wars.

As these big-picture social trends and emotional hot buttons are identified, marketing departments at the automakers and their advertising agencies are running focus groups and one-on-one interviews with consumers. They then use the consumer sentiments, and in some cases direct quotes, from these conversations to create advertising images and write copy that tells people with similar wants and worries exactly what they want to hear. As Wendy Wahl put it, "The consumer is fed back what's in their mind, and the hope is that they then think: that product is for me." Of course, consumers who are not targeted by the ads might well tune them out. For automakers, this makes it imperative to direct their appeal to the people likeliest to buy their brand. "To align people to the right brand and the right car has been the real challenge in the last couple of decades," Kevin Hill said.

This challenge is being met by various automakers, although rarely these days in Detroit. For example, Nashville, Tennessee, is now the head-quarters of Nissan North America, where marketing decisions are made for the resurgent automaker. In 2008, Nissan celebrated fifty years in the American market. When the company brought its first Datsuns to the United States, in the late 1950s, taking on the monolith of the Big Three, it helped usher in an era of unprecedented competition that would weaken the American manufacturers' hold on the U.S. market.[1] Once the number-one Japanese brand in the United States, Nissan was overtaken by Honda and Toyota, but hit a rebound just prior to the recession, gaining its largest share of the U.S. market ever in 2006.[2]

That same year, Nissan relocated from Los Angeles to new head-quarters in downtown Nashville, twenty-five miles from its Smyrna, Tennessee, plant, where it has been assembling cars since 1983. When members of the marketing staff agreed to be interviewed, they were still adjusting to the move. Offices and cubicles were in the process of being set up, and, perhaps unsurprisingly, the dizzying pace of change in the industry quickly became the topic of our conversation with public relations executive Darryll Harrison and Fred Suckow, then director of marketing. Harrison, a friendly, down-to-earth young car enthusiast who had written his senior thesis on the auto industry, was more than willing to relocate from southern California, where he had grown up and gone to college, to continue working at Nissan. Suckow, a large, imposing man, explained that Nissan lost market share in the 1980s and 1990s when its product lineup did not change in the face of increasing competition from other brands. It forged an alliance with French automaker Renault in 1999 and worked to reshape the company "to be all things to some people."

Suckow echoed the belief that smart car marketing means directing separate, distinct messages to those who buy using their head and those who buy using their heart or gut. "There is a big selection of people who view cars as appliances," he stated, describing the more rational buyers out there, such as Jeff and Elizabeth at the beginning of this chapter, who logically calculate need against cost and carefully compare modestly priced cars. But, he went on, "Then there's a ton of people who view them as an emotional connection." Suckow seemed to imply that by going for the mass market, Toyota and Honda are selling primarily to the "appliance" people who care more about practical features such as cargo space, safety, and mileage, and that Nissan's niche strategy is to target "emotional connection" people who are swayed more by speed, gadgetry, and styling.

The Nissan marketing strategy was to appear as a "young brand," and in fact its customer has a lower average age than Toyota's or Honda's. It also has an enviably diverse customer base, doing a higher percentage of its business with groups that are forecasted to grow, including African Americans and Latinos, and garnering more buyers who make their purchases based on emotion.

Nissan had homed in on its young, diverse target the same way other companies only now routinely do. For years, products were marketed to broad demographic groups defined by age group and gender because this was the way media was sold to advertisers. If you wanted to reach men aged 25 to 39, for example, you might buy spots on *Monday Night Football* or space in *Sports Illustrated.* In recent decades, "lifestyle clusters" became the method by which companies identified the people most likely to buy their products. While network television buys still depend on demographic marketing, more targeted media channels such as cable, satellite radio, and highly specialized magazines and web sites allow marketers to deliver specific messages, even about the same product, to different groups of customers.

Market segmentation has been refined to the point that demographic and geographic data enables marketers to tell which few brands you are likely to choose between. Market research company Claritas provides a variety of these kinds of segmentation systems to advertisers. Their PRIZM data can tell an advertiser, for example, that in the Boise, Idaho, neighborhood in the 83704 zip code, most residents fall into a few types with catchy labels like "Bright Lites, L'il City" and "Middleburg Managers." "Brite Lites, L'il City" folks are mostly white college graduates, have a median income of $69,380 from professional jobs, and are homeowners aged 35 to 54 years old. Further, they are more likely than the average person to attend college sports events, eat at Bennigan's, read *Macworld* magazine, watch the Independent Film Channel, and own Volkswagen Passats.[3]

Of course, this makes plain that as much as we would like to think of ourselves as individuals, not consciously trying to keep up with the Joneses, our street address or our Facebook page is all that is needed for someone to closely guess, through the income, ethnicity, and education we tend to share with our neighbors and friends, what our family size, hobbies, television viewing habits, and brand preferences are. With startling precision, marketers can predict what type of car, not to mention brand of toilet tissue, we are likely to buy.[4] Marketers know what we don't like to admit to ourselves: we are a lot like a lot of other people.

Nevertheless, Fred Suckow explained how Nissan is able to forge an emotional connection with huge groups of individual consumers, which makes them feel like, well, individuals. "We actually use anthropological research. We do 'in-home invasions' through our Advance Planning Group and we ask people about their met and unmet needs. For example, with heavy-duty truck owners, we ask them what they love about their truck and if they could build the perfect truck, what they would change. That's how we find out where there are holes in the market."

Once they find a "hole" or an opportunity, Nissan designs the product and its marketing campaign around the ideal consumer for that vehicle. Suckow explained that, in the company, as the vehicle moves from design to factory to market, executives continually refer to this ideal consumer by the name of a real person from one of the early focus groups, in one case, Sue. So they are always thinking, what does Sue want in her car? What advertising campaign will Sue find appealing? What kinds of incentives will she respond to? While they have larger sales targets than people exactly like Sue, Suckow stated, nevertheless "we have a laser-dot-on-the-forehead kind of focus" on the type of people who are likely to buy a particular car and how to forge an emotional connection with those people.

That emotional connection is cemented when advertising feeds back to the consumer messages expressed in focus groups about what they want, elevating their concerns and validating their desires.

This method paid off with the third-generation Altima, launched in 2001. As Suckow put it, "People would say, 'Altima was built with just me in mind.' It was really our first breakout, big-volume car, in terms of cars that sold a lot not just based on price, but we sold more than 200,000 in one year based on emotional connections. People were saying about the Altima, 'Not everybody has one, and it feels like it's got a lot of my personality in the car.' We got that from male and female, African American, Hispanic, and they would say they bought it because of the performance, the design, and the styling. And we'd go, 'Boy, we've married them up.'"

PITCHING WOO

Once they've figured out which group of consumers to woo, car companies start marketing to them continually and in earnest, even though only a small percentage of them are, at any given point in time, poised to buy a car. This expenditure makes sense because although car purchases can be emotional and impulsive, as mentioned earlier, they are "high-consideration products" that require research and reflection, which means that we are all, to some degree, always shopping for our next car.

Some take this to an extreme. A realtor named Marc had owned 25 cars by his early forties—a car a year since he started driving. Long commutes in the past and lots of driving on the job now account for some of this, but Marc admitted, "Oh, I'm always looking." He reads all the major car magazines and *Consumer Reports* and is so knowledgeable based on his own experience of buying and selling cars that friends and family rely on him to help them decide what to buy, to locate a car, and in some cases to negotiate a price. Other buyers are more typical, such as Maurice and Mark, who visited a recent auto show. Maurice, an outgoing New Yorker in his twenties, attends shows frequently and keeps up with the new models even though he just bought a new car in the past year. He likes to stay abreast of design trends and new technologies and options. His friend

Mark, admiring the concept cars nearby, also had, as he put it, "a fairly new car," by which he meant a two-year-old model.

Auto marketers spend seemingly ridiculous sums simply to expose consumers to their product. But frequent design changes provide the news and images for publicity and advertisements that keep car buyers interested in looking. And the automakers know that although their advertising and promotion may not lead directly to purchase, it does create desire for the category as a whole and shapes attitudes about individual brands and vehicle types.

American consumers like to think of themselves as immune to advertising—our belief in our individualism and independence makes us reluctant to admit that we are swayed by it. But dollars tell the truer tale. Corporations spend huge amounts each year on advertising in the welter of media space: on network and cable television, in newspapers and magazines, on the radio, on the Internet, on billboards, buses, and other "outdoor" advertising, and through the mail. Group account director Gary Exelbert of advertising agency DDB smiled knowingly at the idea that people think ads don't affect them, but noted, "When it comes to creating brand image, nothing does it like advertising."

If it didn't, the more than $18 billion spent on advertising by automakers and dealers in the course of a recent single year just wouldn't make sense.[5] Even in the industry-rocking year of 2008, when national ad spending declined, five automakers made the list of top ten advertisers.[6] Most of the ad dollars spent by the automakers go toward television commercials, making it impossible to channel surf without landing on an ad for a car, SUV, or truck.[7] In fact, automakers spent an average of $630 in advertising for each car they sold in 2005; some luxury car brands spent much more, including Aston Martin, which spent $3,698 for every one of its cars sold.[8] While these ads are so pervasive they can seem like background noise that we tune out, the money behind them is not spent casually. Meticulous research and detailed analysis of past sales is what leads auto executives to approve and allocate these enormous sums.

Marketers are well aware of our belief that it is always *other* people who fall prey to advertising. In fact, they have played on this in their commercials. A perfect example is the Volkswagen ad that follows a couple driving in their Passat. As they pass other cars, they notice drivers, each with a megaphone in hand and hanging out the window, announcing the different insecurities that led them to buy their vehicles. One expensive car's driver announces, "Because Daddy didn't love me." A male driver blurts out, "Because I'm making up for my shortcomings." A woman in a flashy sports car announces that she bought hers because attention from men validates her. Finally, the drivers of the Passat realize that they don't need their megaphone because they bought their car for the right reasons: it has the "lowest ego emissions" in its class.[9]

Advertising is just one component of the automotive marketing plan. Additional billions are devoted to factory incentives, promotion, product placement in movies and on television, special events, and publicity. One increasingly important part of the marketing mix for car companies is the auto show. Although these shows have been around for years, helping car companies to introduce new models to the press and directly to potential buyers, attendance numbers at the dozens of new car shows held around the nation each year have been mounting.

Fast-talking, fast-driving cabbie Zeeshan was enthusiastic as he delivered visitors to the 2007 New York International Auto Show. He had already been to see it and seemed hugely relieved that his passengers wouldn't miss it. "It's the last day, you know!" he shouted before zooming away from the Jacob Javits Convention Center. Inside, a small portion of the show was free to the general public, but the 1.2 million visitors were mostly there to pay $14 for full access to several floors of new cars and trucks, concept cars, and car accessories like the Bumper Bully for parking garage protection or high-tech car polish.[10]

Over a loudspeaker in the Nissan area, an attractive product specialist gave a crisply confident pitch for the Sentra parked alongside her as dozens looked on. In the adjacent Honda area, a woman posed happily in the driver's seat of a sporty model for the company's photographer at a "free photo" station. As she left the car, she was handed a laminated card on which was printed a unique web address directing her to find herself posed as the model in a Honda ad. In this way, the potential consumer literally enters the advertisement and is able to visualize him- or herself as the owner of this car, something traditional advertising seeks to do psychologically.

For some consumers, auto shows provide a real service; they are a way to learn about and compare cars without the sales pressure they would find in a dealer's showroom. For the overwhelming majority of attendees, however, the auto show is viewed as entertainment, a fun and relaxing day out with the family or friends. At the New York show, kids scrambled in and out of driver's seats while parents looked on, amused, and took their pictures. Cameras—digital and phone—were everywhere as people took shots of the cars to share with friends and family who couldn't make it. It was a vivid reminder that marketing so suffuses our culture that we hardly notice the tide of marketing messages with which we are continuously swamped and even assist in the job ourselves by providing word of mouth.[11] In the case of marketing that entertains us, we are willing to seek it out, pay the price of a ticket for it, and pass it on to others. This is why auto shows are so attractive to automakers, who want to reach consumers when their cynical ad filter is turned off.

SELLING CARS TO THE BLUE'S CLUES SET

In every business, it is cheaper to keep a customer than to develop a new one. Every automaker would love to have a host of return customers like Tim, a construction worker who declared his devotion to his Ford Fusion and lifelong attachment to the company that produced it: "I love the car, I love the car. . . . Ford has come a long way to develop that kind of car. . . . I've always had Fords ever since I graduated from high school, my dad had Fords, my grandfather had Fords, so it was like a family tradition. Ford is heading in the right direction. They did a really, really nice job on that car." A year away from his lease being up on the Fusion, Tim has already test-driven a Ford Escape Hybrid, with which he was quite impressed. Then there was the retiree in his eighties who had owned three Pontiac Bonnevilles in a row; he was checking out what GM had to offer since they had stopped making his favorite model. (In fact, a year later, in 2009, GM would close down the entire

Pontiac division.) Seeking to increase their chances of keeping lifetime customers such as these, automakers are targeting one key demographic group: children. "Get 'em early" is the plan, according to one marketing executive.

Real early. Car companies try to influence kids' brand preferences as early as middle, elementary, or even preschool because research has shown that children form their automotive preferences this young. In a famous study, Russell Belk found that by the second grade, children had developed well-formed stereotypes about the kinds of people who owned different makes and models of cars. Second graders in Belk's study saw, for example, the owners of large cars as wealthier, "luckier," and more successful than owners of small cars, and they viewed owners of newer models as "smarter," agreeing that they would rather be like them than like the owners of older cars.[12]

Based on the research of Belk and others, several car companies have, despite arousing a small spark of controversy, embraced a strategy of advertising to children. In 2005, Chevrolet announced that it had reached a multimillion-dollar deal with Nickelodeon to advertise and promote its Chevy Uplander on the company's television channels and web site and in its magazines.[13] As a result, kids watching *SpongeBob SquarePants* or *Blue's Clues* could learn about the Uplander SUV and its "PhatNoise-powered" digital entertainment system for playing music, videos, and games. Car companies also reach young people by running ads during the sports, comedy, crime, and adventure programs that the whole family watches.

Marketing automobiles to children has a payoff now and in the future. Today, kids exposed to car marketing influence their parents' buying habits to a shocking extent. J. D. Power and Associates found that more than half of parents surveyed admitted that their children had meaningful input into the decision to buy the family minivan or SUV, with children aged six to eight most influential in the process.[14] As though to validate this statistic, as her parents discussed their potential new car purchase, seven-year-old Ohioan Natalie piped up, though she didn't initially seem to be listening to the conversation: "I want the Tribeca." When asked why, she responded confidently, "I like the interior." It turned out that Natalie, an only child, had been on a mission to convince her parents to make their next car a Subaru Tribeca. Asked to elaborate on the advantages of the vehicle's interior, she explained the value of its third row of seats. The third row would mean she could take more than one or two friends with her. Her mom agreed, although with a "we'll see" tone in her voice, that yes, the third row would be great. Not too long after this conversation, Natalie's parents bought the Tribeca.

Beyond helping children like Natalie to influence their parents today, marketing establishes brand awareness and interest that children then carry with them into adulthood. One ad executive explained that teenage preferences are an excellent predictor of later car purchases. Corroborating this, many adults talk passionately about the car they *always* wanted. (Even some teens maintain they have "always" wanted a certain car; 17-year-old Michael proclaimed, "I've always had my eye on a 1972 Mustang.") Some had finally acquired it; others still had their sights on that childhood dream car.

Of course, advertising isn't the only medium through which children come to desire automobiles. Films like Disney/Pixar's *Cars* (and all the merchandising and cross-promotion that go along with them, including toys, food, even Kleenex boxes) and toys such as Mattel's Matchbox cars encourage children as young as toddlers to see cars not just as fun and exciting but as anthropomorphic friends with distinct personalities. Children who ate a Happy Meal at McDonald's during the summer of 2006 received a tiny version of the monster-sized Hummer to play with on the drive home.

Older children and teens are reached increasingly through product placement in films that glamorize fast cars and associate them with nonconformity and rebellion. *The Fast and the Furious,* a wildly popular movie about sexy Los Angeles street racers, starred a customized Toyota Supra and a Mazda RX–7; its sequel, *2 Fast 2 Furious,* showcased Mitsubishi and Nissan sports cars, among others; and *The Italian Job* introduced American teens to the new Mini Cooper S.

More and more children of all ages are attracted to the fast-growing sports of NASCAR and Formula One racing. And there is the MTV hit *My Super Sweet 16,* in which wealthy teens are thrown extravagant parties to celebrate their coming of age. In most episodes, the gift given—to the astonishment and envy of the guest of honor's teen friends—is a very expensive SUV or sports car. In one, a sixteen-year-old girl squeals with joy when her father presents her not with one but two vehicles. Her friends gasp in excited disbelief; Dad looks on as a proud hero.

Like the rest of us, children and teens like to think that they are resistant to advertising. So, cars are being sold to them through word of mouth, product placement, video games, merchandising, social networking sites, and other promotions that kids don't always recognize as marketing or that they don't regard with the same cynicism they might traditional ads. Watching an attractive teen on a reality show or a well-liked celebrity driving or admiring a certain car can have a profound impact on the child viewing it. In fact, this type of marketing can be very powerful with both children and adults because, as marketing guru James Twitchell put it, "In reality people often do not know what they want until they learn what others are consuming. Desire is contagious, just like the flu."[15]

Finally, because kids tend to be less rational than adults in their decisionmaking and because they are engaged in the full-time job of figuring out who they are, they are prime targets for marketers' image-based appeals. When DDB's Gary Exelbert was asked why consumers and watchdog groups don't seem to be objecting to the automotive industry's directing its appeals to children, he responded in an interesting way, having worked for many years on the Hershey account. "These groups have lower-hanging fruit to go after," he said, such as fast food and snacks, which are seen as unhealthy for children. Marketing cars to kids, no matter how young, passes muster because most people think, like Gary, that cars "are not bad for you."

But cars are more dangerous to teenagers than they are to people in any other age group, and nothing—no other kind of accident, homicide, suicide, or disease—is more fatal to teenagers than cars, yet teens remain an intense focus of the car companies. Currently, adolescents, like many adults, embrace the notion of individualism but don't always live it. By far the number one reason teens give for disliking a brand of car is that it "blends into the crowd."[16] Teenagers say they want to stand out and be individuals. Because today's adolescents think that "being cool now means shunning what's cool," or, in other words, rejecting what they perceive as having mass appeal, advertising executives recommend that brands position themselves as creative, individualistic, or customizable.[17] At the same time, appearances and approval from peers remain important. Teens prefer car brands with appealing exterior styling and brands that their friends will admire.

Luckily for parents, the brands teens want aren't always the most expensive ones. In a recent survey, the pricey BMW 3 Series sedan was in the top tier, but so were the modestly priced Honda Civic and Volkswagen Beetle. In fact, one teen volunteered that in a scenario in which he was given a McLaren F1, a supercar with a million-dollar price tag, he would sell it, buy a more practical car, and keep the rest of the money for other things. He said, "I guess if you had more money than sense, you could buy a car like that."

It will be up to the car companies, once they've secured these seemingly pragmatic teenagers as customers, to trade them up over time to more expensive models as they earn more and learn to want more.

THAT CAR IS SO YOU

Bearded, middle-aged, and six feet tall, with a lankiness that makes him seem taller, Alan is a director at an auto museum. Although it comes as no shock that he is a car enthusiast, the breathless, almost giddy excitement with which he described why he recently purchased a brand new Mini Cooper was nevertheless surprising: "I said to myself, you know, if I am ever going to buy a new car, here are the things I'm going to want in it, and it should really kind of say something about me and how I look at things. I bought a Mini because it is one of the most unique cars around." In Alan's view, the unusual styling of the car has an aura of individuality that rubs off on its owner. "It is a quirky little car and it has a certain amount of style to it but it beats all expectations people have. People expect this big guy is *not* going in this small car—he's going to have his knees up to his neck! There's a quirkiness to it, and if you meet other Mini people, they have the same kind of quirkiness to them."

Seventeen-year-old Luke didn't yet have his hands on his own car when he was interviewed but was working an astonishing five part-time summer jobs to save the money to make it happen. His ideal vehicle: a pickup truck. Luke grew up in the comfortable suburban Connecticut home of his well-off parents but prides himself on being different from other kids in his school. Instead of trying to compete socially by flaunting his parent's wealth in a Mercedes or a Lexus like some other teens in his affluent town, he proudly labels himself "blue collar." In an environment in which many high school students are imagining careers in banking, law, or business, Luke wants to become a firefighter and has been quietly volunteering for years at the local firehouse.

He believes his pickup would reflect this rebel identity: "I'm going to buy a pickup truck—I don't care what people think. I'm going to put a new turbo in it and an exhaust and it's gonna be *loud*. I'm gonna stick out. That's fine with me. I'm going to pull into the school parking lot next to someone in their little BMW and I'll be in my big pickup truck. It's who I *am*." A group of Luke's friends who were listening in nodded their heads at the notion that cars should suit your personality. Stepping out of a certain car in public advertises who you are, these teens agreed.

It is true that some Americans buy cars with little thought about the message it sends to other people. Nonetheless, the rest of us read meaning into what they own. Take Julia, who drives a fourteen-year-old Volvo station wagon. The boxy shape and the yellowing white paint of the wagon make it stand out in a parking lot of mostly newer cars. To get into the passenger seat, it is necessary to toss children's books, baseball hats, and sports equipment aside. More of the detritus of family life fills the door pockets, the backseat, and virtually every inch of floor. Inside and out, Julia's car reflects her, although she doesn't consciously intend it to. To outside observers, it might say that she is an unpretentious, busy mom who probably isn't bringing home a large paycheck.

Car enthusiasts can be dismissive about frugal people like Julia, who drive the same old cars forever, and about people who buy unassuming models such as Toyota's Camry or Ford's Focus. These are people, they sniff, who just view cars as transportation. But even people who seem not to care about cars live much of their lives in them, and we inevitably read their values and identities not just in their car's make and model, but also in the color, condition, and care.

In a recent study, researchers asked participants to match photos of people with photos of the cars they owned, and they were able to do so correctly more than two-thirds of the time.[18] Age and apparent income were among the key factors that helped people to accurately connect owners with their cars; facial expressions, grooming, and other minor details also had an influence.

These associations are partly born from experience—we have seen certain people driving certain cars—but are also hatched from marketing messages the automakers have delivered to us about who *should* drive a particular car. Because we make these judgments about others, often harshly, we know we too will be judged. We don't want someone to get the wrong idea about, for example, our politics or sexuality based simply on our choice of vehicle. One young driver with family ties to the oil and gas industry was adamant that he would not buy a hybrid because he would "not get any satisfaction from driving around, y'know, a hippiemobile." A gay man with fairly conservative political views explained that he wouldn't want to date someone who drove what he saw as a stereotypically flashy "gay car" like a bright red Mazda Miata. These judgments can extend to overt moralizing. Although one college student stated, "I would never judge someone by the car that they're driving; I think that's really not a very moral thing to do," just a few minutes earlier he had described the parents of peers who drove expensive cars at his prep school as "stupid" for letting them drive those cars. He went on, "I think it's sort of—it's ostentatious. It's pretentious and I find it a little morally reprehensible and unnecessary. Extravagant."

With all this social approval and disapproval at stake, the automakers toil to create distinct images for their cars and to congratulate those who buy them. Honda taps into our desire for individuality by marketing its Element as a car for mavericks. "The Element embodies a unique attitude—call it a freedom from convention," a Honda brochure explained. "And not trying to fit in has made the Element just the thing for almost anything you're up to. So load it up, get out there and live your own unique way." The Element comes in offbeat colors like "Tangerine Metallic" and is often pictured in unusual, outdoorsy, and sometimes kitschy locales, helping communicate its image of nonconformity. Element owners echo the message, referring to themselves in an online owners club as "a rare breed" and the car as "a state of mind." Another Honda brand meant to appeal to our individualistic outlook is the Ridgeline pickup. Targeted at suburbanites tired of driving the same SUVs as their staid neighbors, the Ridgeline was shown in one television commercial following a group of trucks moving like cattle on a frenetic drive through the frontier. The Ridgeline cut off from the pack as the voiceover intoned: "Separate yourself from the herd."

Mazda, on the other hand, crafts a more mainstream, younger image, claiming it knows "how real people live, work, and play" as it targets fun-loving drivers with its "Zoom-Zoom" campaign. Mazda's cars produce "the emotion of motion," "exhilaration," and "adrenaline" because they are "spirited" and "fun" for people who want to stay young or "recapture that feeling." The cars are likened to amusement park rides for their youthful drivers. Mazda families know how to live, too. They are the market for its minivan, the Mazda5, a sales brochure for which shows a young surfer couple snapping their own picture in front of the vehicle, which is loaded with surfboards. The cute infant-sized wetsuit they've just purchased tells us the van will soon carry a child seat. The message: having kids doesn't stop Mazda owners from having fun. That's just the kind of nonstop adventurers they are.

Having absorbed these differentiated marketing messages, many consumers think of the car not just as a mode of convenient, individualized transportation but as a form of self-expression. As marketing materials for the Ford Fusion put it, "The STREET is your STAGE." And corporations have spent massive sums researching consumer psychology and have produced a raft of studies showing that the desire to express ourselves is not just one factor in consumer preferences but the key to why we choose one product over another.[19] This can help explain why the automakers offer consumers a plethora of models, even though many of them are quite similar in how they work and look. We don't just buy products that match our personalities, but to express who we think we are, who we think we should be, or who we want to be.

Also, because cars are used "across situations," in the words of one professor of consumer behavior—we use them with our family, at work, and in social situations—we try to send multiple messages to the world with them.[20] This helps explain the growing market for "crossover" vehicles, which are positioned between an SUV and a car, vehicles such as Chrysler's Caliber or Toyota's RAV4. An accountant with two kids who also plays in a garage band on the weekends can express his work identity (practical), his family identity (caring), and his social identity (artistic) by buying a crossover, which costs less and gets better gas mileage than an SUV, has plenty of cargo room and safety features, but has cooler, sportier styling than a minivan.

Americans' reliance on spending to help create and communicate a sense of self has become increasingly entrenched. While the 1950s was the era of keeping up with the Joneses by consuming what they consumed, by the 1970s, marketers began to help Americans to shift to today's motivation for spending, which is to distinguish and differentiate ourselves.[21] As sociologist Judith Schor explained it, what became important "was to consume in a personal style, with products that signaled your individuality, your personal sense of taste and distinction. But, of course, you had to be different in the right way. The trick was to create a unique image through what you had and wore—and what you did not have and would not be seen dead in."[22]

Any doubts as to whether this trend is still strong and deep can be dispelled by a simple test. Just ask a group of American males whether they would willingly drive a Subaru wagon, widely known as a "Lesbaru" based on its reputation for being popular with gay women, to their weekly pickup basketball game. In their quick and vehement answers, you will hear the power of what has come to be called identity shopping.

SIGNALING SUCCESS

While few car buyers like to admit that status motivates their purchases, consumer experts like marketing executive Wendy Wahl agree that "conspicuous consumption" is still alive and well in the twenty-first century. When this term was coined by social scientist Thorstein Veblen at the dawn of the twentieth century, he was describing how America's then tiny upper class consumed "freely and of the best" products in order to tele-graph their wealth and social superiority.[23]

But according to Wahl and other marketers, conspicuous consump-tion has become more pervasive in our current era of "mass affluence." The very upper tier still exists, but now there is a second, larger layer of quite wealthy people. The wealthiest 10 percent of the United States in 2008 in-cluded 15 million households with an average income of $289,000 and net worth of $3.1 million.[24] Add to that those people who can buy cars on credit, and a great number are able to afford the luxury cars that the rest of us, through media exposure, know to mean financial success and high social status.

Paul Hartmann, an automotive veteran with more than thirty years in the business, summed it up more simply: it's not that there are rich peo-ple in America; it's that there are a lot of rich people in America. Within this group, distinctive automobiles are a key way to compete for attention and create a sense of individuality. By way of example, Hartmann, who was an area manager for Porsche North America from 1985 to 1992, re-called the furor that was caused when the Porsche Cayenne was about to be introduced.

High-end consumers were excited about an SUV from Porsche. It was not substantially different than other SUVs available on the market, but it was a first for Porsche, the maker of luxury sports cars. The enthusiastic early adopter, who needs to be a trendsetter, is a much-sought consumer in any fashion- or technology-based industry. Hartmann explained, "It was very common at Porsche: people would call up and say, I understand you're going to build this car. I want the *first* one. Put me down for the *first* one. They wouldn't even ask for the price. They'd ask for a range. And we'd say, well, we don't know exactly, but it's got to be somewhere in be-tween $85,000 and $100,000. And they'd say, that's okay as long as I've got the first one."

Because they are mobile and we wear them like our clothes wherever we go, cars are even more effective than our homes in transmitting a mes-sage to the world about our social class. Jessica, a successful business-woman, has upgraded her vehicle with each promotion through the upper ranks of a Fortune 500 company. Pulling her expensive car, currently a

Mercedes, in next to her male colleagues' in the executive parking lot is one visible way she communicates her power and competitiveness in the workplace. Without such a car, she thinks she might be taken less seriously as a competitor or peer in the upper reaches of the company.

One teenager understood that cars are a means by which people seek to communicate not just personality but wealth and status: "If you see someone driving like a '98 Camry compared to like someone rolling down the street in an Aston Martin DB9, it's like you can tell their background or where they're from. It's not always the case because I know that some people can live in a two-room apartment and have a really nice car but it's normally the way it is."

For people in certain careers, the image of success (or lack of it) that they feel they display through their vehicles is terribly important. Marc, like many real estate brokers, came to the profession after a change of careers (he used to be a competitive sailor). He built his commissions and, as he could afford to do so, he traded up to a more impressive car in which to take his clients house shopping. Marc is a self-described car nut for whom his career choice has served in part as justification for owning his dream car, a BMW 5 Series with a V–8 engine. "Isn't that convenient?" he asked, laughing. He explained that in his field he needs "a car that has a certain amount of gravitas—cachet—so that if I pull up to a $3 million house to make a proposal, people think, oh, this guy could be one of us." The car gives Marc the confidence he needs as a salesman to the affluent and creates an impression of wealth, "even though," he joked, "I live in the ghetto."

When he made his midlife career change to real estate, another broker, named Rick, refreshed his wardrobe with designer ties, Brooks Brothers blazers, and tasteful loafers. But he realized, after his first visit to a brokerage to pick up the keys to a property he planned to look at, that a new car would be even more important. The real estate office's parking lot was a glittering sea of silver Mercedes and Audi sedans. There are other things that Rick would prefer to spend his money on, but he knew that it would be better for his career to invest in a luxury car. It might seem logical that people looking to buy or sell a house would prefer to feel as though they were not overpaying for the help their agent provides. Yet, driving the wrong car, brokers know, can send the message that they are not all that successful; this can cause clients or potential clients to doubt their ability to negotiate the best deal. So Rick traded in his beloved, decade-old Honda Civic hatchback for a brand-new Acura TSX sedan, complete with buttery leather seats and polished wood trim.

The car must fit the job, and the driver still must deliver on expectations to their boss or clients, or this career "investment" will become just another depreciating asset. The simple fact is, for most Americans, unlike realtors, their car can't charm those making decisions about their worthiness for promotion or hire, so the magical carriage is just a simple pumpkin.

———————

As we have seen, Americans tend to view cars as a form of self-expression and a signal of success. And because we see ourselves as individuals, we believe that self-expression to be internally motivated and unique. Depending on what we drive, and whether we're able to find or afford the kind of car that best represents who we are, our cars may communicate our personality, interests, gender, class, age, politics, occupation, and ethnicity. Nevertheless, it is the automakers and their marketing specialists who create the opportunities to express ourselves in this way. How the automakers market to us and how we choose to spend our automotive dollars reveals that Americans are not nearly as free spirited and individualistic as advertised.

And once each consumer—whether a status shopper, or an identity expresser, or someone who genuinely has developed some savvy pragmatism and marketing resistance—makes his or her way into a showroom, stand back. Because here comes the fastball.

Chapter Four

THE PITCH

HOW WE BUY

In 1972, Chris, a fresh-faced young college graduate, proudly drove a brand-new Ford Maverick off the lot and home, eager to show his wife and in-laws the super vehicle he had purchased at a fantastic price. At first, he couldn't understand the tepid reaction he received as the family stepped slowly, hesitantly around the vehicle. His father-in-law was even wincing a bit. So Chris quickly jumped to explain the car's horsepower, mileage, and features, and then unveiled his big surprise. Through his sharp negotiating skills, he had bargained down the asking price by several hundred dollars: yes, he had wangled an amazing deal. That's when they all broke up laughing, because what Chris didn't yet know was that the Maverick was a hideously garish shade of chartreuse. What the dealer plainly had figured out—reassuring him, "Yeah, it's yellow, it's yellow"—was that Chris is color blind.

There are innumerable tales to be told of car purchases gone awry, not all of them cute or amusing. In some, the blame is readily placed on the dealer who knowingly sold a lemon; in others, a momentary lapse in consumer judgment is admitted. But more often than not, Americans buying cars don't even realize when they've been deceived—by a dealer or by themselves.

"THE BUYER IS A LIAR":
EMOTION VERSUS REASON IN CAR BUYING

"The buyer is a liar" is how dealers explain the difference between what consumers say they want in a car and what they end up buying. Our checklists are often lengthy and mostly practical, but our ultimate purchases are often based on a boiling stew of rational needs, emotional wants, and impulsive acts encouraged by high-pressure sales tactics.

Paul Hartmann, who shared his memory of the commotion over the Porsche Cayenne in the last chapter, has spent most of his adult life in the automobile business. In addition to his seven years at Porsche, he started his career as a Volkswagen dealer in the 1970s and most recently worked for Saab, rising to oversee much of the company's North American operations. Now retired from Saab and working as an industry consultant, Hartmann said one of the most important changes he has seen over the course of his career is the increasing tendency of buyers to stretch financially and spend more on cars. This started in the early 1990s, when SUVs broadened the market for passenger vehicles and the range of options available to the consumer swelled. No longer were buyers choosing between just economy and luxury, two and four doors. Suddenly, choices abounded. Was the right purchase an SUV, minivan, wagon, or pickup? Hatchback, coupe, sedan, or convertible? Sports car, luxury, or military?

Sources of financing also expanded, and with these convergent factors, buyers, encouraged by dealers, changed their approach. Instead of narrowing their choices based on a prioritization of needs, say, to a group of comparably sized sedans or to cars with strong safety records, buyers started thinking in terms of a specific retail price. People would come into a dealership and say that they could spend so many dollars a month and they could write a check to put so much down. Then they would ask, what is the most car that I can get for this? The overriding goal became to get the most car not for the least money but the most car for the most money they could afford to pay.

The dealer has no obligation or incentive to show the buyer anything at a price below this point, even if there are cheaper cars on the lot that might satisfy the buyer's articulated needs and desires. In fact, salesmen are compensated on an escalating commission structure that gives them the incentive to increase the dealership's profit on each sale.

As in other businesses, dealerships set prices to maximize sales by using the psychology of the price-end of nine. It is impossible not to notice that advertised leases almost always end with the number nine: $299, $359, or $449. Hartmann explained how dropping the price of the Saab soft-top, for example, just $30, from $529 to $499, could boost sales by 30 percent. People who weren't even thinking about a convertible before they stepped into the showroom, but who had come in thinking they could spend in the $400s, were quite likely to drive off the lot in a new convertible. And as Hartmann pointed out, no one really *needs* a convertible.

Although in the previous chapter we said that cars are "high-consideration products," consideration is relative: car buying has become a much less considered decision than in bygone days, when the norm was for consumers to save to buy a car, place an order, and wait for the car to be delivered to the dealer. This practice (still common in Europe) gave buyers plenty of time to consider and reconsider their decision before it was too late. By contrast, an important component of transactions today are "sign and drive" promotions, which give buyers the ability to drive away that day in a new car without even having to write a check. This makes impulse car buying possible, even likely.

And because American consumers have come to expect not to have to wait for a car, dealers must operate like fast food restaurants, ready to quickly hand over the hottest, freshest product. As a result they have huge inventory carrying costs, part of which, of course, gets passed on to the consumer. In our interview, Hartmann focused on the thinness of dealers' profit margins. Most will make 10 percent on a typical sale, which, he argued, is much less than retailers reap in other industries. And, he asked, for what other product do customers feel comfortable asking the seller how much he or she paid for it? No one would go into a shoe store and ask the owner how much he paid the manufacturer for a pair of Italian loafers before he would agree to pay the price being charged. Of course, no one spends a year's salary on footwear, either.

To pad their profit margins, dealers push financing products. Financing, extended warranties, and other add-ons can make up three-quarters of a dealership's profits, leading the cash buyer to feel unwelcome at some dealerships.[1] A cash buyer has probably decided exactly what he or she wants to spend on a car, but a credit buyer might be encouraged to spend more based on creative financing. Financing has become so prevalent and is marketed so shrewdly that these days only a fraction of buyers pay with cash.[2]

THE LURE OF THE NEW

The fact that even the most educated car owners habitually underestimate the ongoing, total cost of a car—which goes far beyond the purchase price and credit costs, as we will see in a moment—is just one reason why we are buying more cars and more expensive cars than we need. We are also buying cars more often than we should. A minority of consumers who are looking to buy a new car are doing so because their current car's lease is up or because it no longer runs. Buyers are much more likely to be in the market because they are "tired" of their current car, are interested in the style or advertised features of new cars, or are buying yet another car for the household.[3] Legendary General Motors head Alfred P. Sloan would be pleased. "Stimulating sagging sales in a replacement market by inducing the consumer, long before his present car's useful life was over, to trade it in for a newer and higher-priced one" by changing models annually and providing a range of makes at different prices was an idea Sloan introduced in the 1930s.[4]

Sloan's marketing strategy lives on—gloriously. Until the most recent increases in gas prices and the advent of the recession, Americans were holding on to their cars for shorter periods and buying a new one on average about every five years. A University of Michigan study estimated that an increase in the turnover rate resulted in an additional 800,000 new vehicles being sold in this country in the six-year period from 1999 to 2005.[5] Auto industry executives, among others, expect this trend to resume when the economy brightens. While there is hope in some quarters that the recession that began in 2007 will produce a permanent shift toward frugality, others anticipate that consumers will return to trading cars in and out of their personal fleet. This is the case even though keeping your car as long as you can, despite increased repair costs for an older car, is far more financially sound than buying new cars and swallowing the high early depreciation.

The appeal of newness to the American car buyer helped shorten the buying cycle in recent decades and increased the sales frenzy over the very latest innovations, resulting in the dealer's axiom that "anything you can sell you can't get, and anything you can get you can't sell." The dealer's fantasy is having on hand almost enough of the hot car of the moment: the Mazda Miata in the early 1990s, the Porsche Boxster in the late 90s, or the Toyota Prius in the mid 00's. One auto executive explained that during the summer of 2007 the hottest-selling car in America was the newest Jeep Wrangler. "It's pretty cool. It looks like a classic Jeep—but it's got four doors," he said. When pressed on why this represented something new, he responded, "Well, it's almost the same but it's different. It's got a soft top and you can put the top down and you can take the doors off." Of course, the two-door Jeep has a soft top and you can put the top down and you can take the doors off. But this car expert understood: "It's just like a two-door Jeep except—it's got four doors. And, wow! Jeep's never had one and no one's ever had one. Wow. Wow. So now the dealer knows that people are going to pay full sticker."

The four-door Jeep Wrangler highlights how the lure of the new sometimes clouds buyers' judgment: at the end of its introduction year, this momentary sensation topped *Consumer Reports'* list of worst cars, with a score of 17 out of a possible 100.[6]

When automotive executives talk solemnly of their mission to address consumers' "unmet needs," this has often translated to minute tweaks, like a new style of cup holder or the addition of a light over a passenger makeup mirror. Enough of these small tweaks and an old car can be sold as "new" and generate amazing market enthusiasm. Cars that actually offer something meaningfully new, such as the first hybrids, can create a feeding frenzy that inflates prices and encourages some of the most reprehensible, but not uncommon, dealer behavior—like the good old-fashioned bait and switch. What follows is the story of the buying experience of one of the authors during the spring and summer of 2006, a time when rising gas prices had spiked demand for hybrid vehicles, and the automakers weren't making enough of them to meet it.

DESPERATELY SEEKING PRIUS

By the time we entered the parking lot of the Toyota dealership, we had already made several attempts to price a new hybrid sedan—attempts that had left us wary. At the time, unless we wanted a hybrid SUV, which seemed like an oxymoron—a fuel-efficient gas guzzler—there were only two automakers to choose between, both Japanese. The first Toyota dealer had quoted a $28,000 price for the Prius, which was more than five thousand dollars above sticker price, had required a deposit of more than a thousand dollars, had no car available for a test drive, and held a waiting list two months long.

So we decided to make an online request for a price quote on the Civic Hybrid. When the local Honda dealer emailed the quote, it was a few thousand above sticker, but he stated we could have a car in one or two months. When we emailed back to set up a time to come in for a test drive, the response came that there were no cars available to test drive, and, suspiciously, the wait had now, a few days later, stretched to three to four months. But we weren't ready to give up. We headed to a dealer a few counties north, where demand for hybrids might be less ferocious.

As we approached the door of the dealership, two salesmen in crisp shirts and ties advanced toward us. One shook our hands, speaking as though he had been expecting us, and waved us inside. "An old trick," he confessed. "I tried to make [the other salesman] think I've spoken to you on the phone before so I could beat him to the punch." Now he was our salesman and our new jovial friend, whom we'll give a pseudonym for reasons that will become clear. Pete ushered us to his desk and we made introductions all around. As we expressed our interest in purchasing a Prius, we couldn't help but notice the photo on Pete's desk. It was of Pete with a toddler, presumably his son, both of them smiling happily, the very picture of familial bliss. We couldn't help but notice it because it was strategically placed on the very front edge of the desk, facing away from Pete and out at us.

After a few moments of getting-to-know-you chit-chat, Pete explained how hard it was to get his hands on a Prius to sell, but affirmed that he was absolutely determined to help us. Just an hour away, Priuses were selling above sticker price but Pete was throwing around sticker prices in the low $20,000s. We sort of liked Pete, despite his disconcerting habit of declaring how honest he was. We tried to shrug off some discomfort: as a member of a profession that has a tenuous reputation for integrity, maybe Pete was just a bit defensive.

Pete rummaged through his desk and produced a brochure. After reviewing the eight different options packages available, we chose a more basic, level 3 package. Pete would have to go see what his inventory manager could locate and left us for a few minutes, returning to tell us that we were in great luck! He could get us a level 4 Prius in less than two weeks. Were we interested? Yes, we were, but we needed to know how much he was asking. Pete thought he could get us the car for $25,000. Were we interested? We told him we needed a few minutes, so Pete left us alone. To someone who had paid about $15,000 for their last vehicle, $25,000 seemed like a lot of money for a car. Pete explained that there was no state sales tax on hybrids, and we could apply for a federal tax deduction, so the premium over sticker should not concern us. We were committed to buying a hybrid and the price was a lot better than the $28,000 the first Toyota dealer had quoted for the exact same car. When Pete returned, we told him yes.

"Great," he said, "let me just go check with my inventory manager."

We were excited. We were going to get a new car! This wave of euphoria quickly disappeared as Pete returned with bad news. The Prius he had for us was not a level 4 but a level 8, the fully loaded model. It would be nearly $28,000. How could the car suddenly change from a level 4 to a level 8 in the course of twenty minutes? The level 4, Pete gave us by way of very limited explanation, was gone. Now all they had was a level 8. Did we want it? It might be weeks or months before a level 4 would turn up again. When we told Pete that we would keep our humble six-year-old

Civic rather than pay $28,000, he finally asked us, "How much do you want to pay?"

This seemed like a ridiculous question. What was the right answer? Nothing—we want a free car? Sticker price—we want to pay what Toyota intended and keep the government incentives intended for consumers trying to be eco-conscious citizens? We explained that we had been able to wrap our minds around $25,000 for a car with more options than we needed but anything more than that meant we would happily keep our Civic. Pete told us he would call us as soon as a level 4 reappeared, and we left the showroom feeling deflated and manipulated.

About a week later, while we were traveling, Pete left a message on our voice mail announcing that he had a Prius.

When we called him back two days later, he scolded, "You really need to get back to me right away. I had to give that car to someone else."

"What level Prius was it?" we asked.

"A level 8."

We reminded Pete that we were interested in a level 3 or 4 and hung up the phone. Two weeks later, another message from Pete arrived.

When we called him back, he whispered into the phone. "I have a car for you, but it isn't here," he hissed.

"Okay," we responded uncertainly.

"Call me back on your cell phone," he continued. "If anyone knows I'm doing this for you I'll be fired."

It turned out that an old buddy of Pete's at another dealership a few towns away—we'll call him Rob—had a Prius level 3 on the lot, but we needed to call our insurance company immediately and get up there right away and buy that car. Again we had to ask Pete for the price, and several phone calls later we finally had a number we could live with. Within twenty-four hours we were driving home in a new "Driftwood Pearl" Prius for which we had paid $25,700, a figure $1,800 above sticker price.

The entire experience made us feel like we were adopting a baby through less than legal channels. And now that we own it, we do love that car like a child, one that consistently produces 50 miles per gallon in lieu of report cards full of A's. We can't help but wonder, though, how much of the money we paid over sticker went to our baby trader "Rob" and how much went to honest Pete. We also wonder how much of that premium resulted from our poor negotiating skills.

Fortunately, we were able to find out online how much people in the area were actually paying for the same level Prius, something a smarter buyer would have done earlier. The average price paid, according to Edmunds.com, was $26,069. After all our effort, we were only $369 better at negotiating than the average Prius buyer in the state. But most of us were paying far more than Toyota was charging.

PAYING $34,000 FOR A $17,000 CAR

Across the country, car buyers are paying more than they should and more than they know. A handful of whistleblowers, including Duane Overholt, have helped to reveal the myriad methods dealers use to keep buyers in the dark about exactly how much they are paying for their car and credit. Overholt was a car salesman for many years, one who eventually became so uncomfortable with industry tactics that he abandoned sales to form an organization called Stop Auto Fraud in order, he told us, to do "penance" for the damage he feels he inflicted on car buyers. Informing the public, representing whistleblowers, and filing suit against dealerships are just a few of the organization's activities. Overholt sees his group as helping to right the balance of power between consumers and dealers, who often hold great sway in local, state, and even national politics, keeping fraud enforcement at bay.

Some of the questionable tactics Overholt sheds light on are legal: dealers in many states are allowed to make credit contracts for several percentage points over the interest rate for which a buyer qualifies from the bank. In Connecticut, for example, if the bank makes a loan at 16 percent, the car dealer can add an additional 2.5 percent. Dealers can also simply rush loan paperwork past buyers, sometimes even after the car has been driven off the lot, all with legal impunity.

Murkier activities include shielding information from buyers that would help them make a sound purchasing decision. A popular car dealer software package, ProMax, allows dealers to print out proposals in two different versions: one for the dealer and credit agency that includes the details on what is being purchased and the amount of the finance charges, and another for the prospective customer that is much, much sparer. These ProMax proposals allow salespeople to hide line items from customers, including how much they are paying for options and accessories; lease fees; the amount the dealer expects to receive for the trade-in; and, most importantly, the total cost.

Instead, customers' attention is redirected to a few monthly payment choices they are being offered. But, as the ProMax web site notes, "The most important thing when presenting [the] proposal is to take the customer's mind off the price by giving them choices and assume the sale" has already been made. As ProMax also points out, the choices to be presented (between say, a 60-month term with $800 down and $225 a month, or a 60-month term with $1,300 down and $215 a month) make no difference in the dealer's profit, but deceptively suggest that the buyer is in control of an important financial decision.

In addition to craftily written proposals, car dealers rely on a variety of sales techniques to push buyers into making poor financial choices. Many work with the premise, as does one Massachusetts car dealer, that their job is to "make friends first, sell cars second," because "it is easier to sell a car to a friend." This salesman begins, he told us, by asking buyers how much they can afford, and advises them against paying with cash, "because it is a depreciating asset, and if you buy it all today, you will never get that money back." That linguistic sleight of hand apparently works to get more people into purchasing credit along with their depreciating asset. It is also not unusual for a salesman to act as though he is doing a buyer a favor by taking his old car off his hands when in fact he is obtaining it for a price far below the wholesale value of the car and the amount the buyer would get if he sold it himself.

Dealer tactics that are not simply unethical but baldly illegal are unfortunately not rare. These include selling "ghost items," which are invisible products such as undercoating or warranty extensions that may never have actually been added or for which the dealer has greatly overcharged. Other common scams include giving the buyer a false credit score and charging them a higher interest rate as a result, or telling a buyer that the dealer will pay off their existing loan but then proceeding to fold it into the new loan. While the Florida attorney general recently found that 34 percent of automotive purchases and/or lease deals in one class action lawsuit involved predatory lending or deceptive sales methods, Duane Overholt's independent research suggested the real number was closer to 65 percent.[7]

In cases where dealer fraud has been discovered and litigated, it becomes clear the extent to which car buyers can end up spending more than they know or intend. Take the case of a Nissan dealer in North Carolina who sold a local warehouse worker a new 2002 sedan with a sticker price of $17,627 and add-ons that took the price to $19,442. However, the dealer then turned around and reported to the financing source that this vehicle's value was not $19,442 but $26,292, and the buyer's loan was based on this inflated number. After a $1,500 down payment and five years of $547 monthly payments, the warehouse worker would have ended up paying fully $34,320 for his car, roughly double the sticker price.

ENOUGH ISN'T ENOUGH

Perhaps the most compelling evidence that Americans are led to buy more vehicle than we really need is the fact, noted earlier, that there are more cars and trucks in the United States than licensed drivers, according to the Bureau of Transportation Statistics. As we have seen, the one-car household is increasingly rare. One owner of multiple vehicles responded to an online article reporting this data with a defiant post: "Proud member of a two person household with 1 pickup truck (with camper, oh the mileage horror), 1 evil SUV, 1 John Deere tractor, 1 Grizzly ATV. All paid for by hard work, thank you very much." Many people reported various practical uses for an extra vehicle, including a driver who has found having a backup car in the garage essential in the middle of cold Michigan winters. Maurice, in his twenties and the owner of two cars, is the only driver of both. He explained that each car serves different purposes: one car sportier and a hatchback; the other, with more cargo space, is for utility errands and when he has passengers. While most households' second, third, or fourth vehicles aren't the expensive ones in the stereotypical millionaire's vanity collection, the extra car has become not just the norm but an expectation.

The fact that many families now include two income earners accounts for an increase in the number of vehicles we feel we need. But the very idea of family members finding ways to share a car, carpool, and adapt their schedules to others' has become unpalatable. A 2006 Pew Research study found that in response to higher gas prices, only 21 percent of Americans said they had started ride sharing or carpooling more often. In this survey, "more often" was not quantified, but might mean sharing a ride to work once a week or more. Since then, the amount of carpooling has risen only slightly.

Increasingly, the second or third car is for the teenager in the family, who is seen as needing a car to get to school, activities, or to part-time work, even when walking, school buses, and public transit are possibilities. And often a new, rather than a used, car is justified for this teenage driver with the argument that it is safer. Parents want to ensure that their child drives a car with all of the latest available safety equipment and one in the best possible condition. Some parents also mistakenly believe a bigger vehicle is a safer vehicle. As a result, American teens drive an unnecessarily big, new, and expensive fleet, when statistically the age of the driver is a more significant indicator of driving danger than the age or size of the car.

Regardless of how many vehicles they own, Americans tend to buy vehicles for peak needs rather than typical needs. SUVs are a terrific example of this. Most of the time, their owners are driving alone or transporting one or two passengers and the amount of groceries a hatchback could carry. But the purchase is justified (or rationalized) by the occasional needs of the family vacation, the weekend ski trip, or a few spring trips to the garden center. One working mother defended her purchase of an SUV, which serves largely to enable her solo commute to and from work, as a necessity because her two children are taller than most teens. She feels her kids, who will be off to college in a few years, shouldn't have to fold themselves into a smaller car for the short trips they take.

Obviously, a few SUV owners do use their vehicles for the rugged four-wheeling purposes they are pictured being used for in commercials, but the reality is that, as one auto executive admitted, less than five percent of the American public ever goes off-roading. And even those drivers who say they use their SUV "a lot" or "often" for this kind of driving, when pushed for specifics, count using the vehicle this way at most once or twice a month. Renting an SUV for those occasions would be the financially smarter choice. Nevertheless, with the automakers' push in the 1990s to sell more large, high-profit-margin vehicles to Americans, by the end of the decade, almost half of all vehicles sold were SUVs, light trucks, and vans.

While some have become more sheepish about owning or buying SUVs in light of growing awareness of environmental concerns and others have become discouraged by the cost of filling up one of these vehicles, plenty of suburban parents in particular continue to argue that they "need" one. Those with younger children tend to make the compelling case that child car seats take up a great deal of space. Those with older children point out that kids are physically bigger these days than they used to be, although the more modest station wagon sufficed to transport the numerically larger families of the past. And more than a few, like one father of three in the process of researching his next vehicle purchase, contend that "no one makes station wagons anymore." The fact is, as the automakers have focused their marketing dollars on SUVs and crossovers, roughly three dozen vehicles classified as wagons were on the market while this man was looking, vehicles that were invisible to him. Many of these vehicles, such as the Ford Taurus X and Chrysler Pacifica, provide the seats and cargo space but lack the styling we have been conditioned to admire or the image we wish to project.

It is true that as gas prices have risen and increased in volatility over the past few years, some consumers have been moving to smaller cars. Relatively tiny cars like the Honda Fit, the Toyota Matrix, and the Mini Cooper have all seen healthy sales since they were introduced. But industry experts are skeptical about a large-scale shift to compact and subcompact cars. Some people are adding these cars as a second or third car, but most are still holding on to the SUV. Gas prices and hard economic times have loosened, but as yet have been unable to fully break "the American fascination with big vehicles," which, one auto executive argued, "is here, will always be here, and that's not going to change." His explanation for this: moving to a small car feels like descending the social ladder. "Americans look at it as a step down. As you moved up in life, you moved to a bigger car. Americans are very status conscious."

THE LUXURIFICATION OF THE AUTOMOBILE

Perhaps most significantly, cars have been subject, like many other product categories, to the "luxurification" of America. The American consumer has gone upscale, and a rash of books instructs advertisers and marketers on how to take advantage of this trend. In her book, *Let Them Eat Cake: Marketing Luxury to the Masses—as Well as the Classes,* consumer marketing expert Pamela Danziger advises companies: "Today consumers everywhere at every income level want more luxury and are willing to pay for it." Indeed, they are willing to borrow for it. As a result, she explained, "the only strategy that will really work and take a company and its brand into the future is to continually enhance and build more and more luxury into the company's products, its service, the brand."[8]

When it comes to cars, this desire for luxury means that premium brands like Jaguar, Mercedes-Benz, and Lexus saw significant growth in the U.S. market in the early years of the new millennium. In 2005, *Ward's Dealer Business,* a magazine for automobile dealership professionals, noted that 100, or one in five, of the top 500 dealers in America in terms of sales were luxury dealerships, up from 81 the year before.[9] These included 26 Mercedes-Benz dealerships, a group that hit record average sales.

But, as Danziger points out, consumers in the new millennium began paying more for luxury at every level. As a result, cars as humble as the Honda Civic can be ordered with a leather interior, a satellite-linked navigation system, and an MP3 input jack and playback capability. A young Swedish representative of Volvo noted that, unlike European consumers, Americans demand that their cars be "fully loaded," even when options on Volvos (extras built in at the factory, such as heated seats and headlights that angle as the car turns) can add up to between four thousand and seven thousand dollars to a car's price. Accessories (even more extras added on after the car leaves the factory, such as mud flaps and bicycle holders) can add thousands more.

Car dealers note that "everyone" wants the latest personal communications, entertainment, and comfort technology with them wherever they go. Elaborate choices and packages seem like requirements, not options, for American consumers who have quickly grown attached to every bell and whistle the automakers have developed. And, in fact, many features once offered only as options have become standard, helping to drive up the base sticker prices. Air-conditioning, AM/FM radio, a CD player, cruise control, and power door locks were once largely available only as options and now almost universally come standard. By 2005, these were the top five non-safety features considered by Americans to be "very important" to have in their next vehicle. By 2009, buyers desired a whole new set of options, including wireless internet connectivity and premium surround sound. To better compete, auto makers are likely to make more of these expensive features standard, wrapping them into the base price.[10]

These days, having luxury doesn't just mean purchasing pricey goods, it means pampering yourself. Many people justified their purchase of a new, expensive car in interviews as something they *deserve*. They might deserve the car because they work long hours, because they have a long commute, because they are careful with money otherwise, or because they do so much for other people and this is one thing they do for themselves.

The message of much car advertising is—why not? You should buy the RL, argued one Acura ad, because it is "a personal assistant, beautifully disguised as a car. It's a luxurious, attentive environment where your needs are the number-one priority." Ad copy for the Hyundai Azera encourages: "Reward yourself. The all-new Azera is everything you deserve. And although it's anything but standard, the Azera is loaded with premium standard features. . . . So go ahead. Indulge." And if you have really earned it, suggests the advertising for the Rolls-Royce Phantom, go for "the world's gold standard for luxury for over a century. For those who have set the highest standards for themselves, there is no more authentic reward than to drive a Rolls-Royce." This attitude of entitlement is closely intertwined with notions of class, but also with the value of individuality and our disdain for conformity. To this end, Audi of America's tagline is "Never follow." In its pitch for the Lincoln Town Car, Ford proposes that because the vehicle "rewards you with the essential luxury car experience," you will "move distinctively." If you own the Cayenne S Titanium Edition and lose it in the parking lot, one ad maintains, you will find that the new, "head-turning ad-dition" to the Porsche line of SUVs is so unique that "everyone can direct you to it."

At a special event before the opening of one major auto show, the Aston Martin display was surrounded by a glass enclosure with an entrance presided over by a beautiful young female gatekeeper. The scene produced the same kind of discomfiting insecurities and gnawing questions that the burgundy velvet rope at an exclusive nightclub can invoke. Passersby were left wondering how the select handful of people surveying the sexy British sports cars got inside the glass and who would be turned away.

When asked why America appears to have become an ever-growing market for new and grander vehicles, the advertising agency DDB's Gary Exelbert suggested something else is at work: the American spirit of com-petition is creating "this insatiability, this thirst to always want to outdo, always trying to be better and bigger" than the next guy. Nothing else could have explained the success of the Hummer in a 1990s car market al-ready flooded with oversized SUVs and trucks, he argued.

Even those not pulled in by a message of entitlement or driven to compete socially can succumb to the appeal of luxury once they are in the showroom. John, a father in his thirties, described how his usually prag-matic and frugal wife became quickly convinced to buy a minivan loaded with extras like heated leather seats, a 300-watt Bose sound system, and a DVD player. "And I'm looking at her thinking, this is not you," he said. But the couple happened to be in the showroom when the dealer was run-ning an aggressive year-end incentive program and ended up spending more for their minivan than they had intended. They got so much for their money, they thought, using the rationale of good value rather than that of good price to justify the buy. And they were already paying so much for the vehicle, why not pay just "a little" more to get a lot of lux-ury? John was not specific about how much they paid above what they originally budgeted; however, although he said they "can swing it," he added "it's a pretty tough nut to pay."

The value rationale is one echoed by many car buyers, and it can be a logical one: a cheap car can actually cost more to maintain. The truth is, though, that reliability is no longer a factor for the vast majority of vehicles being sold today. In fact, in 2006 J. D. Power and Associates reported that the gap in long-term quality between luxury and nonluxury vehicles had been cut in half over just the previous four years.[11] The decision to spend "a little" more, often made in a moment of heady exuberance or heavy pressure in the showroom, is rarely a practical one.

Automakers and dealers have encouraged Americans to take the value concept beyond the common sense from which it sprang into the realm of luxury, emotion, and rationalization. When productivity gains meant that it should have been cheaper than ever to manufacture a car, Americans were spending more and more for them as they piled on options and accessories and upgraded to more expensive models.

Consider Jason, a science teacher with a tremendous passion for cars. Interviewed in his classroom, he shared his love of cars, often gazing into the polished ebony lab tabletop and speaking in a hushed and thoughtful tone. Jason explained how, each time he buys a new car, the next car is always in his sights. There is always the car he thinks he can afford right now and the car he knows he really wants: his "halo car," as he dubs it, his current image of automotive perfection, one that is always just out of reach. He demonstrated this by taking us through his personal automotive history. When he bought his first car with money from his first job, it was an Infiniti G20, although it was the VW GTi he really wanted, and when he finally owned the GTi, he lusted for the BMW he couldn't yet afford. Now that he owns the BMW, it is the Porsche 911 he wants. In some sense, the 911 has always been Jason's Holy Grail.

The patient yearning in Jason's voice is similar to that of many others who say that their dream car is the car they've wanted ever since they could remember wanting a car. The Porsche 911 was Jason's very first Matchbox car, given to him by his father, along with the sales brochure from Porsche for the real thing, when he was just eight years old. He told us he can "very vividly remember how brilliantly exciting" this gift was and that he can still visualize himself being presented with it. While the Matchbox version sits on his bookshelf in his bedroom, it is Jason's "life goal" to own the real deal. "One day," he confidently asserted, "I will own it, God willing."

In ever desiring the next and better car, Jason is not unique. And he is the car industry's favorite kind of customer, always stretching for as much car as he can afford. Jason is fairly unusual, however, in the care he takes not to assume too much debt, and not to overspend on other things so that he can indulge his love of cars. Unfortunately, the advertising-desire spiral he illustrated, in which consumers trade in their cars for increasingly expensive vehicles, has proven financially disastrous for many American families.

While we may believe our car says something about who we are, we would benefit from thinking of it simply as a mode of transportation. Only then would we buy the car we really need and can really afford. Ultimately, our individuality is stripped away as we succumb to automakers' ideas about what and how much we need in a vehicle, many of which look quite a bit alike, and all of which have the same basic function of transportation. When we buy these cars, we think we are taking control by making well-researched choices, but we often ignore our research and bend to our emotional needs for attention, status, or power, and our desires to please our families or impress our friends—drives with which the auto industry is very familiar and which make it easier to sway or even swindle us at the point of purchase.

As we will see, because many of us are going into debt to buy a vehicle that we think says something about us, we are limiting our options for self-expression in other spheres. We must work hours and hours longer to pay for our cars, and we have fewer dollars and hours left to spend on other things that might make us happier or more fulfilled. The papers we are drawn to sign in the supercharged encounter in the car salesroom have eroded our financial security, put our ability to retire at risk, and helped plunge the nation's savings rate into its current deep well.

Chapter Five

THE CATCH

WHAT WE REALLY PAY

owena learned the hard way that owning a car is no simple matter. She grew up in northern California, in a happy if carless home with her young sister and their single mom, an immigrant from the Philippines. When Rowena graduated from college and got a steady job, she marveled to find that she could afford to lease her very own car. For just $199 a month, she was in a beautiful new Honda. Three years later, she was convinced to turn in the lease and buy a somewhat nicer car, one with "just $299" in monthly payments. When the car was repossessed a year later because she could not afford it, she figured she had given the dealer and the loan company over $15,000. She can't remember now how much she spent for insurance, gas, parking, and tickets during those four years, but she gasps when she does the math and figures it was probably about $12,000. Four years and a total of $27,000 later, she had no car, no savings, and ruined credit.

Rowena was surprised when she got into trouble because, like most Americans, she far underestimated the true cost of car ownership, and found car sellers less than eager to inform her of it.

ONE IN FIVE DOLLARS OUT THE TAILPIPE

Food, clothing, and shelter: we grow up learning this litany of the three essentials for supporting ourselves. But this trinity no longer represents the top costs of running a household. While housing remains the most expensive essential, transportation is now a close second. By 2003, it swallowed one in five dollars spent. That's in sharp contrast to 1960, when just one in ten family dollars went to transportation. Why such a difference? In part, it's because back then, communities were built in less sprawling style, public transportation was more available, cars were less expensive, and people were more likely to decide to walk to their destinations or put their children on the school bus.[1]

Medical care, on average, does not even compare as an economic burden. Health and food come third and fourth on the list of household expenses, and even combined they do not equal the cost of transportation.

But most Americans have a shaky sense of the scale of their car's impact on the household budget. Moreover, they tend to focus on gasoline prices, and perhaps repairs, but often take for granted significant fixed costs such as insurance and car loan payments, and ignore altogether the more invisible cost of depreciation and the tax burden that comes with a car-centered society.

The average price of a new vehicle in 2008 was $26,477.[2] Often, in the consumer's mind, once the car is driven home from the dealership, this cost is behind them. One woman contended that only one of her family's two cars constituted an expense to the household: "We paid for the BMW with cash, so I consider that paid for." But even if a car has not been financed, the costs of owning and using it just keep on coming. The U.S. Department of Energy reported that the typical American household drove its average two cars a total of about 22,000 miles per year.[3] Most recent estimates calculate that driving costs the average American 66 cents a mile, or almost $14,000 a year per family to drive their two cars over that distance.[4] Parking and tickets can add hundreds more.

The variation in car expenses among families can be great, depending on the number and size of cars they own, the miles they drive each year, and whether they live in a rural, urban, or suburban sprawl community.[5]

Cars driven more miles depreciate somewhat more rapidly, of course.[6] But there are not many other financial incentives, besides saving on gas, to drive less: toll roads are rare, most insurance companies and the tax man (in his role as the financier of infrastructure) charge the 1,000-mile-a-year driver just as much as the one who drives 30,000. One encouraging development, however, is the emergence of low-mileage insurance. The current system operates like all-you-can-eat restaurants: heavy users' driving risks and social costs are paid for by light users, and the system as a whole encourages more driving. Pay-as-you-drive insurance would save most households an average of $500 annually, according to a Brookings Institution economic analysis.[7]

Location is another big source of variation in car costs. Families in sprawled-out metropolitan areas such as Houston, Atlanta, or Phoenix spend roughly $1,300 more a year getting around than do those in more compact communities.[8] This difference has little to do with variation in the local prices of gasoline or car insurance. Instead it is the outcome of people having less public transit available and thus needing to drive longer distances, with the resulting higher costs of depreciation, gas, and repairs.[9]

Even when depreciation, car loans, gas, and other direct costs are added up, the full price tag for the family car still hasn't been tabulated. When buying homes, car owners in many parts of the country often look—and pay extra—for a garage with one or more bays. Half of the new homes sold in the Sacramento area in 2007, for example, included three-car or even four-car garages. To figure this into the family budget would involve costing out what proportion of a house's down payment, mortgage, property taxes, and maintenance goes into this portion of its square footage. A two-car garage can add $30,000 to the price of a house and account for 10 percent of the property tax bill.

The car is not only a major component of household spending, but its costs are often very unpredictable, giving families a sudden and painful financial kick in the shins. Surveys show that one in three Americans in the past year had "unexpected expenses that created financial trouble," or "seriously set them back" and, of those, fully one quarter was car-related.[10] While medical expenses outflanked the car in negative impact, people's cars created more unexpected financial trouble for them on average than their homes, children, or life events such as weddings and funerals.

A Brooklyn high school teacher described the breakdown of his Volkswagen, too expensive to fix, as one of a series of financial setbacks. "I was driving a VW and it died. The engine just basically came apart. Right now it's not a very good time economically for me to buy a car. I've been hit with a lot of big expenses this year, so we're just kind of going through a kind of rocky time economically, so buying a new car is probably not high on our list of priorities. In a normal year, where my finances were straight, I think I would be buying a car pretty much without hesitation." Both he and his teenage daughter described the car's role in getting them to family vacations as the toughest part of the loss. "We drove all the way to Canada and back in that car," the daughter added. "We took some great trips in that car. It was sad to see it go." They were lucky, though, to be able to fall back on New York City's excellent bus and subway systems for their day-to-day needs.

Middle-class families can have their budgets busted by the sudden need to put $1,600 into a new automatic transmission or by a $700 bill for a clutch replacement. In fact, the economic crash of 2008 and resulting job losses left many people unable to repair their cars. Several Rhode Island area shops reported the (at least temporary) abandonment of broken autos at their shops as struggling owners waited to somehow accumulate the needed money. Even in the best of times, many families have faced the financial risks of unexpected car repair as well as automobile collisions. We take these budget dangers for granted, dangers that are part of the more general phenomenon of the increasing privatization of risk in the United States, of which reliance on the private car rather than public transportation is but one example. When a train breaks down, passengers are inconvenienced, but the wider public will sustain the cost and the risk of its repair. When your car breaks down, you assume the risk individually.[11]

Most Americans see these expenses as inevitable and normal, but rarely do they think of them as dictatorial. While they note that we drive to work, less often do they recognize that we increasingly work to drive. Some teens jump into these expenses with both feet: one energetic young woman from New Jersey told how, to the pride of her family, she drove an hour and a half round-trip to a job every day after school and on Saturdays. Ironically, this is a job she took mainly to be able to buy gas and insurance for her car. Many would celebrate her determination, as well as that of the Connecticut teenager who took on five different small jobs to save for his first car. But the kudos these teens received were not as often matched by adult reminders that the car is a rapidly depreciating asset, expensive to own and use, as well as a financial risk that may suddenly entail a maintenance or deductible expense of hundreds or even thousands of dollars.

While plenty of Americans correctly see their car as a straight-out drain on their budgets rather than as bearing any resemblance to a stock or a savings account, many are encouraged and motivated to see their car as a wise place to invest money. Car salespeople often encourage this way of thinking: one Cadillac salesman was more ventriloquist than objective observer when he said his customers think about whether to pay more for a hybrid model by asking themselves, "Do I get a return on my investment?"

How is Jamie, a working-class man in his early forties, faring with his car investments? He bought a "2005 Ford F–250 Super Duty Pickup, extended cab" that he said cost him $48,000; he put down $9,500, and then took out a loan for the rest—"8.9 or 9.8 percent," he wasn't sure, but he does know he still owes $7,700. At first, Jamie thought he could afford the pickup; he was earning a good income driving big rigs. But then he lost his job, and, to try to make ends meet, he started driving a cab. But the ends were not meeting: he was having to decide whether to pay his child support or make his monthly truck payment. Jamie had purchased loan insurance, but at the time of his interview, he wasn't sure if it would pay out, given that he had gotten another job, never mind whether or not it paid much. His plan was to try to negotiate with the loan company; yet chances were good that his truck would soon be repossessed. Jamie knew how it would happen because he'd seen it on television, maybe on the mock reality show, *Operation Repo:* "They send somebody to come with a tow truck to spot your truck and hook it up," and it's "see you later." Ironically, he was hoping as a last-ditch effort to be able to pay off his remaining debt obligation with the settlement from a crash he'd had in a different vehicle.

Repossession is common and getting more so, but a multitude of families who haven't experienced the tow truck treatment live in fear of it, feeling the strong, sometimes extreme pressure that vehicles put on their monthly outflow. Only those who have not felt this strain can persist in believing that cars are a financial investment.

THE BALLOONING AMERICAN CAR LOAN

Cash savings as the route to major purchases is going the way of the polar ice caps. With the aggressive marketing of credit by all sorts by banks and stores, families are now more indebted than ever before in U.S. history.[12] Personal credit card debt alone averages $8,500 per family, and a typical family spends fully 20 percent of its earnings in interest payments, from which the financing institutions, including auto lenders, reap astounding profit.[13]

It was in fact the sale of cars on credit, introduced in the 1920s, that led the way in getting people used to the idea of buying things before they had the money to do so.[14] When consumer credit really began to take off, right after World War II, car loans contributed the major part of the twenty-fold increase in indebtedness from 1945 to 1960.[15] By 1955, 60 percent of car sales were on credit, and today, relatively few people purchase new cars straight out with cash.

The amounts of debt that households carry to own a car can be staggering. Auto debt has skyrocketed due to dealer offers of "zero interest and no money down," pushing up the average amount financed for a new car purchase to nearly $25,000 in 2009. That amount, until the recession of 2008, was 95 percent of the total cost of the car. With the recession, worried dealers and creditors began to demand somewhat larger down payments from their buyers, but even then the amount financed was an average of 88 percent of the car's cost.[16] The average monthly payment for new car buyers in 2009 was about $470, or $5,640 a year. Given that most households have at least two cars, a family's yearly car payments alone (before gas, insurance, etc.) can easily total $8,000 or more.

Lenders have extended car loans from an average of three- or four-year terms in the early 1990s to six- and even seven-year terms today. The loan period has increased for a number of reasons: one is that car prices have risen beyond the means of many, as real incomes have dropped or remained stagnant while other costs have risen. Despite 80 percent productivity growth in the United States since 1973, 90 percent of American workers' wages dropped in that same period by 11 percent in inflation-controlled dollars.[17] New car prices have risen by 23 percent since 1980, taking inflation into account, while used car prices declined in inflation-controlled dollars in the same period. [18] Loan periods now average more than five years—due to the strenuous efforts of car manufacturers and dealers to get people into their more expensive models, and as consumers come to regard people at ever-higher income levels as their status reference group.[19] As one marketing analyst put it, "Thanks to the credit card and boilerplate leases on big-ticket items, you can have just what the millionaire next door has. Not the money but the stuff."[20]

With these longer-term loans, increasing numbers of car owners now find themselves in the "upside down" position—the new term for a car whose current retail value is less than the amount its owner still owes to a lending company. Over one-third of people trading in their cars in 2004 to buy new ones found themselves upended in this way, owing *more* than the car was worth.[21] The solution for many is to simply fold their old debt into a new car loan, either increasing their debt burden or getting less car for the same amount of monthly outlay.

When Peter, a Boston construction worker, was asked how much his current car cost, he answered "$400." That, of course, was not the $22,000 price of the Saturn he bought new in 2003, but the monthly payment that he makes on it. Peter's thinking about car costs is typical, a habit of reasoning that he and other Americans have acquired from the car dealers who often begin by asking them how much they can afford a month and working it out from there. A writer for Edmunds.com who went undercover to take sales jobs in several car dealerships reports that he was advised in each place to begin by asking buyers how much they could afford to pay each month and to then ask "and up to . . . ?" He was also taught to keep drawing potential buyers' attention to that monthly payment figure, which makes it much harder to keep track of how much one is actually paying for the car overall.

A recent innovation in the car loan business, designed to eke more profit from the millions of annual borrowers, is the bimonthly loan. For "just" a $399 "enrollment fee" (split among the dealership, the loan company, and the salesperson), a buyer can take his monthly car payment, split it in half, and pay every two weeks. Paying twice every 28 rather than once every 30 or 31 days means you end up making one additional payment each year, paying your loan off sooner. Theoretically this is a good thing for consumers, allowing them to become debt-free more quickly, but because most buyers trade in their cars well before their loan expires, many will still end up being upside down when they close out the loan. One salesman promoting this loan repayment program in the Midwest drives 45,000 miles a year going from dealer to dealer, where he is finding the job a relatively easy sell given that the dealer gets additional money up front and given how many buyers are "payment thinkers" for whom two $198 bills look better, somehow, than one $399 payment per month, even though the annual payment total will be larger with the biweekly system, and the total interest paid no smaller an amount.

Ellen Stark, former senior editor at the personal finance magazine *Money*, notes that when real estate values rose sharply in the 1990s and 2000s, many people began "dipping into the piggybank of home equity" to finance cars they couldn't afford. Further, while many Americans are making too little to save, there are many who could, but don't, make maximum contributions to their 401(k)s or contribute to IRAs. Because "they'd rather have stuff now than save for later," as Stark said, the personal savings rate of Americans dropped dramatically from the double digits in the 1980s to eventually turn negative in April 2005 for the first time since 1933.[22] As a nation we now live beyond our income, and we are led there in some large part by car spending.

The crash of 2008 has undermined the faith of many Americans in the stock market, and the collapse of home prices has wiped out much of the equity that had been the route to car ownership for a good number of people. The alternative of saving rather than borrowing to buy a car now looks more attractive and sensible than ever.

OIL OBSESSIONS: OUR UNDUE FOCUS ON GAS PRICES

The majority of car costs are in depreciation and loan interest, yet most owners continue to focus on the price of gas. This is partly because the price of gas has been rising so fast: it tripled in a decade, from $1.16 a gallon in 1998 to over $4.00 in 2008, and after dropping sharply, crept up again.[23] People's attention is riveted on gas prices because they are so visible as people drive up to the pump. Imagine, though, if cars came equipped with a "depreciation gauge" that told the owner, each time he or she turned on the car in the morning, how much less it was worth than the day before. Or what would happen to our sense of the burden of car insurance if we had to drive up to an agent's storefront every week or so to hand over $50 to insure the family cars.

Instead, consumers see only those ever-changing numbers above the pump, and ask why. Many see price hikes as the result of gouging by the local gas station owner or by the oil corporations. Others focus on the foreign countries that they see as setting an exorbitant price on each barrel of oil. Still others see the price as a natural market mechanism, reflecting the iron laws of supply and demand, with demand inexorably climbing along with economic growth in India, China, and at home. But to GM spokesperson Tom Wilkinson, the breathtaking gas price volatility of the past few years acts as a barometer of national and personal security. Suddenly spiking gas prices created great anxiety "because of the uncertainty. I don't think a lot of people believed energy prices could move so much and so quickly. People think we're big Americans, we're ruling the war in the Middle East, there's no way we can be harmed. When gas hit $4, I think it was a realization that things are fundamentally changing in this world, and it set off a huge panic attack. 'If gas can go up that far that fast, what else is going on that I should be worrying about?' . . . It's just part of a realization that we can't control everything going on in our lives. . . . It seems like it's just the sense that life has gone off its axis, and nobody knows what to do about it."

What people imagine as a sensible solution to high gas prices is also quite variable. The *New York Times* reported in 2007 that, in response to the rising cost of gasoline, hundreds of thousands of families had bought new, smaller cars, including hybrids such as the Toyota Prius and high-mpg vehicles like the Honda Civic.[24] However, many were not replacing their SUVs or other low-mileage cars, but simply adding them to the two cars already in their driveways. As a result, the new car's depreciation, loan interest, and insurance charges more than ate up whatever gas savings they achieved. Other, less affluent families are driving fewer miles, or reducing the speed at which they drive in order to save on gas. Mainly, though, they are spending less on other things, including vacations, clothing, and gifts, in order to continue to have gas for their cars.

Those intent on remaining in light trucks and sports vehicles have been drawn like moths around the new hybrid SUVs, which have suddenly appeared on offer from almost every automaker. Many customers talk of better gas mileage as their prime motive for buying one of these hybrids, not environmental concerns. But hybrid SUVs cost thousands more than their nonhybrid versions and much more than a more gas-efficient sedan, while still only getting miles per gallon in the low or mid-20s.

Chevrolet, for example, began selling a hybrid version of its Tahoe SUV. At $52,000 fully loaded, it is nearly $13,000 more than its all-gas twin and is rated at 21 city and 22 highway mileage, compared with the regular Tahoe at 14 city and 19 highway. A buyer would have to drive many years on $4 a gallon gas to make up the price difference, and would still not have accounted for higher insurance, depreciation, taxes, and other expenses, minus tax rebates, for that higher-priced hybrid. Many SUV drivers refuse to consider the more fuel-efficient options out there, such as the Honda Fit station wagon, rated at 27 city and 34 highway, or the hybrid sedans, which can get as much as 50 miles or more per gallon. When asked why they need an SUV, people mention their dog, their twins and twin strollers, the snowy winters of Vermont or Utah, or their desire to tow their boat to a lake in the summer. Some will admit to other concerns: women who say they like the power of being "high up," or men who explain that their SUV shows their outdoorsy side to the women they date.

These consumers will pay more for the hybrid erroneously thinking this price premium will be offset by gas savings, allowing them to retain their SUV ride in a world that seems to be going green.

The automakers happily enable this thinking. Vigorous green-washing and promotion of gas mileage improvements were everywhere in evidence at the 2008 and 2009 auto shows, where the Cadillac Provoq concept car, based on hydrogen fuel cell technology, sat up on a green carpeted dais. Emerald neon lights and flat-screen forests provided virtuous backlighting to the 22-mpg hybrid SUVs and heavy horsepower alternative-fuel sedans. Despite this spectacle, each technological innovation to raise gas mileage in recent years has been offset by the production of heavier, greater-horse-power, high-tech fleets. The result is a household budget—and environ-mental—burden that remains the same or worsens each year.

When it comes to the cost of gas, a variable more important than pump prices is how much you drive and how far you live from work, and as a result, how *much* gas you use each week. As Americans have decided where to live and work over the last decades, they have made trade-offs be-tween shorter commutes from more expensive houses closer to urban or suburban jobs and longer drives from cheaper suburban or exurban devel-opments. People increasingly made the latter choice with the boom in housing prices of the 1990s and 2000s, particularly when the price of gas remained low. Some people overextended themselves financially in both directions, however, by taking on larger homes and mortgages in the ex-urbs and an expensive long commute in an SUV.

These individual household budget choices are part of the giant set of feedback loops between the price of oil, the price of housing, and national gasoline consumption rates and commuting lengths. As Michael T. Klare, an expert on resources and international conflict, has argued, the combi-nation of cheap oil and rising housing prices, plus the failure to regulate Detroit's fuel efficiency and the heavy marketing of gas-guzzling SUVs and trucks, resulted in a rise of petroleum consumption from 17 million bar-rels a day in 1990 to 21 million barrels in 2004.[25] When oil prices shot up from under $20 a barrel at the end of 2001 to over $100 a barrel just six years later, and banks raised their interest rates, this helped burst the hous-ing bubble, cut dramatically into people's ability to buy new cars, and helped push the country into recession. What became unsustainable on the household level became unsustainable for the nation as a whole. The result is what Klare identifies as "a massive, irreversible shift in wealth and power from the United States to the petro-states of the Middle East and energy-rich Russia." Those countries collectively took in $750 billion in oil revenues in 2007, much of it from Americans at the pump, from Davenport, Iowa, to Binghamton, New York.

Gas prices grab the most attention and generate the fiercest agitation at least in part, it seems, because we have come to think of gas as a birthright and a necessity. Like water, it should flow easily and cheaply, as it has long done. More consumers have come to understand the concept of peak oil— that world reserves are finite and that production may have already reached or will soon reach a peak and begin to fall. They have also heard or read extensive news reports about the rise of demand in China and India. Yet they also tend to believe it should be a top national policy priority to keep oil economical. Cheap oil is still valued more highly than environmental preservation, reduced traffic congestion, or breathable air.

Drivers differ on whether keeping their tanks full requires repealing gas taxes or investigating price gouging or drilling in the wilds of the Arctic National Wildlife Refuge (ANWR) in Alaska. The assumption reigns, though, that something could and should be done to control that price. Two gray-templed brothers from New York we interviewed argued that there is currently plenty of oil for our cars, and to get it the nation should just drill in ANWR. They are more than ready to jump into an electric car, though—if priced no higher than a gas-fueled car—in order to be able to continue to drive economically as gas prices predictably rise again in the future. But they sharply contrasted their rationale and identity to what they call "the greenies": "I'm not going to buy a hybrid to save the world," one of them scoffed. Of one environmentalist leader, he noted, "Ted Kennedy is a hypocrite: he's against the wind farms off Cape Cod."

In the shadows remain the many other routes to less expensive driving: more durable cars and tires, more affordable insurance, higher fuel efficiency standards, and better land use planning. Carpooling, public transit, doing multiple errands on a single trip ("trip chaining"), and shopping online rather than schlepping back and forth to the mall have all, until recently, seemed inconvenient, unreasonable, or unrealistic. Such cost-saving options have not been up for public discussion in part because the world of cars, insurance, and solo driving—the car world as currently organized—just seems normal, timeless, and unchangeable. The car and all its entailments are not like a cup of latte or a night out for dinner. As driver after driver reiterated, cars are viewed as a necessity: one has to drive to work, to shop, and to take children to school. Mammoth car expenses are accepted as the unavoidable price of the freedom the car is imagined to provide.

Rising gas prices can and have trimmed the amount of driving people do, but when those prices drop, it is expected that people will "naturally" return to driving more miles and buying cars that gulp more gas. In fact, the car system continues to set up incentives for the purchase of gas, despite rising or volatile prices. This has everything to do with the power of the oil industry and trends in suburban and exurban real estate development. However, the severe economic downturn and the financial unsustainability of exurban mortgages and commuting may be the first "good news"—at least in terms of balancing household transportation budgets—to arrive in a while. They just might result in the reduction of some of these transit costs over the longer-term.

THE HIGH COST OF CRASHING AND CONGESTING

Hundreds of thousands of people each year are involved in car crashes. The ensuing costs can range from a simple $500 deductible for a fender-bender with no injuries to bankruptcy or the loss of a home resulting from an un- or underinsured crash that permanently disables a parent and unleashes a torrent of medical bills and legal fees, all in the face of lost wages. The National Safety Council estimates the average cost of a crash in 2001 was $1,040,000 for a fatal crash (including lost wages and productivity and property damage) and $36,500 for just the medical expenses for the average injury, expenses that are much higher for lifelong care of the severely injured.[26]

The total annual cost to the nation of automobile crashes has been estimated at up to $433 billion.[27] This includes medical costs, property losses, emergency services, rehabilitation, legal costs, and lost productivity. About one-quarter of overall crash costs fall on individual families to pay, while the remaining three-quarters comes from the public at large through their taxes, insurance premiums, and higher costs for health care.[28] Striking numbers of Americans each year incur steep medical bills from car crashes, despite being what is considered "fully insured." One 1998 study conducted by Congress found that, on average, crash victims whose medical and car repair bills were between $25,000 and $100,000 were reimbursed just over half of those costs, while those whose costs topped $100,000 recouped less than one-tenth of their total bill from their car insurance.[29] While Medicare and Medicaid sometimes step in to make up some of the difference, for many, the crash becomes the beginning of a descent into deep indebtedness.

Job loss after a serious crash is also common. Wendy Colletti's car crash story, which appeared in the *New York Times,* began in 2000, when the car she was riding in was hit from behind by a van towing a trailer. The force sent her into the dashboard, shattering her knee and damaging her spine. Taking multiple sick days from her position at an equipment leasing company and weekend waitressing job, she was soon fired. Three years and multiple surgeries later, she was still in a struggle over the medical bills with her insurance company, with which she has a no-fault policy. She had by then reached the point of not having paid her gas and electric bills for several months, and ended up, like many others with car crashes as part of their tales of woe, on the *Times*'s "Neediest Cases" list.

To the costs of crashing must be added the ramifying costs of congestion. The Texas Transportation Institute, in a 2007 study, calculated the total cost to business of traffic jams in America's major urban areas. It found the bill for lost time/lower productivity and excess fuel consumed was $78 billion annually, and that was almost double what it had been just over a decade earlier.[30] In addition, businesses absorb other car-related costs, including dealing with turnover for those who burn out on long commutes and providing parking for workers. A parking garage engineer's informed estimate of the cost to construct and maintain a single parking spot in an urban garage is about $19,500 a space.[31] These costs are passed on in higher prices to consumers or lower wages to workers. In some cases, traffic costs have led businesses to leave a community altogether, taking jobs and tax dollars with them.

Families, like businesses, are bleeding cash on the highways. In 2005, commuters in urban areas lost a total of 4.2 billion hours and plenty of fuel to traffic delays.[32] In addition, for almost everything a family buys—from food to toys to clothing—prices are higher because of the cost of transporting those goods to your local store through traffic-choked roads.

THE TAX AND SPEND EXEMPTION

While most of us could, if pressed to dig through our receipts, quantify the high cost of car purchase or lease, insurance, repair and maintenance, and gasoline, or see what happens to our savings after a car crash, a good number of the total dollars drained from household budgets by the automobile are hidden in our tax bills. Each year, massive outlays of tax money go toward road construction and maintenance, bridge repair, police to monitor drivers, first responders to rush to and clean up crashes, and traffic management equipment and maintenance. While some of these public monies have already come out of the pockets of drivers through gas taxes and tolls, parking tickets, and vehicle registration and license fees, some come from additional charges to the general public (whether drivers or not) through local property and sales taxes, special bond issues, and general tax funds.

Over and above this, the average household pays additional taxes to refill public coffers emptied by federal subsidies to the auto, insurance, and oil and gas industries, and for environmental cleanup of car-related pollution. The first, most visible such subsidy was the Chrysler bailout of 1979, with federal loan guarantees worth $3.8 billion in today's dollars. Today's economic climate has once again led the government to subsidize the floundering American auto industry: as of May 2009, General Motors and Chrysler had been given a total of $30 billion in bailout funds.[33] An additional 2009 federal program (dubbed "Cash for Clunkers") was intended to benefit the car industry by subsidizing thousands of dollars of the purchase price of a new auto for qualifying owners of older, lower-mpg vehicles.[34] The oil and gas industry has historically received massive tax breaks as well, with $3.6 billion in tax incentives received in 2005, according to the Government Accountability Office.[35] In addition to the tax breaks are reductions in the royalty payments that the oil and gas industry are charged to drill on public land, and industry research and development subsidies, which together add another $6 billion a year to the public financial burden.[36]

Where do the tax dollars go, exactly? First there are roads and bridges. At all levels of government, a total of $74 billion was spent in 1999 on road construction and maintenance.[37] Despite a large and somewhat successful effort by the transportation reform movement to reorient spending priorities (for example, to grow public transit, put repair of existing roads before new highway building, and to create pedestrian-friendly communities) and their demonstration that community economic prosperity is enhanced by better public transit systems, there continues to be relatively scant funding for it.[38] These reformers are drawing attention to how much and how many kinds of local expenses could be eliminated or reallocated with less car dependence. Businesses would benefit from lowered costs resulting from a reduction in the road delays that slow workers and deliveries; from improvements to poor freight rail systems and connections to other modes of transit; as well as from lowered taxes due to reduced government spending.

A large portion of an individual community's budget often comprises wages for local firefighters who act as first responders to crash sites, police who manage traffic and parking, and public works personnel who keep up the roads. One study found that 40 percent of Denver's police activities, 15 percent of its fire department deployments, and 16 percent of its paramedic services are centered on automobiles.[39] And it is not just those police specifically devoted 24/7 to traffic departments who spend their time and energies on managing the flow, theft, and crashing of vehicles. As one retired New Jersey officer put it, "Every police officer on routine patrol is technically doing traffic enforcement because they are expected to enforce the law and stop anyone they observe breaking it." He went on to explain that most officers in any department spend at least part of their day dealing with crashes and violations. In more affluent communities around the country, some police officers are used just to manage the high volume of cars navigating around buses and each other to bring children to and from school each day.

Public works is another car-centered area of local government expense. The city of Sacramento, California, for example, budgeted $33 million for parking services and street maintenance in 2006.[40] In addition, traffic lawsuits, judicial actions, and the incarceration of perpetrators of DUI and other major traffic violations together put $11 billion annually onto local tax bills across the nation.[41]

Like spending on the military, spending on roads has remained one of the few federal budget items to avoid the chopping block with the rush to downsize government and turn its functions over to the market since the 1980s. Road spending was a key element of the stimulus spending rushed through after the economic crisis that began in 2008.

It is a rare public figure who suffers if he or she pushes for more spending on roads. In 2005, members of Congress were able to bring their districts more than $10 billion in transportation pork in the form of earmarks to the transportation bill, the vast majority for highways and roads. (This was the year former senator Ted Stevens brought home millions for Alaska's notorious "Bridge to Nowhere."[42]) With much profit to be taken by entrenched interests in the asphalt, construction, and engineering industries, spending has only increased over time. For example, Boston's Big Dig (begun in 1991) became the single most expensive civil engineering project in U.S. history, at almost $2 billion per mile of tunnel and highway. Its main contractor, engineering corporation Bechtel, managed to glean $180 million in profits for its work.

Even this vigorous spending on highways has not been adequate. Periodic bridge and road collapses due to poor maintenance—and regular trips for car repairs and tire alignment after driving along potholed streets—are reminders of the government's tendency to buy new roads before repairing existing ones. Current estimates are that a quarter of U.S. bridges are "structurally deficient or functionally obsolete" and a third of our major roads are in mediocre or poor condition. A huge bill is about to come due: anywhere from $155 to $375 billion, it is estimated, will be needed for their repair.[43] In reaction to this, California, as well as some localities in other states, announced an intention to end new highway construction and focus instead on maintenance, repair, and alternative solutions.

THESE GAS PRICES ARE KILLING ME

In a conversation about the tax dollars that go to maintaining the auto way of life, the true elephant in the room is not the local first responders' salaries or even the high price tag of bridge fixes, but the financial and human cost of using a giant military apparatus to secure access to cheap oil to fill our tanks. Successive U.S. administrations have regularly sent the U.S. military to wield a sword or offer the carrot of arms deals and military training to governments sitting on oil reserves. Major oil producers in the Middle East, Latin America, and elsewhere tend to appear high on the list of countries receiving military aid. An oil-for-protection arrangement with Saudi Arabia was first worked out by Franklin Roosevelt in 1945, and continues through today. In 2007, for example, Saudi Arabia received a $20 billion package including high-tech satellite-guided bombs and fighter jet upgrades (with the entailment, to placate Israel, of multibillion-dollar increases in military aid to that country).[44]

It is difficult to calculate precisely how much the military budget could shrink if it stopped being deployed to ensure that we have plenty of gasoline. This is not only because the military and its spending are so vast and shrouded in secrecy, but also because debate swirls as to what other strategic goals, along with access to oil or control of oil prices, we might be pursuing simultaneously with the same funding. Nonetheless, a number of economists have tried. By some calculations, 10 to 25 percent of the annual military budget—at $700 billion in 2009—should be allocated to the line item of oil resource control.[45]

These figures represent just a fraction of the actual cost of this oil protection service to the nation, as economists Linda Bilmes and Nobel Prize–winner Joseph E. Stiglitz demonstrated in their study of the eventual total costs of the Iraq War.[46] They put its price tag at $3 trillion, a cost that figures in the macroeconomic effects of international insecurity and higher oil prices, lifetime disability payments to veterans wounded in the war, the economic costs of withdrawal of the civilian labor of the National Guard and Reserve, the lost economic productivity of those who died (the notorious VSL or "value of statistical life"), and the health care costs for the tens of thousands of soldiers with such serious injuries as brain damage, blindness, burns, nerve damage, disfigurement, and post traumatic stress.[47]

Many Americans who were reluctant to believe back in 2003 that the invasion of Iraq had anything to do with oil now say that our involvement in the Middle East is motivated by the desire to keep oil flowing our way.[48] One middle-class New Yorker named Lars reasoned that we couldn't have gone to save the Iraqi people from tyranny because, in his view, Americans don't feel as culturally connected to Middle Easterners as they do to Europeans, on whose behalf they fought in World War II. So, he said, other than oil, "I don't know how else you can explain our interest in the Middle East. We wouldn't have gone there if there weren't a huge economic imperative."

Many are frustrated that the strategy backfired. Said one politically moderate man, "It's clear that the current system and the policies that the policy makers have clung to have engendered these kinds of fuel prices, with the fact that the first Gulf War and the second Gulf War are pretty much—let's cut to the chase—about making sure that the U.S. has access to cheap oil. But now that things are getting bogged down there, the repercussions are sort of a backlash and it looks like we are paying what is actually closer to the actual cost of a gallon of gasoline than we have been for many, many years." This man, like many other Americans, focuses on the failure of the government's plan to control oil, but unlike many others, he understands gas prices have been artificially depressed in the past.

Even more compelling is what the people sent to fight the war have to say about this. When asked why the United States was in Iraq, one war veteran from the Bronx responded, "It's obviously some economic gain. And the only thing that I can think of that is logical is to police the oil. If we police the oil and we can have some type of ownership—whether it's actual ownership or just as far as a contract with the new regime there, or the new administration in Iraq—then we can secure the wealth that the oil creates, and pretty much own the global economy, you know?" A wide range of opinions exists in the military, according to polls as well as to one Army National Guard medic from New Jersey, Pat Resta, who was there. "Especially as a medic, I would rotate through units, and one day I would be in a unit where there was this really conservative Republican guy from North Carolina, and he was there to liberate people. And a couple weeks later, I'm in a unit from Cleveland, Ohio, and they're talking about how this war's B.S. and it's about oil. It was kind of weird to go back and forth."

The war has prompted Americans—civilians as well as soldiers—from across the political spectrum to speak of their wish to escape from "dependence on foreign oil." While most of the problems caused by the car system—debt, inequality, pollution, and fatalities—persist whatever the national origin of the oil that fuels our cars, the public's recognition of the connection between oil and the costs of preparing for war or supporting dictatorial petroleum-exporting regimes represents a hopeful step forward.

ALTERNATIVE HOME ECONOMICS

America's household budgets are already groaning under the weight of their cars. In a lifetime of, say, fifty years of car ownership, an American family will likely spend almost $1 million on its vehicles.[49] And those are only the dollars that go directly to the car dealer, gas pump, garage, and insurance agent. Add the more invisible and sometimes externalized costs of taxes, crashes, and traffic. Take a deep breath and then add the costs of the wars and arms dealing to secure oil, and the coming health and environmental cleanup costs.[50] The total rivals anything we as a society take on as a task or goal.

A small but growing number of families in the United States are determined to spend less or even nothing on cars. There are some, including the quite wealthy, who wisely see this as a route to greater retirement savings. Journalist and personal finance expert Ellen Stark argues that short of downsizing to a smaller house or apartment, taking control of spending on cars is the single most effective and painless way Americans can trim debt and save for retirement. A young American family who might spend that $1 million over the course of their lifetime could cut this in half by buying cheaper cars, used cars, or fewer cars, driving far fewer miles, and investing the rest, building a nest egg. When *Money* magazine profiles smart investors, Stark said, these individuals invariably own and drive older cars, resisting the lure of the latest and greatest vehicle. Stark lives the gospel that the magazine she long worked for preaches and remains the proud owner of a 1993 Buick LeSabre.

This strategy can be taken even further, for financial as well as environmental reasons. Art Ludwig is the owner of a small environmental business in the mountains near Santa Barbara, California. He is not a fan of the car, joking that he has long imagined a sequel to *Guns, Germs, and Steel,* the best-selling account of the rise of modernity by Jared Diamond: it would be called *Nuclear Weapons, TV, and Cars.* Because he categorizes the car as a liability rather than an asset, and because he focuses on separating out the ownership versus operational costs of the auto, his family has one car, very old and rarely used. When he sees a new car, he says, "all I can hear is tick, tick, tick" as the car ages and loses value. Over the years, he and his wife have put their money instead into their home, which as a result is much more luxurious than the homes of other people in their income bracket. They plan on drawing on their home equity to help pay tuition when their two young children are ready to go to college.

To really understand what Americans pay and what they forego to own a car, however, we need to take a detour through a diverse set of the nation's neighborhoods, because while all men and women may be created equal according to our political ideals, the American automobile discriminates between us based on whether it's parked in the driveway of a double-wide trailer, a middle-class bungalow, or a gated mansion.

Chapter Six

THE CATCH
THE RICH GET RICHER

"Only one reason buses have such big, wide windows," insists Anthony, a character played by rapper Ludacris in 2005's Oscar winner *Crash*. "To humiliate the poor brothers reduced to riding in them." Anthony voices something understood by poor urbanites—many, people of color—and by the 10 percent of the country's population who are carless. Americans living without a car, especially in sprawling communities with weak public transportation, face limited mobility, restricted job options, more expensive goods and services, and, as Ludacris's character sharply points out, a powerful stigma in a car-based society.

However, it is not just lack of a car, but car ownership itself, that is helping to make the poor poorer and the rich richer. This established but little-known truth rubs against the conventional wisdom that owning a car is positive by definition, generating not obstacles but opportunities. But the average costs of owning and using a car do not tap all budgets equally. Although the rich buy newer and more luxe cars, their expenditures on them represent a far smaller portion of their household budgets. And the poor and working class pay much more than the well-to-do for the same cars and automotive services.

The car system redistributes wealth upward, magnifying inequality in the United States. How exactly does it do this? In three critical ways. First, people in poor, carless households often face extreme difficulty in getting and keeping employment because it is challenging for them simply to get from their homes to available jobs. Second, working- and middle-class people are being held back from economic advancement or pushed further into debt through car ownership. Cars are an expensive and depreciating asset for which there remains pervasive discrimination in pricing and financing. What these first two factors mean is that the poor can't live without the car and they can't live with it. Third, at the same time, the car consolidates and elevates the status of the wealthy. Some of the very wealthiest families in the nation are or have been the beneficiaries of the auto industry, or of windfall gasoline and banking profits reaped from the car- and gasoline-buying public.

SOCIAL AUTO-MOBILITY: THE CAR'S INFLUENCE ON RISING INEQUALITY

For the first several decades after World War II, the United States was a country with a large and relatively comfortable middle class. The rising tide of affluence in those years lifted most boats, and economic measures showed slow gains in levels of equality until the mid-1970s. For a variety of reasons—most of them having to do with public policy changes initiated during the Reagan years, related declines in the strength of unions, and the oil shocks of the early 1970s—this began to change. The idea of a government safety net for those excluded from a living wage was shredded by the notion that the market would more efficiently solve such problems. Wages and benefits for the working and middle class flattened or declined, corporate profits rose, and CEO salaries went through the roof: where the ratio of the highest- and lowest-paid workers in the United States was 50 to 1 in 1965, it was 800 to 1 by 2005.[1]

In the process, the fundamental social contract between government, business, and American workers was radically changed. Wal-Mart became the largest corporation in the country, and its mostly minimum-wage, no-benefits, nonunion workforce gradually took the place of the iconic auto industry workers and their high wages, pensions, and union protections. As anthropologist Jane Collins has pointed out, "If Henry Ford paid his workers well so they could afford to buy his cars, Wal-Mart pays its employees so badly that they can only afford to shop at Wal-Mart."[2] The question became whether the giant retailer's employees could afford to buy tires, much less the car to put them on.

The rise in inequality has been such that by 2004, the wealthiest 5 percent of the country owned nearly 60 percent of household wealth. Median family income, controlling for inflation, has been going down as the share of income by people at the very top goes up. And with personal savings disappearing and debt rising, that wilting standard of living means the majority of families cannot experience even small setbacks without falling further behind or even into bankruptcy and homelessness.

Many Americans do not see a problem with this kind of wealth and income inequality in the abstract, even when it is pointed out that the United States is now a more unequal nation than India and is an outlier from most other modern industrial countries such as Japan or France. In part, this is because, as one poll showed, a large number of them believe they got the lucky end of the stick: forty percent of Americans either think they are in the richest one percent or expect to be there in a few years.[3] Almost as if they are choosing to believe that the nation still enjoys the relative equality of its past, the majority of other citizens label themselves middle class, including some people whose incomes put them either far above or far below the median.[4] The real story of a tiny upper class and a majority struggling to meet expenses[5]—and of how the last decades' massive transfer of wealth up the class ladder is tied into the car system—is barely understood.

When it comes to the car, a snapshot of growing inequality looks like this: there are now outfits that rent, yes, *rent*, tires to the poor who cannot come up with the $200 or so they need to replace their tires in order to pass state inspection. And there are luxury car dealerships in nearby zip codes that do a brisk business in $200,000 Bentleys.

It is not just the poorest Americans whose downward mobility is accelerated by the car system. For the great majority of Americans, owning a car can be a financially draining experience. This is the striking conclusion provided by the U.S. Department of Labor. Its consumer spending data shows that transportation costs take a hungry 15 to 28 percent bite out of household budgets in all but the top one-fifth of households by income, and a proportionally bigger chomp the further down the income scale one lives.[6]

TO BE POOR AND CARLESS IN
THE UNITED STATES OF AUTOMOBILES

A relative handful of people are carless by choice. They mainly live in compact cities where walking and public transit usually can get them anywhere they need to go. Most of the carless, however, are America's poor—families who are destitute and simply cannot afford to buy a car, not even a clunker, and the gas, tires, and insurance needed to get it on the road.

The consequences of not having a car in a society built around it can be devastating. First, for many, no car means no job. The poor often live in rural areas or inner city neighborhoods far from the areas where jobs are now most plentiful, in the suburban rings. There are many people like Andrew, a recent high school graduate from a working-class neighborhood in Providence, Rhode Island. Lacking a car and the thousands of dollars needed to break in to the market for one, even at the entry level for a beater, he lamented: "I was offered an assistant manager position at Circuit City [in a nearby suburb], but I couldn't accept the job because I had no way to get up there." While in some states it is illegal to ask an applicant whether he or she has a car, prospective employers often pose the question anyway. They may do so because they are afraid the applicant won't show up reliably to work or because the car is a work tool, as for pizza delivery. Having a car is also often essential for starting a small business; so, to be carless is to be denied access to that important route to the American Dream.

The growth of big-box shopping around the suburban ring also allows those with a car to pay less for groceries and other necessities. By contrast, the absence of supermarkets in many poor inner-city neighborhoods and the paucity of fresh food and exorbitant prices in the stores located there add to the financial and health costs of being simultaneously carless and poor.

Medical care is also more difficult for the poor to find without a car. Beth Adler, health service program coordinator at Boston Medical Center, is just one of many professionals around the country working to get health care to the indigent. Even in Boston, which has one of the best public transit systems in the country, being carless can mean being two hours away from a medical appointment. While the city has a van service that can pick up patients and get them to medical offices, clinics, or hospitals, "the person or their health-care provider has to take the time to call, be put on hold, and ask for a transportation request form to be faxed to them, fill it out, and then fax it back"—assuming that they can even get access to a fax machine. Her clients engage, she said, in a "cost-benefit analysis" before deciding to get care or follow up on it. A several-hour trip to the doctor, even if the cost of the treatment itself were free, might leave an hourly worker without enough money for food, rent, or utilities. Adler also pointed out that if she is writing a grant to fund a health program, budgeting in transportation doubles the cost. A donor who may have $25,000 for her program will balk at the $50,000 needed to finance both the services and the mobility to get people to the services.

A variety of organizations, from individual churches sprinkled across the country to national programs such as the Milwaukee, Wisconsin–based Ways to Work, are striving to make cars more affordable for the poor. At the same time, environmental activists have recently been pointing out that the poor are the greenest among us. As consumers of less of everything, including cars and gasoline, and the heaviest users of public transit, their behaviors and impact should be celebrated. While *Crash*'s Anthony is right—there remains a stigma to riding the bus in most cases—that shame could and should be transformed into pride in being environmentally responsible citizens. The ultimate goal should be to create more equality of opportunity without making additional car-dependence part of the solution.

THE WORKING POOR: ONE PAYCHECK AWAY FROM CARLESS

One step up from these poorest households cut off from jobs, health care, and reasonably priced goods are the working poor or near poor who, by rough estimate, include about 50 million Americans. These are individuals with low-wage jobs without benefits and families with two minimum- or low-wage earners. The near poor are those who, as Katherine Newman, an expert on poverty and mobility, has said, are "one paycheck, one lost job, one divorce or one sick child away from falling below the poverty line."[7] They are one car repair or car crash away from poverty as well.

These families usually buy their cars used and often at inflated prices and on expensive credit. Gasoline alone can take a double-digit percentage of their income. They may drive with a broken windshield or a spare tire permanently on one wheel or they may periodically be without use of the car when it breaks down because they cannot afford the repairs. Parking tickets can push a person living on the edge out of automobility: a study of nondrivers in Milwaukee found that most of them lost their licenses or registrations due to unpaid traffic fines rather than for serious moving violations.[8] In traffic court in Providence, Rhode Island, a large number of cases involve unpaid fines on cars needing repairs. As one of the defendants, a young Hispanic man in his early thirties, explained to the judge: "I received a 'fix it' ticket." This was an $85 fine he was given because the policeman who pulled him over discovered his interior light was not working. But because he could not afford the fine and the interest on it kept growing, his car was towed away.

Take Amy, a woman in her thirties with two children, working two jobs, one in an Au Bon Pain restaurant near the local college, and the other as a clerk at a downtown mall. We met her in traffic court, where she'd come to pay off a pair of tickets, one a $50 fine for having a missing plate and the other for driving without insurance, the $76 monthly cost of which was too much for her small budget. As a result of her failure to pay the tickets initially, the state had suspended her license—a full nine years earlier. However small those fees were at first, the cost of the tickets and of renewing her insurance were insurmountable on her paychecks. She gave her car to her sister. Things just got worse, though: the initial $50 ticket for the missing plate had swollen to $325. With the other fine, the new license and registration fees, it would have cost over $1,000 to get Amy back in a car, and that's before even buying one. As with many of the working poor, a tax refund was the only thing that counted as savings, and she eventually had one large enough to show up in court that day.

Amy should get a "going green" award for her use of public transit throughout that period (her husband, too: he carpooled with his boss or rode a bike to his job). Luckily she lived in a city with what counts as reasonably good bus service. But she spent over four hours a day in transit, first on two different buses to take her kids to day care and school, then to get to each of her jobs, and repeating everything in reverse later in the day.

A harder tale belongs to Lori Denton, a woman with three children living in a suburb of Detroit, who was making $13,500 a year in 2001 when her 1983 Mercury station wagon began to periodically fail.[9] Each time, she scraped together money for repairs, but with no quality public transit options, she was regularly late to work. Lori's boss eventually fired her, and she and her children soon ended up in a homeless shelter.

Studies of welfare-to-work programs show that Lori resembles literally millions of other people for whom being without reliable transportation is a more significant barrier to getting and keeping a job than any other single factor. It is a barrier even higher than lacking a high school diploma or special job skills. And she is among the 28 percent of low-income workers in Michigan who sometimes miss work due to car trouble or public transit delays.

Tragically, those for whom the car is an economic lifeline find they pay more to hold on to it than their better-off fellow consumers. The used cars that poor buyers can afford come with higher loan rates than newer cars or cars purchased by people who have had the financial cushion to avoid credit problems. Even with their best rates for clean credit records, banks charge more in interest for used cars: average rates in Rhode Island on a four-year loan to buy an older model are nearly twice those for a new car.

Much more significant, however, is the fact that people in the market for cheap, high-mileage cars—often in the odometer range of 150,000 to 200,000 miles—are at a significant disadvantage in negotiating prices for the car and for credit. They are often more desperate to buy, as they are without a working car (their previous high-mileage car is already broken), while wealthier buyers can afford to wait for another dealer and a better price. Buyers without a credit history, such as many immigrants and young people, or those with bad credit ratings must shop at "buy here, pay here" lots, where the lot owners themselves make the car loans. In addition, the independent lots where the cheapest cars are found are often fly-by-night, sly-by-day operations, trading in cars with salvage or junk titles. Down payments are high, interest rates deserve to be called extortionate, and prices often far exceed the Blue Book value, factors that account for the much higher profitability of high-mileage car sales—on average, they extract a gross profit of $3,800 per car (and this on simple lots out on the edge of town with very low overhead).[10] Loan rates for these used cars can soar as high as 35 percent, costing buyers a full $4,044 in interest for a two-year loan on a $10,000 vehicle.

J. D. Byrider is one of the more respectable-looking of the buy here, pay here used car lots that extract much more from the poor. Decorated with cheerful blue and orange signs, an upbeat tagline ("Good Cars for People Who Need Credit"), and a brand name that seems to offer a quality assurance, J. D.s are clustered in depressed neighborhoods in about two dozen states around the country. Their outlets mainly sell to people who have poor credit ratings or those who cannot get car loans because they haven't yet held a credit card or borrowed any money—people like Inna, an Israeli immigrant to the United States who was told at a variety of used car lots that they couldn't give a car loan to someone who was a "ghost," that is, someone with no credit history. J. D. Byrider's customers get the dubious opportunity to buy American cars of five or so years' vintage at prices far surpassing the Blue Book value, and with loan rates far above even the worst of the used car lots that use bank financing.

For instance, the day we visited, J. D. Byrider was selling a 2004 Hyundai Accent with 96,000 miles for $9,000. As with other cars on the lot, the true Blue Book value of the car, even in excellent condition, is much less, at $2,880. The cheerful salesman boasted that he helped people not just into a car, but into the American Dream of home ownership: "We help you establish a good credit history," he said. "We offer short-term loans, so that people can prove quickly that they have good credit and then they can go ahead and buy a new car, or even better, a new house. But I always tell my customers: 'If you buy a new car, you have to come here and show it to me.'"

Chances are better you will get into financial trouble rather than into a new car.

One woman who did was Carlotta Henderson, a Guatemalan immigrant who cleans houses around Houston and whose husband works for a lawn service. She went to Sunshine Motors, which buys most of its cars for $2,000 or less, does minor reconditioning, and sells them for between $5,000 and $8,000. Carlotta bought an older model minivan with 132,000 miles for $7,000, overpaying by about $2,500. Sunshine made her an offer she couldn't refuse, a 23 percent two-year loan, which brought the price up to $8,500. Her down payment of $1,000 covered half of the car lot's cost for the van, and the first three months of weekly car payments covered the rest. Everything after that—another 21 months of $240 payments—was Sunshine's profit. And of course, the company could repossess and resell the car if she missed a payment.[11]

Poor and working families are more likely to own older cars that guzzle gas and oil and have higher maintenance costs. Drive through any poor urban neighborhood in America and you will find a striking number of auto repair and body shops working on the old, unreliable cars that have "trickled down" to these neighborhoods. Behind these official shops are more informal but not always reliable networks: one working-poor Baltimore man, Dwayne, described his typical struggles with an older car. To afford the repairs his auto needed to get back on the road, he took it to the backyard garage of a neighbor with mechanic skills. Two weeks later, he was still badgering the neighbor to get to work on his car and scrambling for rides to work.

In the current economic climate, things are getting worse. At one Massachusetts auto repair shop, the owner pointed to a car parked outside in his lot that belonged to a young woman: "It's been here for a couple of weeks now. It was only a $200 repair, but she doesn't have the money to fix it, so she just left it here."

The intersection of widespread poverty and predatory, underregulated business practice means that, as mentioned above, people now even rent tires, especially when their bald tires cause them to fail state inspection and threaten their ability to get to work. Rent-A-Tire has 68 stores around the South and West that offer car owners the opportunity to pay for their tires in installments. When the cheapest set available at Wal-Mart may be $450, many drivers are forced to accept Rent-A-Tire's terms. With weekly payments of $32 for a set of four, plus a $5 weekly "club fee"—"sort of tire insurance," we were told by a Rent-A-Tire salesperson—and taxes, a customer will end up paying $2,059 for four tires by the end of the agreement's one-year term. And for all the buyer/renter knows, the tires she drives off with may be used: the company passes off its customers' repossessed tires (taken as soon as seven days after a missed payment) among the new ones.

The poor also pay more for insurance. Families in the bottom fifth of the income distribution spend seven times the percentage of their household income on car insurance as do families in the top fifth. (See figure 6.1 in the endnotes.) Car insurance in inner city neighborhoods, in particular, can be extremely expensive, whether provided by mainstream insurers or fringe outfits. Even when their driving record is unblemished and they are in the lower-risk, middle-aged years, car owners living in some of Los Angeles' poorer areas, for example, can be charged as much as $3,500 per year for insurance, sometimes more than the total value of the car. Carlotta Henderson of Houston, who went to a local insurance agency, Alamo, was charged $2,100 a year, or more than 40 percent of the value of her used minivan.

Great controversy rightly surrounds the fact that in California in 2005, African American drivers were being charged on average much higher insurance rates. A Consumers Union survey of the three largest insurers found that drivers in some African American communities with clean driving records paid nearly $1,000 more per year than did drivers with similar records living in white zip codes.[12] For example, a woman in her forties living in a largely white zip code would pay $1,450 a year, while the same driver with the same car would pay $2,400 if she moved into a mostly African American neighborhood. The insurance scoring practices that result in such skewed rates are a form of redlining that activists are lobbying to have outlawed.

Due to these exorbitant insurance charges, the rate of uninsured motorists is fully 90 percent in some impoverished areas. Because African American and poor families are more likely to drive without insurance, they and others around them are at greater fiscal risk in the event of a crash.

Between the overcharges for their used car purchases, the usurious interest rates they pay, and the gouging by auto insurers and rental firms, millions of working people end up spending nearly as much for a clunker—and then pay out for frequent repairs—as the more well-to-do pay for a newer and more reliable vehicle.

STRANDED BY AGE:
LOSING THE KEYS AND A LOT MORE

The income gap is not the only important and rapidly expanding form of inequality in our car-based transit system—the generation gap is also growing. Older people often become stranded at home when they are no longer able to drive. In urban areas with good transit, elders are among the heaviest users of public buses and subways, suggesting that being home-bound is an imposition on, not a choice being made by, older Americans. On average, one in five people over the age of 65 do not drive, mostly because of health problems or out of a fear of harming themselves or others behind the wheel. By another estimate, more than half of all nondrivers in this age group stay home on any given day because they have no transportation or because they are loath to ask others for rides.[13]

This problem is growing along with the elderly population itself, projected to increase by 80 percent in the next two decades. It will also grow as the suburban population ages, a group almost as poorly served by public transit as the rural one.

Any discussion among a group of older women and men will eventually turn to their negotiations with their adult children over when to give up driving and their frustrations over this loss of independence. Said one woman in her early eighties, "As you get older, your right to drive comes into question. I am going to have to stop soon, and when I do, if I can't get someone to drive me, I'm going to have to move someplace where I don't need a car." Said another who had already lost her keys to the car, "You become a prisoner in your own house. You lose your freedom." While her New England suburban community has a car service for the elderly that she can call on for doctor visits or food shopping, she often has to make an appointment and wait several days before they can come.

Most of us also know someone who we feel shouldn't be driving any longer but is. Ella is an 84-year-old woman who still drives. She says she doesn't much enjoy it, but would be isolated from her good friends in nearby suburban towns if she didn't. She considers herself a safe driver: "I'm very careful," she said, "and I no longer go where I have to read signs and take directions. I know I'm not able to do that." Plus, she added, if she couldn't drive, she'd have to figure out how to take the bus, which she has never done.

The bottom line is this: a car-dependent society ages our old people more rapidly, and infantilizes them more, than a society in which mobility doesn't require that the traveler have the substantial and specialized range of cognitive and physical skills that are needed to drive.

DRIVING WHILE BLACK, WALKING WHILE LATINO

Though it is under heightened scrutiny and legal challenge from civil rights and civil liberties groups, racial profiling has long been a common practice in policing the American road. "Driving while black" or "brown" still means you are much more likely to be stopped for no good reason or for minor infractions for which white drivers are often given a pass. Numerous studies show the practice is widespread. In one study, 73 percent of the drivers that Maryland state police pulled over along one piece of I–95 were African American, even though nowhere near that percentage of the people driving along that stretch of highway were African American. In addition, police statistics show equal percentages of whites and blacks who were stopped and searched in Maryland had no contraband. Crime rates suggest that, if justified at all, racial profiling should be of white drivers: New Jersey police, also found to be racial profiling in their traffic stops, found illegal goods, mostly drugs, in 25 percent of the cars driven by whites, 13 percent of those driven by blacks, and 5 percent of those driven by Latinos.[14]

Cheyenne Hughes grew up in Denver in a mostly poor African American neighborhood. Only 22 when we spoke to him, he estimates he has been stopped, as a pedestrian or driver, 18 times already in his young life. His first stop while driving was in his aunt's car with two friends within a few months of getting his regular license. Two officers came up on either side of the car, their hands on their guns. They ran police checks on everyone in the car. As they prepared to let them go, "I asked why he pulled us over, and he told me it was because I had a low tire. And I was pretty upset, and asked him for his card, because by this time, after so many other incidents [while walking], I knew I could ask." Cheyenne now runs the Colorado Progressive Coalition, which takes on a variety of social and economic injustices.

Also actively combating this practice are the NAACP and Amnesty International. Collecting testimony from contemporary victims of profiling, Amnesty spoke with people such as schoolteacher Milton Reynolds, who is regularly pulled over in his mostly white neighborhood in San Carlos, California. He was once even given a citation before pulling out of his own driveway. After he told the policeman he would be contesting the ticket, he was subjected to several weeks of additional harassment by the patrolman's colleagues. He said, "Between that time and the court date, I had law enforcement officers park in front of my house, [shining] lights into my apartment. My neighbors had begun to ask me, 'What's going on? Why are the cops there?'" Fortunately, his case was dismissed in court.[15]

Although Hollywood stars, overwhelmingly white and wealthy, often make the news for driving while high, this coverage does not reflect the usual class composition of those arrested for DUI and other infractions. While whites admit to drinking and driving just as much as other groups, their arrest rates are much lower.[16] And once arrested for an offense, the accused driver's race and class make a big difference in the legal and economic repercussions. The Associated Press reported on two fathers, both of whom had caused the death of his child by leaving the child in a closed car during the summer. One, a white college professor, was let off. The other, a Peruvian racetrack worker, was given a twenty-year sentence and deported.[17]

For Americans across the color spectrum, laws and regulations relating to the car are the main way they experience the power of government, outside the tax system. Despite being notoriously allergic to the intrusion of state power into our lives, we have come to accept remarkable levels of government control for the sake of the automobile: our driver's licenses are often the only government identification card that we carry with us, car registration is an unquestioned requirement (compare gun registration, which mobilizes massive opposition), and citizen encounters with the police are almost exclusively in connection with traffic stops. The aggregation of power to the state—the growth of inequality between citizen and government—on account of the car is one of the most unrecognized trends of the twentieth century. When that power accumulates in a society with persistent racism, the small and large terrors of racial profiling on the road are a predictable result.

DISASTER IN PLACE: KATRINA REVEALS THE LIFE-AND-DEATH CONSEQUENCES OF CAR OWNERSHIP

White America was to some extent already aware of the problem of driving while black when Hurricane Katrina, with terrible drama, revealed the problem of *not* driving while black. The disparity in car ownership between white residents of the Gulf Coast and their African American, Native American, and Latino neighbors was made painfully clear as whites took to the highways before the storm, and the Superdome filled with people of color waiting for rescue from the devastated area. Only 15 percent of whites in Orleans Parish are without a car, while over 35 percent of African Americans and about 27 percent of Native Americans and Latinos are carless.[18]

New Orleans is not unique in its high levels of racial inequality in car access. Across the nation, the rate of carlessness among Latinos is more than double that of whites, and for blacks the rate is more than triple.[19] Being old as well as African American is a double whammy when it comes to mobility in our car culture. While only 16 percent of white seniors don't drive, approximately 40 percent of older blacks, Asian Americans, and Latinos don't.[20]

Economists have repeatedly demonstrated that being without a car has a more significant impact on African American employment than almost any other factor, particularly in areas of urban segregation where jobs are farthest away. One Brookings Institution study determined that if blacks owned cars at the same rates as whites, it would eliminate nearly half the difference in black and white jobless rates.[21] Without a car, inner city residents, who generally work more irregular hours, must rely on public transit with its scarce service outside of rush hour, leading to their being late or missing work altogether.[22]

In cities with poor public transit, having a car significantly increases one's chances of getting a job.[23] As noted earlier, recent job growth is greatest on the suburban ring, leaving a skewed ratio of workers to jobs in the inner city. But it is no simple matter of an unemployed person changing where he or she lives. The lack of affordable housing and the prevalence of housing discrimination limit that option.

How did this happen? White flight to the suburbs during the post–World War II period was facilitated by massive public investment in the roads to get them there. This radically expanded the existing spatial segregation of minority communities, and was followed by the growth of jobs in suburban locations, which has further disadvantaged inner city African American families without cars, for whom such a commute by public transit is either very difficult or impossible. Moreover, in a kind of parting shot to African American urban residents as whites fled, those highways were often routed specifically through African American neighborhoods, eviscerating them. Take Durham, North Carolina, for example, where Route 147 was built to help connect the downtown manufacturing and business center with land being developed and sold almost exclusively to whites in suburbs to the north of the city. That highway was routed through and displaced Durham's main African American business district, so well known for its cultural vitality and economic success that it was called the Harlem of the South in the years when Harlem was at its most vibrant.

When public transit has been proposed to link inner cities to the suburbs, it has often been resisted by white suburbanites with claims that can be said to be racially coded. In one visible case, when Atlanta's modern urban rail system, MARTA (Metropolitan Atlanta Rapid Transit Authority), was first planned, it grossly underserved the city's African American neighborhoods and public housing developments. After this shortcoming was protested and then remedied with more equitably located rails, residents in several predominately white suburban areas protested against the expansion to their neighborhoods on the grounds that crime would follow the tracks.[24]

Race helps determine whether a family has a car and whether that car is reliable and affordable. It also, horribly, makes a difference in how likely one is to die on account of a car. Because African Americans and Latinos are less apt to own vehicles and so more apt to be out walking, and more likely to be in high-traffic urban areas, they are hit and killed, especially children, at disproportionate rates.[25] Finally, when driving rates are taken into account—what epidemiologists appropriately if ominously call our "exposure"—black and Latino male children are twice as likely to die in crashes as their white counterparts.[26]

PAYING MORE FOR CREDIT: THE DEALER TAX ON THE AFRICAN AMERICANS, WOMEN, AND THE YOUNG

Credit was once extended only to the well-off who could pay their bills promptly—until lenders began to see the road to profit in the late payment penalties and higher interest they could charge less creditworthy customers in a newly deregulated banking environment. In the 1970s, lenders began to reenvision Americans undergoing crises (such as job loss or divorce) as good prospects and began convincing them that credit would help them get over the hump. After mining this group, they went on to target unemployed or underemployed college students for credit cards and student loans, and then, finally, the poor.

Lending for cars followed the same pattern. Come-ons increasingly targeted the most financially vulnerable. Television, radio, direct mail, and the Internet today are crowded with shout-outs to those "with bad credit, no credit," promising to get them into a car. A typical letter sent to such potential customers in some suburban New York neighborhoods began enthusiastically: "Congratulations! You have received this letter because you have been pre-qualified for an auto loan from Westchester Toyota. Even though your credit may be damaged, if you are currently working, you may be eligible for an auto loan up to $19,995." It goes on, "We help applicants with any credit situation. . . . Good credit, bad credit, no credit, slow pay, repossessions and even bankruptcies. Call us today. . . ."[27] Customers with poorer credit, of course, will pay higher rates, thus likely worsening their credit if they take advantage of the offer and fall behind in their payments.

Predatory lenders—found in both putatively reputable banks and shadier institutions—are often charging as much as 17 to 25 percent on auto loans.[28] The differential between these and more competitive rates adds up to $3,000 or more in excess finance charges for a five-year, $10,000 used-car loan.

Car financing is generally done either directly through a lender or indirectly through the dealer. Major lenders include Citigroup, Capital One, AmeriCredit Financial Services, AutoNation, and Cash America, all of which have been key players in a subprime auto loan industry that directly targets the poor and ballooned fourfold to $65 billion a year in loans in 2003. These are not shady, small outfits, but major corporations: Ameri-Credit had more than one million customers in 2004 and loans that totaled $15 billion.

Lenders often work in tandem with auto dealers to defraud consumers or skim along the unregulated edge of what counts as fraud. In a pattern found throughout the country, Crown Pontiac and a group of other car dealers in West Virginia habitually took credit applications, falsified them with higher paystubs and inflated down payments, and sent them on to AmeriCredit, with the latter's (but not the buyer's) knowledge and consent. A previously unqualified buyer would suddenly be eligible for a loan. But as Mike Hudson, a journalist who has investigated this extensively, notes, the lenders "weren't doing customers any favors by playing games with the paperwork": the customers were charged high interest rates, which were then jacked up even higher by the dealer. At one Nashville dealership, GMAC ended up charging a customer 21 percent, while other car buyers were secretly assessed additional finance charges as high as $8,600. Another victim was an illiterate woman on Social Security disability, whose son had just had a heart transplant. She was charged 17 percent annually, along with a hidden add-on fee of $3,000.[29]

The markup on interest rates is racially biased: African Americans generally are given a higher markup than comparable white customers.[30]

One Ohio State University study using national economic census data found that for both new and used car loans, African American families paid 2 percent more compared to all borrowers.[31] Hudson discovered that the most exploited targets of predatory car lenders were not only African Americans, but also Latinos, seniors, working-class people, and those with damaged credit histories. "Many dealers and lenders," Hudson writes, "perceive these consumers as having fewer options, less financial experience, and a diminished sense of marketplace entitlement, thus making them more likely to be desperate or susceptible when it comes time to close the deal."[32] At the same time, these vulnerable customers are also more likely to have salespeople try to sell them superfluous credit insurance, roadside assistance, and extended warranties or service contracts. Low-ranking military personnel—who are often both working poor and young—have also often been particularly targeted for this type of lending.[33]

Car title loans are another means by which people are driven closer to poverty. These loans, maybe better termed car title pawns, are made to people who own their cars free and clear. The loans function much like home equity loans, but the deed at stake is the car's title. Companies such as Cash America and New Century Financial make short-term loans for a portion of the value of the car, with interest rates often as high as 300 percent annually. The lenders hold the title and a duplicate set of keys and, if payments are missed, swoop in to repossess and resell the car. The Tennessee Department of Financial Institutions found that in one recent year, Tennessee title loan businesses had repossessed a phenomenal total of over 17,000 vehicles.[34] In Cook County, Illinois, several hundred car title loan locations, the bulk of them in predominately minority communities, had average APRs of 263 percent. With such outrageously usurious rates, it is not surprising that these outfits then repossessed (and resold) roughly one of five cars on which they made loans.[35]

Buyers of these types of high-risk loans may have their cars fitted with a disabling device that can be activated if the owner misses a payment. Sekurus, Inc.'s version of this device, called the ON TIME, flashes lights telling the car owner when his or her payment is due. When everything is current, the light is green, but as a payment date approaches, the light flashes yellow. The machine gives three days' warning and counts down the time before the car is disabled. ON TIME also has a GPS component so that the car can be tracked down for repossession. Sales of ON TIME are skyrocketing, growing 30 percent in just one quarter in 2008.[36] (With government oversight mostly absent, the only dubious ally that the poor have sometimes had in fighting car title loan companies is the nation's pawnshop industry. It has been the main opponent to these loans, because they have cut substantially into pawnshops' business in poor communities.)

Consumer advocates have to work against the widespread assumption that people who pay too much for cars or for car credit have no one to blame but themselves for being ill informed or incautious when they approach the dealer. As Duane Overholt said to us, "Who of any of us reads the fine print? The consumer cannot be expected to be a lawyer." People's credit scores sometimes reflect irresponsibility in previous purchases, but more often they are simply a measure of one's place in the American class system, and their use to raise the hurdles to car ownership adds insult to injury. Says one critic of exorbitant car loans, "Credit ratings have become the benchmark by which moral probity is judged. Bad credit is the equivalent of bad character, and few politicians are willing to stick out their necks for people with bad character. This partly explains why there's so little legislation to protect the poor from predatory economic activity."[37]

RISK INEQUALITY: THE BANK ACCOUNT CRASH TEST

You don't want to experience a car crash at any income level, but least of all when you are not wealthy: automotive collisions cause greater suffering for economically vulnerable families. While more expensive cars are not necessarily safer than cheaper ones, new cars are, for the most part, safer than used ones, and new cars are more likely to be in the hands of the well-to-do. Recent models are more apt to have such equipment as multiple airbags and antilock brakes. And they are less likely to have dangerous mechanical or maintenance problems, such as faulty brakes or bald tires. Moreover, the driver of a defective car sitting in the breakdown lane is at great risk of being squashed by approaching traffic: some 10 to 20 percent of all crashes are the result of such a preexisting incident on the highway.

State inspection laws, meant to ensure that all cars are safe, are as much or more a boon to the Rent-A-Tire and car repair business than they are a protection for the poor. Some states have wisely recognized the burden inspection places on the poor by eliminating at least the requirement that older cars meet emissions standards.

In the highway arms race that has emerged over the last fifteen years with SUVs' popularity, class makes a difference in who emerges dead or severely injured from a collision. While some SUVs have not had a significantly better safety record than other large cars due to their tendency to roll over and their poorer crash-avoidance ability, they are more likely to kill other drivers. Because SUVs are more expensive cars, they are generally more often in the hands of the relatively affluent. A person in a more affordable car on the receiving end of a head-on collision with an outsize vehicle such as an Explorer or Hummer will not win the battle.

The financial burden resulting from car crashes can be massive, with dizzying medical costs and resultant indebtedness. This is especially true for lower-income families, who are less likely to have auto and health insurance. Such families also have minimal assets from which to draw on to cover these unexpected costs. On top of all this, many car crashes occur on the job, having the greatest effect on the working class in such industries as agriculture, forestry, ground transportation, mining, construction, and, ironically, auto repair.[38]

PROFITING FROM A CAR-DEPENDENT AMERICA: IT'S NICE TO BE AN OIL COMPANY CEO

Rex Tillerson, the chairman and CEO of Exxon Mobil, feels the pinch at the pump just like you and me. It's just that he has more money in his pay envelope to help deal with it ($24 million in 2008).[39] Add to that the millions more that go to other top executives, and you have enough money to pay for the commute to work for a good number of Americans.

General Motors' former CEO Rick Wagoner was lavished with compensation totaling $15.7 million in 2007.[40] The gap between the richest and the rest is evident in how Wagoner was paid as compared to his pre-decessors. General Motors' chief executive in 1969, James M. Roche, made a more modest $4.2 million, adjusted for inflation. Significantly, Wagoner's $15.7 million was paid out in a year that GM lost $39 billion. A year later, it required a government handout to survive, slashed wages, and outsourced its obligation to pay health benefits for its workers to the UAW. Roche ruled GM when it paid its workers good wages and made money for shareholders.[41]

In return for federal bailout monies in 2008, Wagoner theatrically ac-cepted a cut in pay to $1, but was sacked a few months later. While Wag-oner's former company exited bankruptcy as this book went to press, the Obama administration implemented tax credits that represented a massive further infusion into the car companies by subsidizing new purchases of American cars. Given the United States' car dependency, it is expected that the car industry, however reorganized, will return to major profitability after its restructuring and these government assists.

However, oil and auto company CEO salaries—visible and grating though they are—by themselves are not the centerpiece of how the car sys-tem redistributes wealth to the top. Much more meaningful but less visi-ble are the billions of dollars in tax breaks oil companies receive each year. What that means, basically, is that average taxpayers or the less powerful sectors of U.S. business must make up the difference so that we can fund a basic level of government services.

One group that has vocalized the suffering inflicted by a shift in the tax burden from Big Oil to the little guy is the nation's independent truckers. In 2008, truckers across the country participated in a protest organized by Truckers and Citizens United, an organization of transportation workers and concerned drivers. They circled their vehicles around Washington's National Mall to demonstrate against the rising gas prices that were forcing many of them out of profitability and out of business. Among their demands then and now are the repeal of tax breaks and subsidies to oil companies and tax relief for themselves, including the elimination of what they view as double taxa-tion when they are forced to pay both road taxes and tolls.[42]

Just how big are those breaks for the oil industry? By one estimate, the 2005 Energy Bill—which emerged from the secretive Energy Task Force that Vice President Dick Cheney convened on his first day in office—provides $6 billion annually to the oil companies.[43] Tyson Slocum, the director of Public Citizen's Energy Program, estimates that this subsidy total reached $9 billion in 2008.[44] The bill does this by waiving royalty payments for drilling off the coast of Alaska and permitting oil companies to drill for oil on federal land offshore while paying only 44 percent of the previous rate for this access.

This bill, a U.S. Government Accountability Office report warned, also "relies upon royalty payers to self-report the amount of oil and gas they produce, the value of this oil and gas, and the cost of transportation and processing that they deduct from royalty payments."[45] Several court cases revealed the predictable result of this self-policing—major underreporting and underpayment to the U.S. Treasury.

Critics of Cheney's energy bill noted that windfall profits should have been more than enough incentive for oil drilling and exploration. (Moreover, removing tax breaks might improve incentives for those companies to invest in alternative energy sources. Instead, the oil Goliaths have invested in themselves, buying back stock from shareholders at a record clip.) And those recent profits have been history-making. Exxon Mobil's $45 billion profit in 2008 busted the record for a U.S. corporation.[46] Chevron did well also, with total profits for that same year at a record $24 billion.[47]

The power of these companies to influence public policy, and their ability to withhold supplies and otherwise create high prices, has radically expanded in recent years. Consolidation in the energy industry—Exxon with Mobil, Conoco with Phillips, and Chevron with Texaco—means that the top five oil refiners in 2005 owned 55 percent of gas supply in the United States. In addition, energy trading markets were deregulated in the mid-1990s, allowing for new levels of price manipulation.

The oil companies have been particularly concerned about public backlash against their environmental impact and excess profits. Launching a public relations campaign, they produced materials for schools suggesting that everyone profits when the oil companies do well. A message from their industry organization, the American Petroleum Institute, appeared on U.S. op-ed pages all over the country: "If you are wondering who owns 'Big Oil,'" said one such pitch, "chances are good the answer is 'you do.'

If you have a mutual fund account, and 55 million U.S. households do, there's a good chance it invests in oil and natural gas stocks. If you have an IRA or personal retirement account, and 45 million U.S. households do, there's a good chance it invests in energy stocks." What the ads do not say is that those oil stocks represent small fractions of the mutual funds owned by the middle class, and that the funds might pay out at most a few dollars a year per household. The bulk of oil and auto industry shares are still owned by the wealthiest Americans; 81 percent of the total value of all mutual funds and 89 percent of individual stocks are owned by the wealthiest 10 percent of families.[48]

Car-related industries, through campaign contributions to our elected officials and effective lobbying, ensure legislation that provides subsidies, incentives, and tax relief as well as reduced regulation. Congressional committees periodically run hearings at which they make a great show of outrage, shaming the industry executives called to testify, but go on to do little to control their profiteering.

Sadly, the Obama administration's 2009 involvement in the restructuring of Chrysler and GM may be destined to similarly benefit the few at the expense of the multitudes. Taxpayers, laid-off plant workers, and shutdown dealers are paying an onerous price now in return, it is hoped, for a revivified American auto industry. Meanwhile, Cerberus Capital, the private equity firm that bought Chrysler in 2007, escapes,[49] while the American public is likely on the hook for ten billion or more.[50] And the much larger and far more costly General Motors restructuring resulted in the U.S. taxpayers' owning a majority of the company's stock, a $50 billion investment so risky no one else would take it.

HEDGE FUND HANDS IN OUR POCKETS

In the auto sector, as elsewhere in American business, manufacturing is no longer seen as the royal road to riches. Eerily echoing the reviled Gordon Gekko of Oliver Stone's morality tale *Wall Street,* Ray Diallo, founder of hedge fund Bridgewater Associates, noted, "The money that's made from manufacturing stuff is a pittance in comparison to the amount of money made from shuffling money around." 2007 was the year many first learned the terms "predatory lending" and "hedge fund," both of which have come to hit American car owners, not just home owners, with a vengeance.

The housing crisis grabbed the headlines beginning in 2007, but auto loans played a meaningful role in the CDO market that helped precipitate the crisis. CDOs are collateralized debt obligations, also known as credit derivatives, a financial instrument dating back to the early 1990s that is essentially the securitization of risk. When an investor, such as a bank or hedge fund, purchases a credit derivative, he is buying not a bundle of home or auto loans but a portion or all of the risk of that bundle. As the housing market exploded and Americans bought more and bigger vehicles in the early years of the new century, the CDO market blossomed, and some people got quite rich essentially taking Vegas-style bets on whether ordinary people would get to keep or lose their homes or cars.

Hedge funds, which are largely unregulated, have been especially active in the CDO market, where trades are also unregulated. No one knows just how much hedge funds have made in recent years off of loans, good or bad, because they are not required to file their financial results with the Securities and Exchange Commission like other investment firms. And although some hedge funds, like other institutions such as Bear Stearns, have been bankrupted by being on the wrong end of risk play, many hedge funds have benefited greatly from loans on homes and autos, predatory and conventional. The nation's richest hedge fund manager as of 2008 was John Paulson, who racked up $3.7 billion in 2007, in large part betting against the American Dream by hedging subprime mortgage securities and CDOs.[51]

Who are these mysterious moguls hiding in the hedges, adding to their coffers as Hyundai Sonatas and Ford Rangers are repossessed all across the country? They are our nation's new steroidal aristocracy, people so rich, even since the financial crisis, that it boggles the mind. A *Business Week* profile of one such hedge fund owner began with a set of images that says it all: "A gunmetal-gray BMW 745Li sedan slips out of Steven A. Cohen's 14-acre walled estate. The chauffeured car races along the winding backcountry hills of ultrawealthy Greenwich, Conn. At around 8 A.M., it powers into the parking lot of SAC Capital Advisors. Cohen quickly emerges and darts into the front entrance of his gleaming steel and terracotta-slabbed Stamford (Conn.) headquarters. His driver swings the car around to the back and parks in a space with a simple reserved sign amid a sea of testosterone-exuding cars belonging to his traders: Mercedes S600s, Lexus sport-utility vehicles, and Porsche Carrera 4s." The millions that Cohen, his associates, and their ilk made that day alone likely came at least in part from the bundled risk of loans taken on more modest cars in other people's driveways.[52]

Despite its seeming potential as a tool of equality, the automobile has largely cemented and accentuated class and race divisions in America. In his remarkable book, *Energy and Equity* (1974), social commentator Ivan Illich made the counterintuitive point that high per-capita energy use is associated across history with *less* choice and *less* equity, not more. Our notions of progress make this hard to believe, but, he argued, all humans are born equally mobile. We become unequally mobile when the car chases the pedestrian off the road, clogs the bus or tram rider's route, is unaffordable to many, and creates distances through suburbanization that are hard to overcome without it.

In a car system, people begin to build and live in sprawling style and feel free to live far from their families and jobs: they believe the car allows them a quick return whenever they like. But in so doing, the car actually creates the physical distances (and the subsequent social distances) that only it is then able to shrink. And, given income inequality, the car shrinks those distances for some much more readily than others, particularly the carless. A car culture is a society built around private modes of transportation, but with massive public investment in the infrastructure that allows those private uses. Those without the financial means to own a vehicle are dependent on an underfunded mass transit system. Nevertheless, all of us are paying with our tax dollars in various ways to enrich automakers and oil and gas companies and their executives, helping widen the gulf between the top 1 to 5 percent of income earners and the rest of us.

We have come to understand that cars pollute our collective environment, but we have not yet recognized how they foul our ability to create more equality of opportunity and equality of outcome in our communities. It could be otherwise. Investment in public transit can benefit the great majority and reduce inequality. The contrast of Detroit and Toronto provides a vivid example. Detroit spends twice as much on roads as Toronto, while Toronto has spent eight times as much as Detroit on public transit. Those public choices have the private consequence that each of Detroit's residents spends over twice on average what Toronto's people do to get around.[53] Europe, too, shows how much more physical and class mobility are possible with lower rates of car dependence. As Nobel Prize–winning economist Paul Krugman quipped, "Horatio Alger has moved to Canada or Finland," and, we can add, he probably took the train.[54]

Alternatives to the current inequitable car system include the ones that the Alliance for a New Transportation Charter, a coalition of transportation activists, has summarized like this: "The transportation system should be socially equitable and strengthen civil rights; enabling all people to gain access to good jobs, education and training, and needed services. [It] should allow every American to participate fully in society whether or not they own a car and regardless of age, ability, ethnicity, or income."[55]

The reasons to pursue such a vision of a less car-dependent society are not exclusively socioeconomic, as the following chapters illustrate. A more balanced transportation system will improve our quality of life, helping us to spend more time with our families and keeping us happier and healthier.

Chapter Seven

WHAT DRIVES US

When asked to name a sprawling metropolis choking on its own traffic and smog, people probably think of huge cities such as Los Angeles, Houston, or Atlanta. So citizens of Nashville, Tennessee, were surprised a few years ago to find their modestly sized city topping some unpopular charts. First came the 1999 report that awarded Nashville the number-one spot on its list of cities with the worst air pollution from cars and trucks per capita.[1] Then, in 2001, newspapers reported that Nashville had the lowest population density of any American city, making it the country's most sprawling.[2] Over the next few years, names of quaint Nashville-area towns like LaVergne and Mount Juliet popped up on lists of the nation's fastest-growing suburbs.[3]

Developers were buying up expansive swaths of rural land circling the city and converting it to suburban housing. Highway construction–related delays and detours began snarling traffic. Nashville has worked hard to attract large-scale employers such as Louisiana-Pacific, Caremark, and Nissan, bringing in high-income, cosmopolitan migrants from as far away as New York and Los Angeles. But some worry whether all of this growth means Nashville, proud of its small-town courtesies and southern charm, is fast on its way to becoming one of the very impersonal, sprawling behemoths its newcomers are fleeing.

Nashville's expansion runs in every direction. I–65 is one of the busiest highways running south. Its Brentwood exit delivers drivers to one of the city's wealthiest and oldest suburbs; up until this decade the town was suburbia's last outpost. The next town out, Nolensville, was until recently a tiny rural hamlet with as many churches as stores. On the map of Tennessee, Nolensville still looks as though it is in the middle of nowhere, but it was chosen as the site of Winterset Woods, a housing development emblematic of modern suburban sprawl.

On the road from Brentwood to Nolensville, some acres of woods and farmland remain, decorated with the occasional cluster of grazing horses that long characterized middle Tennessee. But the transformation from countryside to suburb is evident on the main road, lined with one new development after another. Grand stone-lined entrances with spouting fountains, freshly shorn lawns, and echoing rows of brick-and-shingle single-family houses have replaced dirt roads, springs, meadows, barns, and idiosyncratic homes. On one seven-mile stretch, no fewer than seventeen newer developments front the road. Some have names connoting prestige, such as Saratoga Hills and the Governors Club, but others have taken their names from the landscape leveled to erect them: Beech Grove, Brookfield, Woodlands, and Winterset Woods. "For Sale" signs dot the remaining undeveloped stretches.

On a visit to Winterset Woods as it was still being completed, we followed the freshly paved road into the development until it ended abruptly at the far edge where an unmanned dump truck stood, filled with tree branches and brush. Behind it, woodland had been cleared and the fresh earth readied for the construction of more houses. It was a quiet Sunday, and with few of the homes occupied, the place had a desolate feel, the aura of a formerly inhabited place rather than of one yet to be peopled. The development was still ringed by forest, but, eerily, on its completed lots it was hard to find a tree.

For Winterset Woods residents who work in downtown Nashville, the commute of less than an hour, without traffic, would be short relative to what many face from some city suburbs. Residents would have up to 2,600 square feet of new living space and access to a pool and clubhouse.

They could wake up in the morning, pick up the newspaper from their driveway, and have a cup of coffee on the deck.

If they needed milk for their coffee, they would get in the car and drive the three miles round-trip to the market in the still-tiny center of Nolensville. Other errands would have to be run to LaVergne, Smyrna, or Brentwood, ten- to fourteen-miles round-trip, not terribly far by today's ex-urban standards. Still, when we visited, there was virtually nothing within walking distance. No park, no church, no store. There were no bus stops. Homeowners with young children would be lucky: the public schools newly opened to handle the expected population boom were within walking distance. But each resident would seem to need a car to get to work, shop, socialize, and pursue Nashville's cultural offerings. Driving into the heart of Nolensville, not a person was seen who was not driving a car or getting into or out of one. The amazing thing is that this is *not* amazing. Many Americans now live this way and don't think twice about it.

Sprawl has become a hot topic at Nashville Metropolitan County Council meetings, planning meetings in the Nashville suburbs, and in *The Tennessean,* Nashville's newspaper, which has published hundreds of pieces on the issue in the past several years. Citizen groups across middle Tennessee have been galvanized to battle the rippling environmental effects of sprawl. In just one example, the Southwest Williamson County Community Association fought alongside the Southern Environmental Law Center and other groups to force the Tennessee Department of Transportation to deal with the damage to water quality caused by muddy runoff from highway construction.[4]

Mary Pearce, executive director of the Heritage Foundation of Franklin and Williamson County, believes that Tennesseans have belatedly woken up to the issue. For a long time, she said, "most people were not that concerned about sprawl because there was so much open space. As farm after farm has been developed—the community is now concerned that some of the rural character of our community be preserved." In part due to the activism of the Heritage Foundation, the city of Franklin has taken actions such as purchasing horse farms to ensure their conservation. Pearce thinks that the community finally understands that controlling sprawl is the key, not just to maintaining the area's character and appeal, but to securing its healthy social and economic future.

SPRAWL AND CRAWL: THE SIX-HOUR RUSH HOUR

While some citizens worry about the varied effects of sprawl, ordinary Tennesseans' complaints about the issue, like most Americans', focus on traffic. Wherever they live, people commonly feel that traffic is worse than it was just a few years ago.[5] They are not wrong. Nationally, the rush hour—defined as those peak hours of travel when roads are most congested—has expanded to span more than six hours a day, making it harder and harder to avoid.[6] Of course, in some cities, such as Los Angeles, the numbers are dramatic: 50 percent of travel hours each day are congested. In other words, the rush hour in L.A. lasts for twelve hours out of every twenty-four.

It is not just big cities anymore that are being affected—cities and towns of all sizes are experiencing longer rush hours and increased delays during periods of congestion.[7] The average trip that would normally take twenty minutes without congestion takes more than twenty-five minutes during rush hour.[8] That doesn't sound like much until the minutes lost each way, each day, each week, and every year are compounded. That extra ten minutes a day, fifty minutes a week adds up to 43 hours a year, or an entire workweek.

Depending on their income, travelers may or may not feel the pain of the hundreds of additional dollars they are paying at the gas station annually as a result of being stuck in traffic. Still, even wealthy drivers feel the aggravation of wasting time on the road. The number of hours Americans spend mired in traffic annually has increased by more than half, accelerating the number of people who say they no longer enjoy driving.[9]

"It's not the 405, y'all," Josh Tyler tells his Nashville friends when they bemoan the city's traffic, referring to southern California's famously congested San Diego Freeway. A musician and retail store owner, Josh relocated from Manhattan, and his experience trying to get around in larger, more congested cities makes him a bit more philosophical than some natives about Nashville's traffic. Still, he reports that traffic has increased "a lot" in his Belmont Hillsboro neighborhood, especially since the neighborhood was bisected by a new interstate. And although his store in the busy Green Hills shopping district is a mere two miles from his home, driving there can take him between twenty minutes and half an hour, making the quirks of other drivers more galling and provoking an ongoing monologue: "Were turn signals optional on your car model? 'Yield' does not mean stop! WTF! Don't pass in the bike lane!"

One thousand miles northeast, in New England, Eric, a hardworking corporate lawyer and father of two elementary-school-age children, is even more exasperated by his commute. A few years ago, wishing to spend more time with his family, he left his job in a city sixty miles away—a job he got to by train in about an hour and fifteen minutes—to take a position with a firm located closer to his suburban home. Now he finds the six-mile commute to his office in the next town can take him up to a full hour depending on traffic, a commute that has been getting steadily worse since he started driving it. Because he works late, Eric's drive home is often swifter, as he leaves the office past the nastiest hours of congestion. This gives him an incentive to stay at work longer in order to reduce his time stuck in traffic, even though this means his kids will be that much closer to bedtime when he rolls in the driveway.

Terence in Maryland has an easier time getting to and from his office because he commutes against traffic; nonetheless, he is not immune to worsening congestion. He described a typical weekend errand run in his town as "just crazy busy with lots of cars and lots of lights and stop and go." He also complained, "The smallest little incident on the interstate can cause a major shutdown nightmare situation. And I've seen that. And I've been in it. But you just deal with it."

Why Americans across the country are forced to "just deal with" such terrible traffic is the result of a combination of factors. Sprawl is just one part of the picture. Another is the sheer quantity of cars on the road, a number that has increased drastically over the past few decades. Overall population growth and the entry of women into the workforce are key reasons the number of workers in the United States doubled between 1960 and 2000, from 66 million to 128 million.[10] Because the number of licensed drivers, car owners, and owners of multiple vehicles also increased, the number of vehicles more than tripled in that same period.[11]

As most commuters no longer take the traditional suburb-to-city commute, according to the Transportation Research Board, the greatest flow of commuters—more than two-thirds—is now from suburb to suburb, and this type of flow has only grown over time.[12] Across the nation, so-called reverse commutes are also growing as companies move out of downtown areas but some of their employees continue to live there.[13]

This traffic-exacerbating sprawl seems out of our control. Dozens of people interviewed emphasized how little say Americans have in how much we must drive because of the way our country is "laid out," as one woman put it, or, in other words, how sprawling it all is. When Dwight, who lives in Queens, New York, and works on Long Island, was asked whether gas prices were leading him to drive less, he exclaimed, "You have no choice! You have to get to work." And while no one wants a long or difficult commute, economic realities for many mean they must accept one. One man who was looking for work in a tight job market said that the commute would be a "pretty important" factor in his decision to take a job, but he was still willing to consider anything within fifty miles of his home, a commute likely to add a minimum of two hours to his workday.

Despite traffic horrors and a pervasive sense that land use is a force beyond individual control, Americans have been primarily basing their decisions about where to live not on the length or difficulty of their commute but on the real and perceived value of their housing. Over recent decades, as housing prices climbed, the lure of more square footage and a yard in new developments such as Winterset Woods made more Americans willing to suffer longer commutes.[14] This has helped lead to the staggering increase in the absolute number of commuters traveling by car—over 110 million, compared to just 40 million in 1960[15]—because, of course, the vast majority of these commutes, roughly nine out of ten, are by car.

Only recently has this trend looked stoppable, and not just as a casualty of economic crisis. Gas prices, foreclosures, and the recession are all contributing to slowed exurban growth, but, the EPA revealed, based on housing permits issued, a meaningful shift away from exurban development back toward urban core redevelopment had already been occurring by 2007.[16] In a survey of Atlanta residents conducted that year, the top reason those who had recently switched jobs or homes cited for their move was the desire for an abbreviated commute.[17] Although some city dwellers will always decide to relocate to smaller towns, more are now choosing older, closer-in suburbs over remote exurbs; they are rewarded not just with a relatively short commute but with the joys of walkability. In 2005, health care professional Sean Ogden moved from Philadelphia to nearby Collingswood, New Jersey, where he can happily still foot it to restaurants and shops.[18] Collingswood, along with other towns in its county, has benefited from the Speedline, a rapid transit line that cuts down on car traffic to and from Philly.

Drivers have lots of ideas about how to reduce traffic, most of them involving increasing the supply of roads rather than decreasing the demand to drive on them. (One Florida retiree, though, not alone, if in error, in blaming worsening traffic on the influx of immigrants, suggested that putting an end to our "open door" immigration policy was the answer.) Americans overwhelmingly support more government spending on roads—adding, widening, and repaving them. And while many believe that adding more trains and buses is part of the solution, others become downright angry at the suggestion that government funds might be better spent on public transportation than roads, which they view as their due as taxpayers. One man thought he understood why people get so worked up on the topic: "I think it's very emotional. It's like the gun laws. This is one of our freedoms. This is why Americans don't use public transportation. We're cowboys—'I ride my horse where I want to go.'"

Traffic experts know that adding road capacity is not a realistic long-term solution to the congestion problem. Historically, when mobility in a region is increased due to new roads and road widening, drivers who have been avoiding peak hours no longer do so and further housing developments are built and congestion increases again.[19] In many already congested areas, expanding road capacity to meaningfully improve speed and flow during the rush hours is a financial and spatial impossibility, as economist Anthony Downs explains: "Key routes would have to be widened so much that huge portions of the entire region would be turned into giant concrete slabs. This would destroy thousands of properties along present roadways, wreaking havoc with trees, open space, and many other aspects of the physical environment. It would also be enormously expensive. In fact, no society could afford the costs involved."[20] In other words, there are more cars on the road than there could ever be roads built to support their continual free flow.

Other proposals to reduce traffic congestion tend to be resisted, such as providing incentives to drivers to change their behavior by charging more at peak times on heavily used roads or in certain districts. Witness Mayor Mike Bloomberg's highly publicized, unsuccessful attempt to institute the kind of "congestion pricing" measures in midtown Manhattan that have been effective in comparable metropolitan areas such as central London. In 2003, the city of London started charging a fee, currently £8 (about $13), to those driving private automobiles in the central area of the city on weekdays, exempting certain vehicles such as those used by the disabled and emergency services and providing a 90 percent discount to area residents. The program has reduced traffic congestion, improved travel speeds, reduced delays, and increased already high ridership on trains and buses in the fee zone, all while raising significant revenue for public transit.[21] Opponents of Bloomberg's proposal argued that commuters who have no alternative routes and times available to them would unduly suffer under the plan. Especially in a recession characterized by volatile gas prices, any traffic reduction strategies requiring American drivers to pay more out of their own pockets to take the most essential trip they take—the drive to work—is politically unpalatable.

Meanwhile, traffic just keeps getting worse.

LOSERS TAKE THE BUS TO SCHOOL

So, many more people are on the road. They are also driving more, taking more trips, and covering more miles. Workers travel farther to get to their jobs than they used to, and in all different directions, but still, it seems like the average twelve-mile trip to work can't be causing all that much additional traffic. And, in fact, commuting isn't the main culprit. Surprisingly, it accounts for only a small part of the country's traffic problem—just 16 percent of all car trips. The numbers of other types of trips have exploded. Most individuals take more than four trips per day to get to work, to shop, to run other personal and business errands, to socialize and for recreation, and increasingly, to get to school.[22]

The amount of school travel has climbed as a dwindling number of kids walk or bike to school. Today, fewer than one in eight students across the nation walks to school.[23] At the same time, fewer and fewer children are taking the school or municipal bus, even when service is provided to their neighborhood. Nationally, more than twice as many trips to school are made by car than by school bus.[24] This has resulted in part from where new public schools are being located as district budgets contract. New schools have been constructed to handle growing school-age populations in expanding suburbs and exurbs, with many being placed even farther from town centers than the new housing developments they are serving because land is cheaper there.[25]

A 2005 University of Oregon study analyzed how students were getting to and from Skyview Middle School in the Bend, Oregon, area. The majority of the respondents lived beyond a one-and-a-half-mile radius, qualifying them for bus service. Of these, fewer than half took the bus to school and roughly half took the bus home. About sixty percent were driven to school by carpool or alone by a parent, most of whom cited convenience as the reason they drove their children to school.[26] Parents found it more expedient, for example, to drop their child off on the way to work than to load them on the bus. And what of the students who lived less than a mile and half from school, a distance readily walked or biked by a healthy middle school student? Almost two-thirds were driven to school.[27]

Handling security at a middle school in suburban Connecticut, Tom was so shocked by the traffic clogging the school lot every morning that he started counting the number of vehicles dropping off students. On an average day, more than a third of the enrolled students were being driven to school, even though the school is centrally located, and the district provides free bus service to every neighborhood. Most of those buses arrive and leave every day less than half full. Some car drop-offs and pickups are by parents whose children have extracurricular activities, but most are more discretionary. One stay-at-home mother who had been driving her children to this school every day for the past few years couldn't even remember why she had started the habit.

There are many reasons other parents give for why they drive their children to school, or why they allow them, if they are old enough, to drive themselves. These include a variety of fears, many misplaced, like the one that kids are in danger traveling by bus. In fact, according to the National Highway Traffic Safety Association, children are eight times safer riding the bus to school than being driven by a parent or guardian.[28] Add teenage drivers to the mix and the risk balloons: children are sixty times more likely to die being driven or driving themselves than if they take the bus.[29]

Similarly, some parents are worried that their children will be hit by a vehicle while they walk along busy streets. So driving to school begets more driving to school. Of course, cars are a danger to all pedestrians, but just 16 percent of the total number of children under fourteen killed by cars were pedestrians; it is as passengers that they are much more likely to be hurt. Sadly, children are also in far greater fatal danger from the childhood obesity that a lack of exercise contributes to than from being struck by a car as they walk to school.[30]

"When I was a kid," one retired man explained, "my parents didn't drive me all over town! I rode my bike. I walked. I played Little League baseball—I rode my bike. I left the house in the baseball uniform with the bat and the ball and got on the bike." Rebutting the common argument that kids today have busier schedules, he went on, "I didn't get dropped off at soccer practice. You know, I didn't—I took piano lessons. I rode buses to a different town to go to school. No one dropped me off and picked me up." This kind of talk can be dismissed as the hyperbole of a doddering grandparent who claims to have walked a mile to school each day, uphill both ways. But it does reflect a very real sea change over just a few decades in how kids move through the world. Today, in many communities, seeing a child walking to school or to play is about as common as seeing one riding a horse there. Getting from home to school or to the ball field has become a commute rather than a respite or adventure.

For parents, the drive might represent a few more minutes with their child, but for the child it extends the amount of time he or she is indoors, sedentary, supervised in a structured activity, isolated from the community, and surrounded by electronic devices. Some parents think they do their children a favor by driving them instead of making them get up a bit earlier and hurrying them out the door to walk to a bus stop. What they are really doing is training their children to drive rather than get exercise or use transit, even when that transportation costs nothing out-of-pocket and shows up near the end of the driveway.

As children get older and are able to drive themselves, getting them to ride the bus is a battle many parents aren't willing to fight if they can afford not to. To teenagers, as to the society at large, the bus connotes lower socioeconomic status. One young man from a wealthy St. Louis suburb told the familiar story of how, when he was growing up, cars were "definitely a status symbol. You had—the social classes at my high school were rather distinct because, well, the school district bused in kids from the city of St. Louis, sort of the low end socioeconomically, and they didn't have cars. And then there was an area of the high school that was pretty much just middle class. So it's not like they didn't have cars but they weren't, you know. . . . And here was this other area of town a little bit to the east that was much, much wealthier. . . . They would drive BMWs and Mercedes, Volvos, things like that, to the school."

So when parents let their children drive rather than take the bus (as when they make choices about which car their child should drive) they are also instructing their children in the hidden curriculum of social class.

THE STARBUCKS EFFECT

Many other discretionary trips or added legs such as driving the children to school have become normalized to the point of seeming essential. Nancy McGuckin, a travel behavior analyst, coined the term "the Starbucks effect" to illustrate that the growth of specific kinds of consumer behavior was worsening traffic, as Americans added to their daily routines stops for coffee or food once prepared in the home or bought at the work site.

McGuckin found that in the six years from 1995 to 2001, Americans made over one and a half million more stops in their cars to get something to eat or to buy a cup of coffee. Of course, Starbucks alone is not responsible for all of this extra driving, but as the reinventor of the coffee house, the company led the foodservice industry in this transformation of consumer behavior. In the time span McGuckin studied, Starbucks increased its North American store count to 3,780, helping to popularize the purchase and consumption of coffee outside the home.[31] The number of Starbucks ballooned to 11,168 by early 2008, encouraging many more trips since McGuckin conducted her analysis.[32]

The irony, of course, is that many of us see these pit stops as one small way to relieve the hassles and pressures of our daily working lives, including the grind of gridlock or the boredom of a long commute. And these stops may also be motivated by a genuine, largely unarticulated desire to share public space and interact with others face to face, even if this socializing is in the momentary gathering of other random consumers/ commuters who, like us, are overpaying for their morning joe. Suddenly that geriatric moron in the Audi who left his turn signal on for three miles turns out to be the smiling, polite older man holding the cafe door open for you. Starbucks founder Howard Schultz has been explicit about his company's intent to tap into Americans' thirst for social unity and kinship, stating, "We're in the business of human connection and humanity, creating communities in a third place between home and work."[33] And yet by rewarding ourselves in this way, we can punish ourselves, and others, by making an incremental contribution to traffic.

The Starbucks effect is spurring extra trips at hours well outside of our commutes, as more stores stay open 24 hours a day. Bill and Sarah, a professional couple with two children, found that a few years ago Bill, even after long days filled with commuting, working, and running errands, started popping out some nights at around nine o'clock and driving a few miles to the local Dunkin' Donuts in their Connecticut suburb. Driving to get coffee is more appealing than brewing a pot at home, Bill says, because it "is bought—out. It is like going out to dinner. You don't have to clean up . . . someone makes it for you." According to Sarah, his motivation may be to leave to her the task of putting the children to bed. Their daughter has another theory: that he likes driving Sarah's car, an Acura MDX. Regardless, once Bill returns with the two cups, he and Sarah can finally sit down and relax a bit together before heading to bed to rest up for another hectic two-income, two-child day.

Despite the growth of Internet shopping, car ownership and driving continue to promote consumerism. As we drive more, we buy more. Of course, so-called trip chaining is sensible; if we stop by the grocery store on the way home from work, we can save gas and time. But much of the shopping we do is more impulsive and some of this is spurred by mobile advertising—ads we see on billboards or hear on the car radio.[34]

It turns out that the more time people spend in their cars, the more the shopping decisions they make are last-minute, unplanned, and influenced by mobile advertising. According to Arbitron, which tracks radio listeners, one in five Americans report that a billboard advertising a sale or special motivated them to visit a retailer later that day, and a third say that a billboard caused them to visit later in the week. Nearly half indicate that a radio commercial promoting a sale or special led them to visit a store the same day. People who drive more miles have higher rates of responding to mobile advertising, and they are responding not just with impulse purchases and food but bigger-ticket items. People who are the heaviest in-car radio listeners, for example, report being more likely to buy or lease a new car in the coming year.[35]

Numerous new drivers have told us that the first trip they took after getting their driver's license was to go purchase something, usually food. One 17-year-old boy described how a light bulb switched on the very night he got his license: "It was nice, like, the first day I got it, I got home and I was like, you know what, I don't want to eat here tonight! I want a hamburger and fries! So I went down to Joey's and I got a hamburger and fries. It was awesome." For some teens, this remains the paramount advantage of being able to drive. Eighteen-year-old Louis takes his mother to work so that he can then have the car to "drive to get things, to buy things." When pressed for details about where and what these "things" were, he replied, "The market—to maybe buy a tuna wrap or some other food. Usually tuna wraps."

The upshot of all these shopping trips is that the busiest hour on our nation's roads is no longer during a weekday morning or evening commute, but at one in the afternoon on Saturday.[36]

It can take keeping a trip diary, something like a diet journal, in which miles and minutes on the road are tracked instead of calories consumed, for drivers to realize just how much time they truly spend in their cars and for what less-than-rewarding or unnecessary purposes. The result surprised photographer Liz, of Oakland, California, who for just a few weeks kept a notebook in her car in which she recorded where she went and why and how long it took. Liz doesn't enjoy driving, considers herself to be eco-conscious, and assumed she drove less than a lot of other people, so she was upset to find that her driving was in line with national averages. In short, she was taking more trips and traveling more miles than she had guessed. When she went back to assess how much of this car time was essential or enjoyable, she immediately saw which types of trips she could cut down on—and did.

The Oregon Department of Transportation, along with other public and private organizations, has launched an electronic trip diary on its "Drive Less. Save More" campaign web site. Logging trips enables registered users to keep track of their success in reducing driving through trip chaining, carpooling, or other alternatives. In the site's first ten months, users of this single online trip diary cut more than 900,000 miles from their driving and could take satisfaction in seeing how much they had saved in emissions as well as in gas and other expenses.[37]

A raised consciousness of just how much say we really do have in how much we drive can be empowering. Rather than wait for outside forces to impose change upon us, we can take control of at least some of the time we spend on the road and the miles we put on the odometer—and do so as an individual choice.

WHERE'S THE PARTY?
A VACATION DAY WITH THE LENNOXES

More and more trips have caused the nation's number of passenger miles—that is, the number of miles logged by individuals, including drivers and passengers—to climb to an astronomical 4.6 trillion a year.[38] (Compare this to 180 billion passenger miles annually for rail and bus travel.) And somehow, despite the increasing amount of driving we feel we can't avoid, and the many trips we take to shop and conduct household business, some people still choose to hop in their cars and drive at least once a week "just for the fun of it."[39] The old-fashioned Sunday drive is not dead and maybe it shouldn't be. Cutting down on extraneous trips to Lowe's and the dry cleaner and putting that time and money toward vacation travel with the family, for instance, would surely be a good thing.

In the parallel America of car commercials, we are mostly out there enjoying exciting outings at the shore and in the mountains. "Make Tuesday a Saturday," commands an ad for Toyota's Sequoia, which "allows you to see a weekend where others see a workday." A group of fun-lovers have taken the Sequoia to a beautiful open meadow to engage in an exotic new sport—rolling around inside huge inflatable play spheres they have rented called "Zorbs." This commercial, titled "Zorb with the Lennoxes," appeared on Toyota's web site in an uncut version, which opens with the father explaining how important it is for he and his wife to be "getting out of the city and getting out into nature and make sure we expose ourselves and our children to, um, oxygen." The commercial is part of a larger campaign that follows Sequoia-owning families on a variety of traditional and quirky adventures in nature, including "Surfing with the Geiselmans" and "Trike Racing with the Robinsons."[40]

Yet the freedom and escape from the daily grind promised by the car commercials is elusive. In the real America, even our weekends aren't spent driving to these weekend activities. Laurence and Suzanne, a young married couple as yet unencumbered by children, listed their most typical Saturday destinations: Costco, Wal-Mart, and out to dinner or to the mall to window-shop. According to a 2004 survey of domestic trip activity conducted by the Travel Industry Association of America, only 11 percent of leisure travelers reported engaging in any type of activity in the outdoors and only 7 percent of respondents visited a national or state park. The number-one activity undertaken by domestic leisure travelers, reported by 30 percent of respondents in TIA's survey, once again was shopping.

Cars *can* enable individuals and families to relax, have fun, and enjoy the beauty and excitement of nature in far-flung locations. Nevertheless, even though most of this kind of travel is undertaken by car, vacation trips account for far less than 1 percent of all car trips and less than 3 percent of all miles driven.[41] This raises the question of why more Americans don't rent rather than buy the SUVs and other expensive, gas-thirsty vehicles many are buying with the idea that they will be used to spend more quality time with their families.

Of course, many Americans can't afford to take their family on the vacation they would like. Even among those who can, a good number feel uncomfortable taking time away from work. A third of Americans, more than 51 million workers, do not take all of the vacation days their employer allows, and roughly one in five have been forced to cancel or postpone planned vacations due to work responsibilities.[42] In a downsizing economy, many find their overwhelming workload or job insecurity keeps them from taking the break time they have earned. And that Tuesday the Lennoxes made a Saturday? Even a day off here and there is increasingly harder to swing as employers squeeze more hours weekly out of their salaried employees and expect more weekend work. One man recalled how, when he was growing up in the 1950s, his father was at home for dinner with the family every night, then lamented the fate of the traditional workweek: "Nine times out of ten, he'd work a forty-hour week. Go in at eight, come home at five. Today, if you're in management, if you work less than fifty hours a week, they don't think you're very good."

We are driving to vacation less and less, but we are working more and more, in no small part, to drive our cars to work and shop.

DRIVE TIME REMAKES US

The nation has long clung to the idea that driving is easier than other modes of transportation, when the overwhelming evidence is that, with the exception of the lucky few who have scenic, short, and traffic-free commutes, it is harder—on our psyches and on our schedules. We stubbornly associate driving with convenience, flow, speed, and pleasure, ideas fostered and continually reinforced by car advertising, which is replete with images of fleet driving and roads empty of other vehicles.

Take the magazine ad shot from the perspective of a passenger sitting in the back seat of a Lincoln MKX who is looking past the driver and windshield onto a panoramic city view. The car might be parked on a peak overlooking the city or it could be suspended in midair. The copy reads: "I used to work in a cubicle. One day I escaped. Now, all of my thinking is done outside the box. My dream is to have an office with a view. I think I'll take this next call at 1,200 feet." A second ad in the same 2007 campaign has an even tighter shot through the windshield, positioning the reader as the driver. This time we see nothing but an empty highway heading into the horizon. The huge sky is beautifully streaked with clouds lit by a golden sunset. "Last I remember," the poetic copy fantasizes, "I was drowning in a sea of yellow taxis. Then I hit the accelerator. Now the only yellow I see is leading the way. *My dream is to experience more freedom.* It's all smooth sailing from here." This car promises the driver will somehow escape from the very traffic conditions that car ownership has created in the first place.

One driver, who clocks about 400 miles weekly—his morning routine alone involves driving his wife to the train, going back home to pick up his children, taking them to school, and driving himself to work—echoed the automakers' pitch that buying a new car could bring back the past, a past when driving was easier: "I have to say, as I get older, I'm getting picky about which car I want to drive, because I'm like, I'm really tired of driving this car. I want to resort back to my teenage years, I want a faster car, a more powerful car." He went on to explain that in this merged future/past, he enjoys driving. "I guess in that sense then, I'd enjoy it if I had a faster car, but if I continue driving the car I have now, I don't really enjoy driving. I just use it as a means of transportation. To get from one point to another." And to another and to another and to another. As one auto executive put it, Americans love "the idea of driving" more than they love the reality of driving.

The positive emotions associated with this "idea of driving" also well from deep in our memory banks, when it was possible to take a Sunday drive and not encounter traffic. Holly Hulfish is the exhibit logistics manager at the Saratoga Auto Museum in upstate New York. Working at the museum and coming into contact with its many members and visitors, Holly sees the love of cars as a universal form of nostalgia: "The automobile is important to everybody, whether you realize it or not, whether you're a motorhead or not, because we all have memories. We all remember our first family car and going on vacations in it. We all remember our first dates in a car, or the first car we bought, or the first car we made out in. . . . Everybody. Whether a car is to get from point A to point B or whether you are madly in love with cars, everybody has memories, everyone is tied into the automobile." Many of Holly's personal memories evoke the intoxicating, aimless freedom of childhood summers. She spent some time growing up in northern Virginia and describes with wistful fondness bumping around in the back of a pickup truck with a load of other kids or zipping along the backcountry roads on a motorcycle or in a car with her older brother when both were well below the legal driving age.

While advertising images and fond memories still cloud our vision of the automobile, our ambivalence toward driving is growing. As Jorge, an urban driver with a new job and a new, longer commute to go along with it said, "At my old job, I used to work ten minutes away. Boom and come back. Now I'm driving like thirty, forty minutes. It's nice if you get to just sit there and the music is like good, it's relaxing." Without pausing though, and with greater intensity, he continued, "I hate traffic though. I think everyone does. I *hate* sitting there. You want to go home. You hate to be just sitting there." For each individual, there is a tipping point when the realities intrude on the dream and the present replaces the past. For our nation as a whole, this tipping point will be reached when we come to grips with just how much driving is shaping our lives and changing how we interact with others—in other words, how drive time remakes us.

CAPSULE LIVING

The average American spends more than eighteen and one-half hours a week in the car, or an astounding month out of every year. Out of our *waking* lives, however, car travel accounts for about one out of every six hours. That is 2.6 hours a day or two full months spent driving.[43]

Though it might not seem like it to the parents who spend their days ferrying children around, much of Americans' drive time is spent alone. Some commuters cherish this "alone time," especially working parents, who can find no other time when they aren't surrounded by and responding to the needs of bosses, coworkers, clients, spouses, aging parents, or kids. To Dave, in his thirties, the morning commute is "a chance to be alone, to think, to listen to whatever you want on the radio, to be alone by yourself." Returning home, it is time to "roll down the windows, let the wind come in." There are healthier, more relaxing, more productive ways to pursue solitude, but for working parents squeezed by responsibilities at work and home, the route between the two can be justified as necessary to both of the competing worlds. It is time alone that is seen as unselfish and cannot be contested.

The rest of us tend to travel alone even when it is the antithesis of relaxing. In most states, between 70 percent and 80 percent of commutes to work, the most regular trips we take, are by solo drivers.[44] In 1980, when gas prices were high but traffic thinner than today, about 20 percent of workers carpooled to work; by 2000, that percentage had dropped to just over 12 percent. Carpooling has increased slightly in some parts of the country since its low in 1990,[45] but sharing rides and taking public transportation are solutions that only a minority is prepared to pursue to reduce their frustrations with growing traffic. Where 10 percent of commuters walked to work in 1960, only 2.5 percent did so in 2005.[46] A 2004 AP poll showed that people were willing to vary their routes and the times they left for work but were unwilling to do much else to avoid traffic problems.[47] When gas prices rose above $4 a gallon in the first part of 2008, miles traveled dropped by 4 percent compared to a year earlier, and 8 percent of Americans changed their commuting patterns in some way, but the changes were not vast; consumers reported being more willing to cut back or postpone spending on major purchases, vacations, and even groceries than to reduce driving in the face of expensive fuel.[48]

This makes some sense, given the effects of sprawl. There may not be many fellow employees of a company who live near each other because everyone is spread out across metropolitan areas, and they converge upon their workplace from many directions. However, workplace bulletin boards or online carpooling exchanges could locate possible partners nearby, if a commuter is willing to give up what seems like total freedom in his or her schedule. All it can take to change long-standing resistance to the idea of carpooling is to try it. After Bryant Whelan joined a carpool at his Atlanta employer as part of a Good Morning America Carpool Challenge, he blogged, "I initially wanted to start carpooling to work because, like everyone else, I was feeling the pinch from the gas prices. The strange thing is, I would say that has been only one of the smaller reasons I stuck with the car pool. After spending a couple of weeks with my co-workers during the commute I noticed that I was always in a better mood when I got to work because I was laughing all the way to work rather than cursing the red lights and traffic that were the bain [sic] of my weekday mornings."[49]

Neighbors can also ride together to the mall or the big-box retailers to which many people drive on the weekends. These still-rare examples of ridesharing could work well in some highly social communities where neighbors already spend time with each other. But many people do not know their neighbors and do not wish to know them. When one couple moved into their new suburban home in 2004, they invited everyone on the cul-de-sac to an open house. A guest in her seventies remarked that it was the first time she had been invited to a party on the block, and she was meeting many of her neighbors for the first time. This woman and her husband had moved into their house when it was first developed—more than thirty years earlier.

Suburban sprawl has done much more than physically separate home from work, neighbor from neighbor, and colleague from colleague. As Lieven De Cauter explains in *The Capsular Civilization*, it has encouraged a literal and psychological "encapsulation" in which cars shuttle individuals in a metal casing, closed off from others, "between controlled and enclosed zones," from office park to shopping mall to gated community.[50] De Cauter explains how this encapsulation results in a "logic of hyperindividualism"[51] that makes carpooling, for example, anathema even if it is highly rational.

Even carpooling with family members becomes something to be resisted as a gesture of individualism. Maria described how she and her husband moved out of New York City into the suburbs, already owning one vehicle. They "immediately bought another car as a train car," although both would be commuting to work on the same line into Manhattan's Grand Central Terminal. In fact, they bought the car before they moved into the new home. Now, each weekday they leave the house separately and pay to park two cars at the station lot. "He takes an early train, I take a little later train." She paused and then laughed, "and I'm not good at depending on him to drive me anywhere." Serious again, she explained, "I'm very independent."

Within our individual "capsules," we have access to more and more technology, some of which we use to stay connected across "capsules" with others who are spending too much time isolated and in transit. But the technologies can be aggravating and unsafe to others with whom we share the road. As one man protested, "We've been driving cars since the early nineteen hundreds, and for the better part of a century nobody thought that they needed a phone when they were driving. You would stop and go to a pay phone if you needed a phone. . . . And now, I see it all the time: people get in the car, and they start the car, and they start to drive away and the first thing you see them do is pick up the phone. Why don't they make the phone call before they drive the car?" Many would agree with this complaint, as cell phones further disconnect drivers from those immediately around them—the others on the road with whom they are supposed to be interacting.

But some understand very well why the call is not made before the drive—because there is no time. Ever-expanding workdays, further elongated by commuting, have cut into our time with family and friends. Thirty-two-year-old Heather is one of these drivers. This working wife, who routinely puts in a nine-hour day at her full-time employer, then travels to freelance jobs that supplement her salary before tackling paperwork she has brought home, uses her time in the car to "build in family talk time." She knows that using the phone, though she mostly uses the hands-free option, makes her less attentive and has at times caused her to "brake suddenly" to avoid collisions. Still, she is willing to take this risk. Heather reported being on the phone "every time" she is in the car, even driving on the highway, where it makes her more nervous to do so. She admits to using the phone in the car for just about everything, including making appointments and shopping, activities her hectic schedule won't otherwise allow. Heather is not just passing the time in the car on the phone. She is living her life in the car on the phone.

As Americans spend more time in the car and lead busier lives, interior creature comforts and ultimately distracting technologies have become increasingly popular. Automakers have responded with a bewildering range of pricey entertainment options, some to make our time in the car productive, some to make it pleasurable. As a result, the American car has gone beyond the mobile living room to become mobile den and mobile office. Some auto advertising goes so far as to suggest that entertainment technology is no accessory but in fact the very purpose of the car. One VW ad touted the ability of a variety of its models to amplify an electric guitar through the car's audio system, and pictured a hip young guy jamming, plugged into his vehicle in his garage, as friends looked on.[52]

One experienced car salesperson saw that people are frustrated with traffic and looking for ways to pass the lost time. She went on to explain how the European automakers had a hard time catching on to how Americans were dealing with this frustration. "Cup holders are so important to Americans. Like it's all about having your water bottle, having your coffee, having your soda. And Mercedes, BMW, and also Audi do not understand that, they don't build their cars with correct cup holders. And people are getting angry and going to other companies. So we would go to BMW and say, 'We need cup holders.'" The BMW management response, she said, in a pretty good German accent, was, "Why, why do they have all this water?!" Although she couldn't explain the cup holder fascination exactly, she told them that people are in their cars more, "needing something to do" and "needing the comforts in their vehicle."

While one grandmother who drives her grandchildren from home to school to activities told this salesperson that she did not want a DVD player in her new car because she wanted to talk to the children, this was a rare request. For many, all the technological "comforts" in the car are a way to distract the passengers, enabling the driver to drive more comfortably. To be comfortable in cars has come to mean separate and isolated, even from our loved ones. The reason why technology keeps being added, according to this salesperson, is that "people on car trips with kids are like 'I have to have a DVD player' . . . having that many people in close proximity for a long period of time, I think that's why technology is inside the cars."

Car technology can reconnect us to the people we have driven away from, but it can also disconnect us from those we are driving with. In either case we remain, in some way, alone.

WHY RUSH LIMBAUGH LIKES SPRAWL

The MP3, DVD, and CD players in many new cars aside, most of us primarily use the good old radio for our in-car entertainment. And as we drive more, we listen more, and one of the media we have been listening to more is talk radio. The talk radio explosion in the late 1980s and 1990s is often credited to the repeal of the Fairness Doctrine, which had previously stipulated that broadcasted political opinion must be balanced. Four hundred stations across the United States hosted shows in the talk format in 1990; by 2008, this number had grown to 2,056—an increase of 500 percent.[53] The audience has continued to grow in recent years, a phenomenon attributable in part to more Americans' spending more time driving and listening to the car radio. As one listener in Pennsylvania put it, "My ride to work, each way, each day, is two hours, and has been for the last eight years. I live for talk radio. . . . There are days I sit in my driveway, after coming home, for up to ten minutes while an engaging discussion is ongoing. It's addicting."[54]

Talk radio has been described by its devotees as the new town square—the broadcast equivalent of a Speaker's Corner or a town hall meeting—where average citizens, not just the powerful, can call in and be heard. Although the phone-in portions of most shows are limited and heavily screened to ensure that the host's point of view triumphs, talk radio still positions itself as the voice of the people, the voice of freedom. One Florida driver vehemently agreed with the talk radio host—Rush Limbaugh, she thought—who she remembered arguing that the real reason why Al Gore was against suburban sprawl was not because it led to increased pollution from longer commutes but because he and his liberal cohorts didn't like it that so many Americans were listening to conservative talk radio. Because American conservatives tend to believe that television and newspapers have a liberal bias, they view talk radio as their counterbalancing political and social voice, which they believe to be otherwise repressed.[55]

And talk radio is overwhelmingly conservative. The top ten hosts are all conservative or self-described moderates who lean conservative. The top two, Rush Limbaugh and Sean Hannity, have by far the largest audiences, with Limbaugh pulling in a weekly cumulative audience of 14 million listeners and Hannity garnering 13 million.[56] These talkers have a considerable influence on their listeners. Just as radio advertising has been shown to compel store visits and purchases, radio ideology has been shown to change attitudes and even voting patterns.[57] That is, conservative radio really can and does sell conservatism. One study of Rush Limbaugh's show demonstrated that "regular listening not only correlates with attitudes that reflect Limbaugh's message; listening also relates to opinion change toward greater conservatism and antipathy toward Limbaugh's favorite targets."[58] As in advertising, repetition of a message works: in this study, listeners were more likely to come to agree with Limbaugh on the dead-horse issues he beat most often.

While listening to moderate talk radio was shown to lead to being better informed, a survey of adults in San Diego found that more exposure to conservative talk radio resulted in listeners being more *mis*informed on issues.[59] For example, an overwhelming majority of conservative talk radio listeners believed the following patently false statements to be true: "Illegal immigrants cause most of the crime in this area," "President Reagan cut the national deficit," "Giving clean needles to drug addicts has increased AIDS in California," and "Most of the homeless in America are too lazy to work." Clearly, depending on your station choice, riding in the car may actually make you less knowledgeable about the world you live in.

Political talk radio is also overwhelmingly inflammatory. One man wondered whether the fiery, hostile tone of much talk radio was a natural for drivers girded for their fight with traffic and highway hazards. But whether talk is angry and explicitly right-wing or—like most morning shows that mix talk with music—is goofy, upbeat, and seemingly apolitical, this kind of radio narrows the messages drivers hear to the viewpoints they already have and want to allow into the controlled environment of their car. As a result, being in the car today can reinforce lifestyle choices and ideology.

Conservatives are not the only drivers who live in the media bubble of their station presets. Air America and NPR provide their worldview to political liberals and moderates. And our multicultural world can remain reassuringly monocultural in the encapsulation of our cars. African Americans across the country can enjoy the Tom Joyner or the Steve Harvey Morning Show on their way to work. Latinos can tune into Spanish language stations in almost every corner of the country on their way home. Meanwhile, immigrants can listen exclusively to programs dedicated to the language, culture, and news of their homeland, be they Russians in Boston, Hmong in the Twin Cities, or Hindus in Houston. And no matter how old we are, we can even stay frozen in time, listening over and over again to the radio hits of our high school and college years.

The irony of the smorgasbord of choice we have in media outlets in the car, which could provide one way to break free from our encapsulated lives and engage in the world, is that rather than sampling the variety available, we tend to restrict ourselves to the world we know and the world we want to know. We can stay safe inside our media capsule, shutting out the rest of the world and other worldviews.

The detachment from society that our layered encapsulation creates—alone inside our cars and inside our heads—has a multiplicity of consequences. Just looking at how it affects our behavior toward other people on the road, however, shows that the ways it remakes us are not always pretty.

HELL ON WHEELS:
ROAD RAGE, OTHER DRIVERS, AND THE POPE

Sartre's much-repeated line, "Hell is other people," may hold as a truism more on the nation's highways than anywhere else in the public sphere.

Americans tend to treat traffic and its related hassles as a problem caused by others, failing to recognize our own role as drivers. When the number of media reports about road rage surged in the 1990s, as Barry Glassner pointed out in his influential bestseller *The Culture of Fear: Why Americans Are Afraid of the Wrong Things,* the phenomenon was almost universally presented as a threat to, rather than a threat posed by, American drivers.

Glassner states, "In just about every contemporary American scare, rather than confront disturbing shortcomings in society the public discussion centers on disturbed individuals. Demented drivers rather than insane public policies occupied center stage in the coverage of road rage. Where reference was made at all to serious problems that drivers face, these were promptly shoved behind a curtain of talk about violent motorists."[60] The sudden focus on isolated cases of extreme road rage became a diversion from the growing systemic problems of traffic congestion and the need to explore solutions to them. It also became a way for politicians to avoid suggesting that drivers might drive less or encouraging them to do so through congestion pricing and other effective but unpopular traffic reduction strategies.

Glassner contextualized the risks posed by road rage by comparing the small number of crash fatalities caused by angry drivers to those caused by drunk drivers. Still, irate drivers do kill, causing thousands of crashes every year.[61] But research studies suggests that traffic conditions, as much as any preexisting mental health issues or other stressors, contribute to road rage. One researcher interviewed drivers on their cell phones as they navigated both heavy and light traffic congestion during a single commute. Drivers reported higher stress and aggression when traffic congestion was high, and showed it, tailgating and honking at other vehicles.[62]

Even measures meant to improve congestion, such as road and highway construction and repair, can get under our skin. Highway construction workers and flag people have always been endangered by drivers who refuse to slow down as they pass work sites, but there have also been reports of highway workers being purposefully struck by cars or shot at by angry drivers.[63]

Angry interactions on the nation's roadways are much more common than these extreme examples, however. It is nearly impossible to find drivers who do not admit to having sworn at or given the finger to others who have upset them. Of course, anger is a natural expression of a very rational fear of being endangered by careless or reckless driving. But drivers also fume at people they feel are driving too timidly or cautiously. Bolder drivers will often describe less aggressive driving as being "just as dangerous" as traveling well over the speed limit or weaving in and out of traffic, although their fury is more likely caused by their own impatience than by any actual threat posed by another driver's perceived pokiness.

One reason ordinarily kind and careful people can behave badly on the road is, unsurprisingly, the mental armor of anonymity that being inside a car provides. In a recent study confirming this factor, college students received random assignments in a computerized driving simulation. Some were asked to imagine driving in a convertible with the top down, visible to other drivers, while others were asked to imagine driving in a convertible with the top up. The students who imagined themselves enclosed in the car with the top up drove at seriously higher speeds, ran more red lights, caused more collisions, and hit more pedestrians than those who were more exposed in the top-down group. In one real-life example, a woman who accidentally cut off another driver was surprised to see that the driver who raced up next to her to sneer at her and give her the finger was a colleague also on his way to work. When she saw him later, he sheepishly apologized for his crass in-car behavior.

Sociologist Jack Katz oversaw a study in which 150 Los Angelenos were interviewed about their experiences "becoming pissed off while driving" in the nation's most congested city.[64] Katz sought to explain why drivers became angry at one another, how they experienced that anger, and how they expressed and processed it.

Katz was particularly interested in why drivers react angrily even when the situation is clearly not one in which the driver was put into any danger, that is, when it is not apparently a fear response. He also took note of the fact that passengers, experiencing the same situation in the same moment, rarely become as emotionally exercised as the drivers. Katz explains that this is so because "driving requires and occasions a metaphysical merger, an intertwining of the identities of driver and car that generates a distinctive ontology in the form of a person-thing, a humanized car or alternatively, an automobilized person"; as a result, when another car cuts us off, we experience it as though our body, not our car, has suffered an "amputation."[65] Katz further explains that this sense of oneness with the car we are driving means that being snarled in traffic or having to slow down or speed up because of the actions of another creates a feeling of "falling out of a flow and being stuck or held back" in which we feel constrained and trapped, the absolute antithesis of the freedom that we fundamentally believe driving should provide us.[66] Those who mess with our driving are messing with us, our plans, our lives. We experience not just a loss of the speed and convenience we associate with driving but also of psychic control.

We can also become angry when we witness seemingly dangerous or incompetent driving that we anticipate will cause a problem for us or other drivers with whom we identify—other good drivers who don't exhibit these antisocial behaviors, such as talking on cell phones. Drivers on phones in fact often drive more slowly and make us take longer to get where we're going.[67] Seeing such driving behavior as a social offense can elevate our irritation to agitation. Recent media coverage has educated Americans about the dangers of driving while talking or texting; risky road behavior like this can turn a usually placid person livid. As one older man explained, "Cell phones and cars. That's my biggest pet peeve. I cannot tell you how many times I've seen someone careening around a corner on the wrong side of the road, not paying attention to traffic lights or stop signs and they're on a cell phone. . . . I know a family that got rear-ended. They were stopped at a light and a girl on a cell phone smacked right into them," he said, clapping his hands together. "Luckily they didn't get hurt. That's my pet peeve. That can drive me almost homicidal. Cell phones and cars." In simply recounting his story, which happened not to him but to someone else, this man's "pet peeve" mushroomed quickly into murderous thoughts.

The fact that so few drivers remain consistently serene on the roadways means it makes more sense to see road rage as our own problem, one that we can mitigate by driving less, driving more calmly, and driving more carefully. Aggressive and cautious drivers alike get angry and get hostile as they react and re-react. Katz's interviews revealed a sweeping tendency for all kinds of drivers to seek to "teach a lesson" to or get back at drivers who they feel have wronged them or misbehaved on the road. Everyone seems to have a story to tell of absurd retaliations on the road. One man we interviewed named Everett tells about the time a driver on an access road, talking on his cell phone, made an improper and illegal turn onto the main road, causing Everett to slow to avoid hitting him. When Everett honked, the driver, left hand still pressing the cell phone to his ear, switched to using his right elbow on the steering wheel so that he could give Everett the finger. Even years later, such memories still stir feelings of outrage.

A number of web sites have popped up that allow people to "out" bad drivers, making plain that even if the stress caused by traffic does not lead to aggressive behaviors on the road, many drivers take their aggravation home with them. Sites such as Platewire.com provide an opportunity to vent to someone other than your spouse about that idiot who cut you off, drove too fast, drove too slowly, stopped too long at the stop sign, didn't stop long enough at the stop sign, had no lights on, kept their brights on, parked illegally in the handicapped spot, hogged multiple parking spots, didn't signal, didn't look while backing up, or honked at you for no reason. You can also reward "good" drivers, but it is hard to find one of those postings on the site. Certainly this is a healthier way of getting back at others on the road who anger us, and could help to break the road rage cycle by providing an outlet for frustration.

Although we don't hear much about bus rage or train rage, traveling by public transportation can have its own frustrations and produce stress. Still, people who choose to take public transportation often say they do so to relax, read, and even nap while traveling. Public transit riders can de-stress by chatting with fellow travelers, at the same time possibly making friends, deepening relationships with neighbors, even finding a potential life partner: Amtrak can take credit for countless first dates. One New Jerseyan shared a litany of reasons for having recently made the switch from driving to work to taking the train, including getting exercise on the walk to the station and no longer having to deal with other drivers who speed and "take stupid chances." His primary reason, though, was that "the unpredictability of traffic makes it stressful." From one day to the next his commute by car could be twenty minutes or forty minutes long.

Research, much of which has been conducted on commuters, has repeatedly shown traveling by car to be more nerve-racking. Because it is more unpredictable and requires a higher level of attentiveness and exertion, driving leads car commuters to report significantly higher levels of stress and a more negative mood than train commuters or those who bike or walk to work.[68] And commuters who experience a demanding commute have a lowered tolerance for frustration,[69] meaning that when they come home, they are likely to be less patient with their children and spouses. One commuter explained that when he gets stuck in traffic on the way to work, he does not get angry with the other drivers on the road but with his wife or kids for slowing his departure from home in the morning, delaying him enough so that he ended up being unable to avoid rush hour. Stuck in traffic, he finds himself "tense" and "unhappy" before he even faces the pressures of his workday.

Importantly, people with longer commutes report "lower satisfaction with life" than those with short commutes—that is, they are simply less happy.[70] These commuters' spouses are also unhappy. This suggests that workers making the choice to take a higher-paying job with a longer commute on the assumption that the extra income for their family will outweigh the costs of that commute should think twice.

To reduce the psychological strain from driving, medical professionals suggest getting more sleep, leaving earlier, listening to soothing music, exercising, drinking plenty of water, and other coping strategies. The car companies, however, use this stress as a device to sell more cars. Advertising for new vehicles focuses on a host of options designed to relieve the pressures of driving, such as satellite radio, GPS technology, voice commands, and cameras for blind spots.

One Infiniti ad is dominated by a close-up of a dashboard with seemingly more controls than a 747. It extols, "At Infiniti, we anticipate that you will constantly be surrounded by things you'll need to avoid. That's why we created the world's first Around View Monitor. The innovation of the RearView Monitor taken to a higher level. With four cameras, it's an unprecedented advancement that offers a virtually 360-degree perspective on the world. Now parking is as easy and intuitive as driving. You won't find the Around View Monitor on an ordinary luxury crossover vehicle, but you will find it on a very extraordinary one." And you won't find it on last year's model; that's why the consumer needs "The all-new Infiniti EX." In a Toyota ad, the landscape pictured is a dark and menacing urban maze, but the copy reassures: "No matter how lost the city makes you feel, it's comforting to know the RAV4 is engineered to handle it all. With Vehicle Stability Control, 166hp and an EPA 27 mpg hwy rating, solving the city has never been easier."

So it shouldn't be a surprise that when Dodge held an essay contest to identify the American with the most stressful commute, they chose Joel Schneeberger of Chicago, a man whose commute was deemed most miserable because he had to carpool—with his mother-in-law.[71] Joel's prize? A chance to "vent his frustrations" by destroying a vehicle with a Monster Truck and to "avenge" his commute by driving home in his own brand new Dodge Avenger.

The surest way to reduce the stress of driving, however, is to drive less, either by taking public transportation, carpooling, cycling or walking, Internet shopping, relocating, changing jobs, or telecommuting during part of the week. Fully understanding how drive time remakes us—into a more hyperindividualistic, antisocial, angry, and unhealthy person—should be motivation enough to drive less.

Short of these moves, changing the way we see driving—as a cooperative social activity rather than competitive warfare—could provide the relief we need to survive in a world built for the car rather than for people. In their book *Road Rage and Aggressive Driving*, Leon James and Diane Nahl clarify that road rage is both a learned behavior and a choice—something we can unlearn as individuals and a community.[72] The authors propose that it is time for a "coming of age of driving society," in which we evolve past oppositional and defensive driving to "supportive driving," which involves re-visioning other drivers as fellow travelers, who like us are capable of error and have the same rights to use the road, whether they be elderly drivers, inexperienced drivers, or visitors unfamiliar with the area.[73]

This re-visioning can be seen as an issue of self-preservation, or, as the Catholic Church views it, one of morality. In recognition of the pervasiveness of global car culture, the Vatican issued its surprising 2007 "Document of the Pontifical Council for the Pastoral Care of Migrants and Itinerant People: 'Guidelines for the Pastoral Care of the Road',"[74] which the media enjoyed reporting as the Ten Commandments of Driving. The missive detailed how driving, especially in light of worsening traffic, represented an opportunity for believers to sin or rise above, stating, "Cars tend to bring out the 'primitive' side of human beings, thereby producing rather unpleasant results. We need to take these dynamics into account and react by appealing to the noble tendencies of the human spirit, to a sense of responsibility and self-control, in order to prevent manifestations of the psychological regression that is often connected to driving." The document proposed, "Motorists are never alone when they are driving, even when no one is sitting beside them. Driving a vehicle is basically a way of relating with and getting closer to other people, and of integrating within a community of people. This capacity for coexistence . . . [calls for] self-mastery, prudence, courtesy, a fitting spirit of service and knowledge of the Highway Code."

It is important, if not moral, for Americans, even if we have never experienced a serious road rage incident, and even if our commute is relatively short, to recognize that we are part of a mobile society that has its own evolving, complex, and often contradictory set of rules and etiquette. We are spending more of our lives on the road; most of us interact with strangers on the road far more frequently than in any other setting, if only briefly. Because this interaction increasingly takes place as a competition for scarce resources—room to merge on a busy freeway, a spot to park in a crowded lot—it is rarely positive but that doesn't mean it can never be.

At seventeen, high school student Michael is in training for the car life. The automobile, he thinks, is "essential for modern life, you almost need one." Two decades further along in his own car life, thirty-five-year-old James, like many others, has traveled well past "almost." A suburban stay-at-home dad dismissed out of hand the numerous studies that show that driving is bad for one's health, on the basis that we "have no choice" but to drive as much as we do.

Our landscape, sprawled out as a consequence of poor urban planning, shifting employment opportunities, inadequate public transit options, and rising housing costs, does necessitate much driving. But certainly not all, and perhaps not even most, of these miles we drive are truly unavoidable, a fact visible once we analyze how we choose (albeit to a constant drumbeat of ads) to use our vehicles, to commute alone, to drive when public transport is available, to fill our days with the business of consuming. We need to rethink what we truly need and reclaim the control and freedom we like to imagine the car has given us.

Chapter Eight

GETTING CARSICK

ot everyone suffers from the sudden nausea and headache of motion sickness, but each and every American is getting carsick—even if we don't feel it yet. We are getting carsick as we breathe in the toxins that, despite much regulatory reform and improved engineering, continue to spew from our tailpipes. We are getting carsick, some hundreds of thousands of us, from exposure to carcinogenic gasoline on the job. Cars affect our national and individual health in significant but invisible ways. If we were less dependent on the car, and a gasoline-based system, we would experience much lower rates of asthma, heart disease, and cancer, and fewer mothers would have babies with low birth weight. And no matter what alternative fuels are developed to reduce air pollution, a way of life less reliant on driving would help contain America's obesity crisis.

While everyone who breathes air or drives is affected, the more vulnerable among us—the elderly and the young, and those with existing lung or heart disease—suffer the most. So do people living next to freeways and higher traffic areas, people who tend to be poor. But all of us are at risk of unhealthy weight gain, elevated morbidity, and the health effects—even fatal effects—of global warming as it begins to take a toll. Some modes of public transit pose health hazards (diesel buses or trains also emit toxic exhaust), but on a per-person, per-mile basis, these do not come close to rivaling the contributions to our collective ill health made by the private automobile.[1]

DOES THIS CAR MAKE ME LOOK FAT?

We would never buy an outfit, no matter how deceptively slimming, that actually caused us to put on weight. And yet our cars, which we buy in part based on how they look and how they make us look, are causing us to pack on pounds. The Centers for Disease Control has placed a good portion of the blame for the problem of obesity in the United States squarely on "our built environment and the transportation infrastructure," that is, on the car system.[2] The problem is bad and getting worse: by 1997, roughly 40 percent of U.S. adults could be labeled "sedentary" because they undertook no physical activity during their leisure time, and in the past two decades, the number of trips Americans take on foot has declined 42 percent.

And we don't just drive to the destinations that are time-consuming or impossible to reach on foot. Owning a car makes short walks seem long. It prompts the urge to circle a parking lot seeking a "better" parking space to reduce the few steps into the grocery store or the office. As Keli Ballinger, director of Harvard University's Wellness Center, explained, the inertia of driving becomes habitual because when people stop moving their bodies, becoming physically active again is difficult. There is a psychological effect as well; we come to believe that driving even short distances is efficient or sensible even when it is not. To illustrate this, Ballinger shared an anecdote from her recent personal experience as a house hunter: "We were looking at one property and the realtors said, 'Let's go to the next property.' We had two separate cars and I asked how far it was and they said it was two blocks away. I said we could walk, and they said, 'Oh, no. They're really big blocks.' So we literally got in the car and drove two blocks."

In contrast to the driver, the public transit rider typically walks between home and the bus stop or down the subway platform, up the steps and a few blocks to the workplace. Even someone who is at home all day is likely to be more physically active than someone strapped behind the wheel of a car.

Cars have also helped fuel the growth of the calorie-packing fast-food industry. Car culture has put a premium on speed and fostered the idea that convenience and efficiency should rule as we make our way through the day. Now, our stomachs are subject to fill-ups more frequently than our gas tanks as we motor past the ubiquitous foodmongers hawking their wares along the highway. These include such delicacies as the 1,420-calorie Hardee's Monster Thickburger, Wendy's 830-calorie Baconator, the 1,050-calorie Jack in the Box Vanilla Shake, and McDonald's Deluxe Breakfast, which weighs in at 1,140 calories—before the syrup and margarine.

One very overweight man in his late fifties from New Hampshire, Benjamin, described what the fast food–driving nexus has been like for him. At first, he said he loves fast food because "it's easy and it's delicious." But, then, after hesitating for a moment, he went on, "Now that you have me thinking about it, when I would drive through, I would vastly prefer to eat in the car rather than sit down in any of these restaurants because the car was really connected to the experience and felt like the most safe and comfortable environment to eat the food in. When you eat fast food, you *get* it fast but you also want to *eat* it fast, and you want to eat it alone and not in front of other people and in public." Because we so often drive alone, and we so often eat on the road, we often eat alone. But as our collective weight balloons, we also eat alone as a way to deal with the shame attached to eating food we know isn't good for us.

Adriana, a woman in her forties, quickly gained more than ten pounds upon relocating from the city to a suburb and buying a car. Although most consider her quite slim, she worries that her husband, whom she married when she was subway-fit, finds her car-borne body increasingly unattractive. She explained, "I never eat fast food on purpose. I mean, I never drive there; I go there when I'm driving by. It's not like that's where I meet friends to eat out." When she succumbs to the temptations of fast food on the road, she takes care to hide the evidence from her husband, leaving the receipt on the counter and disposing of the bag and cup before she gets home.

Another feedback loop between driving and poor health is that as Americans have gotten fatter, it takes more fuel to drive them around.

Since Americans weigh on average 24 pounds more than they did in 1960, one study found, this has added up to an additional 39 million gallons of gas consumed annually.[3] This, of course, is but a tiny fraction of the 359 million gallons that passenger vehicles consume each *day* in the United States. But this study only took into account the impact of increased weight in a passenger vehicle. The impact of obesity on gas consumption and emissions is actually much worse: as people gain weight, they often move to larger cars and SUVs to accommodate their girth, and, in addition, begin to drive more than they would if they were a healthy weight.

There are other vicious cycles involved in pushing Americans into the weight-gain spas of their cars. As we will see, car-produced air pollution often makes exercising outside unhealthy and makes it so the unhealthy have more difficulty getting outdoor exercise. Driving rather than walking contributes to the expanding American waistline, but walking in our smog-laden environment can reduce weight but burn the lungs.

And once people become overweight, they often collect additional health problems, particularly in their back, legs, and joints. This, in turn, makes walking painful and driving more likely. Benjamin's weight problem led to "discomfort in my knees and ankles . . . it was harder to walk upstairs and do anything that required much exertion, and I eventually developed high blood pressure and was very uncomfortable in my chest." All of this makes exercise painful and fast food even more attractive: "You don't have to get out of your car, you just roll the window down, you hand them the money, and they give you what you want."

Staying in the car becomes the cultural norm. Aleks, a young woman just arrived in Tempe, Arizona, headed outside to walk three blocks to a grocery store. She didn't realize that this was quite a radical move in her new town: "This was not normal to walk down the street on the sidewalk. I was the only person walking for as far as you could see. . . . There were cars honking at me, people just yelling things at me. It was very unpleasant and awkward to *walk,* and it wasn't as if I was doing it in the middle of the day at the height of the heat or something. I had waited until it was a lot cooler and darker and sort of a time when I thought that more people would venture outside and walk places, but it was very clear that people just don't walk anywhere. Almost everyone has a car so they drive."

It is no surprise then that active urbanites who can afford to move indoors to exercise are doing so in droves. Gyms have proliferated, seemingly on every corner. Breathe deeply of the air in any number of smog-choked cities in America, and you'll be tempted to buy stock in Gold's Gym, Crunch, or L.A. Fitness.

Studies have shown that people who shift from driving to taking public transit are, on average, five pounds lighter than they were when using their cars to get to work.[4] This might be called the public transit diet, a diet that small legions have been forced on as bus and rail use spiked along with the one-two punch of rising gas prices and the economic crisis. Fortunately, there are models available for planned communities that build in walkability as a criterion, attacking one of America's worst public health problems.[5]

I'LL TAKE A GAS MASK WITH THAT INFANT CAR SEAT

A 2006 ad for the Lexus touts its optional air filtration system this way: the light fluffy seeds of a giant dandelion have been dispersed on the wind and are headed straight toward the car. As they approach the front grill, their slim stems morph into swords, ready to stab at the driver were it not for the car's "purifying technology"—something the ad copy says "you'd be more likely to find in a hospital or high-tech clean room than in a car." Following the theory that the best defense is a strong offense, Lexus blames the victim—suggesting that the environment is attacking cars, rather than the other way around. Seasonal allergy sufferers may get excited about a new option that protects them from an environmental nuisance, but the tiny airborne weapons that they, and all drivers and passengers, should worry about are the toxins released by the materials used to craft their car's own interior—toxins that easily resist current ventilation systems.

That "new car smell" that causes our hearts to flutter also causes our livers and brain cells to tremble; liver toxicity, birth defects, early puberty, and impaired learning are all associated with exposure to the elevated levels of certain chemicals permeating our vehicles. These chemicals include phthalates, used to soften automotive plastics, and PBDEs, used as fire retardants in many interior components such as dashboards, seats, and steering wheels.[6] These chemicals do not remain embedded in the car parts but do what is called "off-gassing." They exhale, in a way. Then they are inhaled or ingested by drivers and passengers in the form of dust. Heat and UV rays speed up the release of these substances and also create chemical reactions that produce even more toxic compounds. These effects are especially important in warmer climates, particularly when closed car interiors can reach 200 degrees. The accumulation of film on the inside of the windshield of a new car is one place you can see the visible results of that off-gassing, a process that slows down as the car ages but occurs throughout the life of a vehicle.

PBDEs (polybrominated diphenyl ethers, if you'd really like to know) can be found on many consumer products, but concentrations in the atmosphere inside the car are up to five times greater than in our offices or homes, depending on the model. (Concentrations vary widely by model; for example, Mercedes' PBDEs are much worse than Ford's, while Hyundai's phthalates are eight times worse in off-gassing than Volvo's.)[7] Car manufacturers use other dangerous chemicals, too, including chromium, used in leather tanning and released as people slip in and out of their seats; lead, used as an additive in automotive plastics as well as in wheel weights and solder; and other heavy metals and carcinogens.

Given how many hours the average American spends in his or her car, and how often we drive with our windows closed, these harmful exposures can be the most significant ones in our daily routine. Health experts advise car owners to park in the shade and use reflectors to keep UV rays out of the vehicle, as well as to drive with the windows open. They also encourage car buyers to pressure automakers to eliminate their use of these materials, even if it ends up costing more to manufacture the car.

It may seem like a grim joke, given the tremendous attention that protective parents pay to selecting and installing car seats, but those child seats have some of the same off-gassing problems as car interiors. Infants and children are at the greatest risk for inhalation of these chemicals. Both automakers and car seat manufacturers are under pressure from groups like the Ecology Center to either redesign their components to eliminate the necessity for these chemicals or to use alternative chemicals, such as flame retardants without bromine, chlorine, or other halogens. Some manufacturers have begun eliminating a few of these chemicals from their newest models, but the U.S. fleet of cars remains a toxic one.

THE HIGHWAY OF ILLNESS

The air that we breathe in the millennial United States is not what the Founding Fathers breathed. While horse manure soiled air quality in Colonial towns, that fact is just a quaint footnote to the story of the devastation produced by the exhaust from hundreds of millions of automobiles. Though its quality has improved since the inauguration of the Clean Air Acts of 1963 and 1970, our air still contains high levels of vehicle-related pollutants. Cars and trucks produce five primary groups of pollutants: carbon monoxide; nitrogen oxides; toxins including benzene and volatile organic compounds or VOCs; ground-level ozone (itself sourced from nitrogen oxides and VOCs, and not to be confused with good, stratospheric ozone, which shields the earth from UV rays); and fine particulate matter. The health effects of exposure to these substances include upper respiratory tract and eye irritation and infection, increased likelihood of heart disease, low birth weight, lung and other cancers, and asthma.

It does not take a great leap to reach the conclusion that living next to roadways teeming with car and truck wildlife is not good for your health. But how bad it is, and who is most affected, are facts that we are just learning. The health hammer comes down most heavily on people living within 150 to 500 yards of major roads, although some studies find these cancer corridors can be as wide as a mile on either side.[8] We now know that people inside these corridors are at higher risk of childhood cancers, brain cancer, and leukemia. One study revealed that women living within 250 yards of high-traffic roads were more likely to give birth to premature and low-birthweight babies.[9] Another found that residents of homes near large roads were almost twice as likely to die from heart and lung disease as those who lived in areas with less traffic. Several studies in Denver showed that children living next to high-traffic corridors were six times more likely to develop all cancer types.[10] Children who live near streets carrying 20,000 or more vehicles per day were six times more likely to contract childhood leukemia. The risk comes from the benzenes and other toxins drifting off the roads, as well as from their being deposited on the lawns and soils in which those children play.

Another study, published in the *New England Journal of Medicine*, found that growing up with smog reduces lung capacity. Following children in twelve different communities in the Los Angeles area over the course of a full eight years, the researchers discovered that children lose one percent of their lung function each year, so that by age ten, they have only 90 percent of the lung function they would have otherwise had.[11] Another study, more hopefully, found that although lung growth, which continues through the teenage years, was stunted for children living in polluted areas, it improved somewhat when they moved to less polluted parts of the country.[12]

Douglas Houston is a young policy researcher at UCLA who has been looking at the health impact of living in high-traffic areas.[13] What he immediately discovered is that poor neighborhoods in Los Angeles and four surrounding counties have road traffic almost twice as heavy as the wealthier areas. Rates of respiratory illness and mortality rates are correspondingly much higher there. The poor in these neighborhoods also have older, leakier homes into which traffic pollution can seep more easily.

Areas with air more heavily polluted by traffic are particularly detrimental for anyone suffering from heart disease. Frank Speizer and his colleagues at the Harvard School of Public Health conducted a controlled study of the effect of air pollution on people who were recovering from acute coronary events, ranging from chest pain through heart attacks, following them for a year after the event. Patients with implanted defibrillators had their heart's health precisely measured, and so it was known whether and exactly when they experienced cardiac arrhythmias. Speizer could correlate those arrhythmias with levels of air pollution, finding that patients are significantly more likely to experience harmful arrhythmias on high-pollution days than cleaner air days, as less oxygen gets to the heart muscle.

Unfortunately, even those who don't live near highways face exposure to the high levels of pollutants along trafficked corridors because they drive along them. Some do in fact worry about the outside air joining them for their commutes. Kelly from Atlanta feels this way: "It's funny—in my car I have an air-conditioning function where if you turn on the air-conditioning you can either recycle it within the car or you can use air from outside the car and, you know, I always sort of have this dilemma every time I get in because I don't know which is better for me or which is worse, because clearly the air within the car has already been outside, so there's probably smog in that too, but I also don't want to be cycling in the air from the smog from outside using my AC."

Kelly is right to be concerned. When we drive in our cars, we are exposed to significantly more air pollution than in any other environment, and turning on a car's air filtration system or closing its air vents, a California Air Resources Board study found, does little to decrease pollution levels inside it.[14] A study looking at California data from more than three decades established that the level of volatile organic compounds, or VOCs, is up to ten times higher inside our vehicles than ambient levels.[15] VOCs are the same group of chemicals found in hazardous products, such as lacquers and varnishes, that consumers are warned to use only in highly ventilated areas. The study concluded that despite the fact that we only spend part of our days in cars, our exposure there accounts for much of the vehicle-related pollution we take in.

Automakers have been under pressure to move the air intake from its location on the fronts of cars. The typical current location is such that the most concentrated toxic gases from the tailpipe of the car in front of you in heavy traffic tend to flow straight into your intake valve. Having the option to buy a vehicle with the air intake on the side or rear can lower our immediate personal risk from emissions, but we cannot escape the overall pollution problem: our exhaust always goes somewhere.

WORKED TO DEATH: HEALTH IMPACTS IN VEHICLE-RELATED INDUSTRIES

Marianne is a pretty woman just entering her fifties. When we met her, she had been a tollbooth operator for the past fourteen years, working at a set of booths on the Boston end of the Massachusetts Turnpike. Recently diagnosed with incurable bone cancer, she was at pains to point out that cancer does not run in her family, and as a result she is suspicious that the fumes she breathes in each day are its cause. She has had to continue to work at the tollbooth as she dies, however: "I need the health benefits," she explained ruefully, but without intended irony. While any one case of cancer cannot be definitively attributed to any one environmental cause, Marianne's anxiety about the effect of her work on her health is well founded.[16]

Another occupational group, truck drivers, are increasingly cognizant of their special risks given how often they drive in a brown cloud of their own and other trucks' highly toxic diesel exhaust. Pollution levels inside truck cabs have been found to be astoundingly high, particularly when trucks are stalled in traffic or idling for long periods on line with other trucks to unload at ports or elsewhere.[17] Levels of particulate matter in cabs are 2,000 times greater than state and federal regulators find acceptable. This bodes ill for the truck drivers themselves, of course, but also for cars traveling alongside them. The highest levels of pollution were found in the oldest, leakiest, and most poorly maintained trucks, suggesting that inequality makes a difference here as well. It is the poor and working people who drive the cars and trucks most likely to emit and admit the highest levels of toxins.

A number of other occupations bring workers in dangerous proximity to car-related toxins. Auto mechanics, parking garage employees, and tollbooth attendants are just a few of the people whose jobs expose them to heavy doses of pollutants every day. Sadly, a car mechanic who is diagnosed with cancer may never realize that his illness could be due to the carbon monoxide and benzene he inhaled or ingested slowly over the course of his career, despite the measures required and taken to clear the air inside garage workplaces. And a parking garage attendant surviving on an oxygen tank is unlikely to receive a penny of workers' compensation for his loss of lung capacity.

Working around petroleum is unhealthy in the extreme. It became even more dangerous as the oil companies began to manipulate the amounts of the highly toxic BTEX compounds (benzene, toluene, ethylbenzene and xylene) naturally found in petroleum. Refiners discovered that raising the concentrations of BTEX raised the octane level. When the government ordered the phasing out of dangerous lead from gasoline in the 1970s, the oil companies pushed BTEX from its natural 2 percent levels to as high as 45 percent. Increasing the octane level increased the price they could charge for a gallon of gasoline, a significant matter when 40 percent of all gas sold in the United States is a premium grade (even though only 10 percent of cars have any need for a grade of gasoline with an octane—or price—higher than regular).[18] Like the cigarette makers hiking up nicotine levels in their products, the oil companies shoehorned more toxins into their gas, putting profit before health and bringing sickness and death to untold numbers of petroleum-exposed Americans.

TRY TO TAKE A DEEP BREATH

Kelly jumped in her car and headed to her job as a legal assistant. Along with tens of thousands of other commuters driving into downtown Atlanta, she noticed that the electronic signs hanging along the freeway announced that this summer day warranted a level yellow smog alert. She had already heard this on the morning TV news, which had given her the smog report along with the weather and traffic. Those three pieces of information told Kelly a lot about the restrictions she would live with for the rest of the day. A regular runner, she said, "I sort of plan my workouts at different hours and try to work out when the smog is less." Even when the report is relatively good, she still may have to stop, though, because she often experiences lung pain when she runs.

"It's kind of creepy. It's not just the heat. You walk outside and once you start walking, once you start breathing, it hits you. You want to get out of it *immediately.* Your lungs get heavy, and it's just difficult to breathe, and you sort of feel like you're in one of those sci-fi movies and should be wearing a mask or something, you know? It's just sort of baseline an unpleasant sensation to even be outside."

Atlantans with children, like many of Kelly's coworkers, have bigger worries than their morning jog. "They talk about smog a lot," she reports. "A lot of them would check these web sites before they left in the afternoon—to check both what the traffic was like to figure out how long it was going to take to get home, or pick up their kids from camp, but also the smog count to see if they could let their kids play outside when they got home."

As residents routinely do in many smoggy cities, Kelly's coworkers can visit any number of online sources reporting the AQI, the daily air quality index. The AQI is provided by the federal government for more than 300 cities around the country, using six categories and colors, from green for "good," through orange for "unhealthy for sensitive groups," to maroon for "hazardous" for anyone with lungs. This regular ozone alert system advises at-risk populations, such as children, older adults, and those with heart and lung disease, to stay inside on most days in many cities, and advises all healthy people not to exercise outside on other days.[19]

And while we adapt to living each day with smog, the amazing fact is that 70,000 people across the country stop living each year as a result of air pollution.[20] Although air pollution comes from a number of sources, car emissions are a central culprit. An estimated 50 percent of that pollution is car-related,[21] meaning that approximately 35,000 deaths or premature deaths per year can be attributed to the amount of driving Americans do. The causes of these deaths are often invisible to the rest of us, as many happen slowly and few are attributed to the car; when we attend their funerals we hear only that an uncle succumbed to lung cancer or a dear friend had a second heart attack. As one reporter put it, "while deaths from heart disease and respiratory illness from breathing polluted air may lack the drama of deaths from an automobile crash, with flashing lights and sirens, they are no less real."[22]

Belying the adage that what doesn't kill you makes you stronger, the vast majority of us who will not die from air pollution will still suffer its effects. Much more than a simple annoyance, ground-level ozone exposure can create shortness of breath and chest pain, bring on acute asthma attacks, and, according to the American Heart Association, increase rates of heart disease and stroke. The EPA has said that ozone weakens the immune system and its ability to fight off infections. Because of this multiplicity of health effects, smog-afflicted cities have more children who miss school for illness and send more children to the emergency room and to hospital admissions.[23] In turn, health problems large and small caused by air pollution levy high costs to society in productivity losses and medical expenses.

Some Americans remain unmindful of AQI warnings, imagining that only those in a handful of big cities are affected. While the air quality in Los Angeles, Houston, and Atlanta is notoriously bad, the problem is not limited to a few of the usual suspects or a smattering of days. By EPA standards, Phoenix had 94 days in 2007 during which it was unhealthy for the general population to go outside—over a quarter of the year. The wealthy and otherwise bucolic towns of Greenwich and Darien, Connecticut, and rural Mays Chapel Village, Maryland, for example, periodically find themselves under a code red alert, as they are downwind of cities with heavier traffic.

And some who are aware of the danger choose to ignore it in order to enjoy their lives, especially when the weather makes it irresistible. Unfortunately, ozone levels increase with heat and sunlight, so they're particularly high in the summer, when otherwise pleasant weather draws people outdoors. A 2002 study by the University of Southern California found that the most physically active kids in smoggy areas—those who played team sports outdoors—were three times as likely to get asthma for the first time than similarly active kids in areas with less smog.[24]

Contending with unhealthy air has become the new normal for some people. Kelly, from Atlanta, noted the surrealism of living in a world with bad air: "You sort of imagine those weird post-apocalyptic movies where some catastrophic event has happened and you have all these signs that are sort of directing people because of some strange ozone problem and the entire city looks smoggy and grimy and things like that. But it's a fair comparison because that is what it feels like. It makes you feel like—you get used to it and you stop thinking about how strange it is, but actually, in talking to you about this, I am sort of reminded of how weird it would be if I came home and saw this for the first time."

Of course, the post-apocalyptic scenario most likely to occur is a future warped by global warming, of which the carbon emissions from cars are one major cause. Global warming has already amplified the intensity of severe storms, such as Katrina, which, turbocharged by warmer Gulf waters, killed almost 2,000 people; scientists also project it is or will soon be increasing the frequency of such storms. Rising sea levels associated with increased water temperatures, among other effects of rising CO_2 levels, have already made refugees of some people living on the low-lying atolls of the Pacific.[25] Global warming is also contributing to the rise in deadly heat waves. In 2003, Europe was hit with a summer more scorching than any since the Middle Ages: it took the lives of 70,000 people.[26]

Progress always has a price, we tell ourselves, and some might argue that the suffering of people with cancer, lung disease, and asthma is a sad but inevitable cost of our beloved cars, our freedom, and our modern world itself. But this attitude could change if we develop a better sense of how massive the effects are now. It will help when we understand the unfairness of how that illness is distributed among us, falling most heavily on the shoulders of the young, old, and poor. It will also help when it is recognized that wealth does not allow people to escape breathing polluted air. If we take this all into account, we might then put more pressure on elected officials to get off oil companies' payrolls and set policies that make gasoline the dinosaur of transportation energy sources. We might demand that the car companies produce zero-emissions and nonpolluting cars, as we already know it's possible to do.

While US emissions standards are strict compared to those set in many countries, our weak standards for gas mileage, in combination with the unrivaled number of miles we drive, mean that we pollute at a more significant rate than any other nation. Stronger regulation is difficult to achieve due not just to corporate obstructionism but also to public attitudes. The existence of emissions limits gives Americans a false sense of security, fostering the illusion that we are adequately protected, while downplaying the direct health impact of cars today and the long-term environmental threats they create. An Internet poll conducted in 2003 showed that car buyers believe that if corporations market an auto or an option, and the government permits it, then the product is probably safe. This faith continues to stand in the way of our health.[27]

Even some regulatory progress has proved illusory. In 2008, when the Clean Air Act was up for review, tens of millions of Americans were living in counties where the average concentrations of ozone at ground level still exceeded the limit set a full ten years earlier. And experts saw that limit,

84 parts per billion, as far too lax. Most experts agree that there is no level that is not harmful to at least some of the population.[28] When the EPA announced new, stricter smog limits, the Bush-appointed EPA administrator responsible for the new regulations, Stephen L. Johnson, used the occasion to boast to the press about his role in this "most health-protective" historic move.[29] In the days following the announcement, the real story of the revision was made public: under pressure from industry and antiregulatory groups, Johnson's EPA had ignored the advice of its own scientists on the Clean Air Science Advisory Committee, which counsels the agency on ozone and particulate standards. The Committee had recommended a new level of 60 to 70 million parts per billion; Johnson went with 75. On its editorial page, the *New York Times* pointed out that the difference of a few points could prevent several thousand premature deaths. One epidemiologist and air pollution expert who has advised the EPA in the past put it to us another way: the agency's recent watering down of limits "would kill more people each year than died on 9/11."

TAKING IT TO THE STREETS

Though maligned by some as alarmists who care more about trees than people, in truth such experts and environmental activists have acted as health educators by letting people know about what coughs out the tailpipe and off-gasses from the dashboard. Environmental groups who have been campaigning for higher emissions standards and less car dependence are not trying so much to save the spotted owl as the human being. Groups such as Public Citizen, U.S. Climate Action Network, and Sierra Club have been at the forefront of decades of efforts to achieve stronger federal auto emissions, gas mileage, and air pollution standards. The Ecology Center, with its Clean Car Campaign, is working to reduce the use of toxic vehicle materials. While some of these problematic materials remain significant threats, some manufacturers have committed to reduce their use as a result of this pressure.

Bicycle promotion organizations and livable streets groups in cities and towns around the country (Transportation Alternatives in New York City, for example, and the Livable Streets Initiative) push for more bike-friendly public roads and routes and for greater investment in public transportation. And members of the Smart Growth Network and the Transition Towns/Transition Network advocate sustainable land use and demonstrate the viability of clustered, neighborhood-friendly housing and work patterns. Some very creative people have been reimagining our communities without cars, or with a greatly reduced dependence on them, and the resulting vision that's beginning to emerge is saner and more humane.

While we push for stricter government regulation, even knowing that the auto industry is using all its muscle to push back, the one thing we can do today to help keep our families healthy is to make the conscious decision to drive less. A day may soon come when *not* strapping a child into a car seat becomes an expression of love.

Chapter Nine

FULL METAL JACKET

THE BODY COUNT

eneral Motors' Milford Proving Ground outside Detroit is a sprawling complex containing miles of roads and tracks designed to replicate real-world conditions of rough and potholed roads, icy or wet surfaces, curves, banks, and hills. On site is GM's Vehicle Safety and Crashworthiness Lab, to which a rollover test facility was added in 2006 after viral publicity circulated about high numbers of SUV rollover fatalities. At the Proving Ground's center is the ominous-sounding "Black Lake," a sixty-seven-acre asphalt expanse whose shimmering surface occasionally fools waterfowl into attempting a soft landing. On one blue-skied day in June 2008, the "Lake" was dotted with orange cones delineating courses for acceleration, turning, and braking tests as GM employees prepared for the busload of journalists to whom they were about to introduce Chevy's newest vehicle, the Traverse.

Along with roughly a dozen automotive journalists, most from regional newspaper chains, we hopped off the courtesy bus, looped "All Access VIP" passes around our necks, and entered a hall where our group was greeted by at least as many members of Chevrolet's marketing, design, and engineering staff before settling in for a PowerPoint presentation. Chevy executives enthusiastically touted the innovations and attractions of this, GM's latest "crossover utility" (crossover being the marketing term invented to avoid calling a vehicle an SUV or a station wagon, even as consumers often cannot tell them apart). The Chevy team compared the Traverse continually and favorably to the Toyota Highlander, the category market leader. In the audience, taking notes with Chevy-supplied pens on Chevy-supplied notepads, the auto writers dutifully scribbled as photographers snapped pictures, although they all knew what one grizzled vet actually grumbled out loud, that the Traverse was basically a renamed Buick Enclave, itself basically a renamed GMC Acadia. The journalists obediently gathered around as the vehicle's designer took them on a tour of the exterior of a Traverse and then watched as a marketing executive displayed the many wonders of the interior, a demonstration that involved packing the cargo space with a series of bulky items including a little red wagon and two large sets of golf clubs. By way of contrast, he ostentatiously showed, reminiscent of O. J. Simpson with the bloody glove, how the same two sets of golf clubs couldn't quite fit inside the Highlander. Despite the staff's heroic efforts, the press corps receiving the pitch was underwhelmed. The Traverse, listed at 17 mpg city/24 highway and $29,000 to $41,000 manufacturer's suggested retail price (MSRP), was a very tardy entry into an already deflated utility vehicle market during that summer of $4-per-gallon gas.

Then it was time to hit the road and put the Traverse through its paces. We were instructed to take the vehicle up to a set speed to veer around tight curves; pull a 4,500-pound motorboat behind us and then try to stop; and head at high speed into a wet-slick lane-change course to kick in the electronic stability control. Timid drivers—of which there were few on hand—were prodded to drive faster to really get a good sense of how safe they felt. As each test driver accelerated, slammed on the brakes, and swerved around cones, the Chevy staff drew his or her attention to how safe the vehicle made him or her feel. So did the spiral-bound flip booklet provided that was chock-full of information about the Traverse. Staff and booklet persistently asked: Did we "feel in control"? Did we "feel the tow trailer pulling us back" or to the side? Did the vehicle "feel planted" as we made abrupt lane changes? Did we, in other words, feel safe?

As with most new vehicles, the Traverse does boast an impressive list of safety features meant to enhance both crash survival for occupants and, better yet, crash avoidance: antilock brakes, electronic stability control and traction control, air bags on front and side, and steel beams in the door panels to prevent crushing of occupants in side collisions. But automakers and salespeople admit that cars are generally sold on the warm, secure *feeling* they give the buyer as much or more than they are sold on cold, hard safety statistics. Ironically, moreover, some of the industry's work to give a car the sensation of safety works at cross-purposes to actual safety: one of Chevy's ride engineers acknowledged that they strive to make the car interior as quiet and the road as nonintrusive as possible, even though doing so prevents drivers from sensing how fast they are going or how dangerous the road conditions are. When nearly one-fifth of the nation's major roads are categorized as poor or mediocre, and when excessive speed is the primary cause of crashes, this is a not insignificant contradiction.

The final cushion tucked around all of the safety assurance offered that day was the frequent reminder that the Traverse comes with the On-star system, an in-car crash and breakdown service plan, at the time claiming five million subscribers. Onstar's promotional material lists all the problems that the product can respond to—and it is a disconcertingly long inventory: "Crash? Emergency of any kind? Out of gas? Flat tire? Stolen vehicle? Locked out? Crisis in your area? Fender bender? How are your vehicle's key systems running? Need driving directions?" If cars were once sold primarily as the route to freedom, they are now as much marketed as the lifeboat in a sea of carjackings, hurricanes, and terrorist attacks. And if security-seeking behavior can itself generate an undercurrent of insecurity (think about what it feels like to walk into a neighborhood and notice that all the homes have bars on the windows), it is surely evident here.

Even on a surface level, though, the attempt during the Traverse launch to demonstrate its safety was only partly effective. For one thing, there was the rumor circulating among the journalists that there had been a death on the test track a few years earlier, a rumor that could not be confirmed. For another, although the questions that were meant to be re-assuring (how did we feel?) kept on coming, it was less comforting to be handed a heavy-duty helmet for one of the tests. This turned out to be less a gesture of excessive caution than necessary protection: within min-utes one passenger's head ricocheted hard against the Traverse's backseat window as a gung ho test driver made a particularly sharp maneuver. This incident spurred a female engineer's conspiratorial aside that male car journalists (and there is hardly any other kind) tend to ignore the speed limits posted on such test runs.

The unspoken backdrop to all the safety talk is that a significant per-centage of all cars manufactured will eventually kill or seriously maim someone, making the phrase "safe car" an oxymoron. The good intentions and hard work of GM's safety engineers notwithstanding, the startlingly high number of crashes each year make it nevertheless an absolute certainty that some number of Chevy Traverses will crash and kill their drivers or pas-sengers or the occupants of other vehicles or pedestrians into which the "bold front-end" slams. While today's cars are safer for their occupants than those of the past, three things have prevented people from being much safer today than they were before these car industry safety innovations.

First is the fact that because drivers put in more hours on the road each year, they increase their exposure to the risk of crashing even if the risk of being hurt once a crash does occur is lessened. Second is the fright-ening reality that safety innovations have caused people to drive less safely: straighter roads, wider lanes, partnered with a "smooth ride" and antilock brakes encourage people to drive faster and leave a shorter distance be-tween themselves and the car in front. Finally, a highway arms race, the outcome of which safety engineers politely call "crash incompatibility," has resulted as many Americans have moved to bigger vehicles. The weight, height, and rigid box of vehicles like the Traverse—the very elements that can make its driver feel safer—are deadlier to others on the road, drivers and pedestrians alike. The excessive height of utility vehicles, for example, means that they tend to run over and crush other cars in rear-end colli-sions. The high center of gravity and relatively narrow wheel track of SUVs make them more likely to have a rollover, the most lethal type of crash. Where at lower speeds regular sedans and coupes tend to clip pedes-trians at the knee, flipping them up onto their softer hoods and the relative cushion of safety glass windshields, the huge fleet of crossovers and SUVs now on the road have heavy and high grills like the Traverse's that barrel into walkers' chests, mowing them down and under the vehicle. Although this event sounds freakish or random, it is not unlikely: approximately 10,000 pedestrians are hit each year in New York City alone, and across the country 4,654 pedestrians were killed in 2007, five times the number of U.S. military deaths that year in Iraq.[1]

THE DEATH TOLL

The fact is that the advent of SUVs has made America less safe. But even if all of our SUVs magically disappeared, cars would still be the deadliest factor in most of our environments. As a nation, we are nearly three times more likely to be killed in a car crash than by homicide, and our children face no greater risk of dying from any cause, accidental or disease-related. If we die at work, it is usually in a vehicle; since records started being kept in 1992, crashes are the number-one killer on the job, with professional drivers, salespeople, and farmers especially vulnerable.[2] Most people are shocked when they hear the annual highway death toll in the United States: 41,059 people killed in car crashes in 2007, or an average of 112 people a day—the equivalent of a nearly fully loaded passenger plane going down in flames every single day of the year.[3] Safety advocates often use this analogy both because it suggests how distorted our perceptions of risk can be—far more people fear getting on planes than into their autos—and because it suggests at least one of the reasons why: the car deaths happen one by one and with regularity, like the drip from a broken faucet. Fatal car crashes are so common and at one level so accepted that they often go without mention in all but the most local media unless they occur with some kind of bizarre twist. A carload of teenage girls piloted by one who may have been texting while driving can get attention; so can a car crushed by a dump truck tipping over; or, as in one recent headline in a Boston paper, when a "Passenger in One Collision Allegedly Steals Good Samaritan's Car." But, typically, because the 112 Americans and 3,300 people worldwide who were killed by cars yesterday, or the 112 the day before that, didn't die together, all at once, they didn't make news.

The numbers are mind-boggling, but the tangible realities behind them are even more difficult to fathom. Car crashes produce deaths that are horrible, or "horror-able" as one woman who lost a good friend this way described it. They are not like deaths that can be assimilated because they approach slowly, as with illness, or like deaths that allow for some dignity and grace. They are instead sudden, unexpected, violent, and gory. And though people of all ages, races, and genders die in cars each day, young people—those with much more life left to live—are far overrepresented. Car crashes thieve more years from more lives than any other single cause. They are the leading cause of deaths for all Americans between the ages of 1 and 34 and have been for years.[4]

Since 1899, crashes have killed 3.4 million Americans, claiming far more victims than all U.S. wars combined. And just as we tend to focus on the dead rather than the injured in war, behind this death toll looms the crash injury total: an estimated 2.5 million people suffered crash injuries, many permanently disabling and some merely financially devastating, in 2007 alone. Those horror-able realities lurk everywhere in American society, though muted, veiled, and denied. It's a war out there.

WOUNDED VETERANS OF THE ROAD

Tim Flynn was supposed to be at work. Instead he was at the house where he lives with his parents, homebound again with one of the frequent urinary tract infections that plague those confined to wheelchairs. The forty-five-year-old crash survivor wheeled himself to the kitchen table where he prepared to share his story. Without hesitating, he went right to the day he became a quadriplegic at the age of 19 when, on his spring break from Ohio's Kenyon College, he spent the evening hanging out with his buddy, Alan. The two had a few drinks at Alan's house before driving off in Tim's family car for more fun at a local bar. "A half a bottle of Canadian Club" later, they headed home and drove off the road.

Though he does not remember the crash itself, Tim said, "I remember the aftermath. I was lying in the road, and our neighbor, Mr. Bergen, who was my friend John's father, was a member of the volunteer fire department, and the first thing I remember was Mr. Bergen—he was the first face that I saw and I remember looking up at him. And he was crying." There, but for grace, he surely thought, could be my own teenage son. And as an experienced EMT, he no doubt knew how grim Tim's future was going to be.

Tim had broken his neck, which would paralyze him from the chest down and leave him with limited use of his arms. During the ensuing eight long months of recovery and rehabilitation at top New York hospitals, often spent staring at the ceiling, he was forced to learn how to deal with permanent loss of bladder and bowel control. He struggled to relearn how to do virtually everything, every basic task of daily life, in a new and much slower way. He eventually returned to his parents' house, but spent the next three years depressed, drinking, drugging, and looking for motivation. But Tim was one of the lucky ones: a car crash survivor with a wealthy, hopeful family and a resilient personality. Those resources helped him slowly advance to where he is today, which is helping run a rehabilitation program in Newport, Rhode Island, for those with spinal cord injuries, a program called, with some ironic verve, "Shake-a-Leg." And by his happy account, his relationship with his girlfriend is a healthy one.

As he told his alternately devastating and inspiring tale, forceful, involuntary spasms related to his urinary tract infection had Tim gripping the arms of his wheelchair to keep from falling out. Still, he kept on, explaining that he still feels guilt for "dragging his family" into the agony of his crash and treatment, and even now, a full quarter of a century later, the burden they have of continuing to care for him in their retirement. Because, he said, "it's not just me that's paralyzed . . . you know, my family has to deal with it, my friends have to deal with it."

Each of us may not know someone like Tim Flynn, but we know someone who does. Tim Flynn is one of millions.

People are injured in a thousand ways, sometimes seriously, every day. But car crash injuries are the most massively traumatic for the obvious reason that, unless we're in a high-velocity vehicle, our bodies are otherwise usually moving no faster than about three miles per hour and have at most a few feet to fall before hitting something. Injuries caused by cars are different. They include broken necks and spinal cord damage, crushed limbs, massive brain and other organ injuries, heart lacerations, and complicated fractures. These injuries are the result of what safety engineers call "the second impact" of the body against the inside of the machine that occurs after the first impact of the machine against an object like a bridge abutment or another car. While seat belts and air bags protect us from many injuries that would have been severe in the past, they cannot protect against other passengers or items in the car hurtling around the interior, intrusions into the passenger compartment, or high-speed collisions that partly or wholly destroy that compartment.

In a small town hospital, the arrival of an ambulance with one or more crash victims sets the emergency room into a blaze of motion, and it is not unusual, as in Tim Flynn's case, for emergency and hospital personnel to directly or tangentially know the person or people who are being rushed in for treatment. In larger, urban hospitals, the daily flow of patients injured in car crashes does not create the same impression of a rare and personal event; in short, it does not have the same effect of seeming "horror-able." Standard operating procedure in American emergency rooms is to utilize a scaled system for triage developed by the Association for the Advancement of Automotive Medicine. MAIS (Maximum Abbreviated Injury Scale) scores allow ER personnel to sort out the incoming. A victim suffering minor injuries such as abrasions, cuts, and broken fingers rates a 1; one with broken bones or having lost consciousness rates a 2; complicated fractures and concussions a 3; massive organ injury or heart laceration garners a victim a score of 4; and spinal cord injuries or crushed limbs score a 5. At the top of the scale, an MAIS score of 6 is reserved for those with injuries that are not survivable, such as a crushed skull or chest. In a country where crashes are ordinary, the honor student, the neighbor's wife, and the bank teller become a 3, a 5, a 6.

The vast majority of crash injuries are scored minor or moderate, and those people will or should check out of the hospital feeling lucky. But 206,000 injuries a year involve complicated fractures, spinal cord damage, and brain damage, injuries that are life-changing.[5] The most common permanent and severely disabling injuries are to the spinal cord and brain; such injuries often lead to lifelong dependency, family disruption, and tremendous suffering. Brain injuries in particular often precipitate other cascading effects.[6] This is illustrated by the case of Peter, a crash survivor in his mid forties.

Peter's crash occurred in 1982. As a friend of his described it, Peter and another friend "got into a terrible accident and his friend was killed, and Peter was in a coma for about six months. He was sort of a miracle: he emerged from the coma, but he had a head trauma, *and* he broke his back. He tried to kill himself on a couple of occasions. You ever see the movie 'Leaving Las Vegas?' Well he sort of did a similar scenario, where he saved all his money, bought a plane ticket and went to Reno, and was gonna kill himself there . . . I think a lot of psychoses developed over the years that sort of led him to this place, probably as a result of the brain injury. He's very isolated now. He did well for 15, 20 years, but then just sort of hit a wall . . . aging in a wheelchair, shoulders start hurting, you get secondary health problems. Peter's had some bad skin problems in terms of skin breakdowns, where he had to be in bed for a year. So, it all contributes to a real depression, and it's tough to work your way out of it. . . . So anyway they managed to trace him to Reno. They had to get the Reno police department, and they cased all the hotel rooms and they found him . . . and thank God they found him when they did. They had to break into his room, they found him on the floor with his wrists cut . . . but he didn't do such a good job in cutting his wrists, thank heavens, so he didn't die. And so then there's a whole new ball game. They had to put him up in the hospital for six months to get him psychologically stabilized. It's just, it's an awful scenario . . . Now he's gone off the deep end, I mean now he hears voices."

Even injuries that are less life-threatening than Peter's can be overwhelming. They include such gruesome damage as "degloving" of the hand or facial disfiguration. Some so-called moderate injuries, moreover, can be disabling. Lower-extremity injuries—usually and especially ankle fractures—can have a huge impact on someone's life, and fully one-fifth of drivers admitted to trauma centers after crashes had at least one such fracture. Six months after a crash, two-thirds of such patients in one study were still having trouble walking, many remaining in wheelchairs or reliant on walkers. Another study found that only 58 percent of those with these injuries had gone back to work a year after their crashes. In a study of people hospitalized in Maryland with crash injuries, 40 percent of the financial costs incurred were to people with leg and foot injuries, injuries especially disruptive to people with jobs requiring physical labor. The families of the injured had often depleted their savings due to lack of insurance coverage, high co-pays and deductibles, loss of work and income, or some combination of the three. Only 17 percent of the group with broken lower limbs had escaped without crash-related financial damage to their families.[7]

For the elderly, even relatively minor car crash injuries can end their mobility and result in a host of other health problems that end up slowly or not so slowly killing them. Allan is one of many such seniors. A brilliant historian and college professor nearing retirement and looking forward to spending more time reading and writing on the deck of his shoreline vacation home, he was in a car crash that wrenched his back. Before long, he required a large male personal assistant to help him up and down stairs or into and out of the passenger seat of his car. But most of the day-to-day care, including changing his diaper, comes from his wife, Sophia. Like legions of other such female caregivers, Sophia could not now easily hold down a job even if she wanted to. Although she seems to handle it all well, and although Allan tosses out a few good ribald jokes about all this, the car crash meant his health and quality of life deteriorated much more rapidly than it otherwise would have.

While Allan maintains a surprising sense of humor, victims of car crashes are susceptible to losing much more than an upbeat attitude. Depression and post-traumatic stress disorder (PTSD) affect many who seem to have been able to otherwise "walk away" from a crash. The American Psychological Association published a study based on close follow-up of survivors of serious car crashes in Albany, New York. When they were compared with a demographically matched control group, it was found that 39 percent of the injured experienced PTSD.[8] Common in combat veterans, this mental injury is, not surprisingly, taking victims in the highway wars. This stress disorder prevents roughly one in seven of those afflicted from getting back in a car, and many more continue to experience extreme anxiety when they do by necessity get into an auto.

Said one woman, who was in a front-end collision just a few years after a family member had died in a crash: "I had a lot of pain for about six months. Initially I just was on crutches, I had some ankle pain. I used to be a very comfortable driver, and that was when I initially felt . . . I wouldn't call them panic attacks, but I went to a psychologist. In my head, when I see something coming, I would hear the crash as though I assumed it would then crash. I still do: it's like sound effects. The accident changed my worldview," she told us, "whereas before I believed everything always works out, not anymore."

Forty-three percent of those in the Albany study who suffered from PTSD also developed major depression. Some of the factors that contribute to both kinds of psychological injuries are the fear of dying as a result of the crash, the wait for a relevant court decision, and the severity and suffering of their physical injury.[9]

The aftermath of a crash is especially agonizing for those who, in addition to sustaining their own injuries, had been behind the wheel and were (or feel they were) responsible for killing or permanently disabling someone else. For those people, guilt can be overpowering and unending. Even when people in such situations feel they are not to blame—explaining to themselves over and over as one such driver does, "There was no street light, and he just walked into the path of my car"—they often continue to be haunted by the death. For those who kill their own passengers, often loved ones, the guilt can be even more dreadful, as they live on to directly witness the suffering of the rest of the family.

Shockingly, no one has collected reliable data on how many Americans have been permanently disabled by crashes, furthering their invisibility. The National Spinal Cord Center has estimated that approximately 79,500 people are living today with spinal cord injuries from car crashes, with about 4,200 more paralyzed each year.[10] Estimates of the number of people who are disabled for at least some period of years after a crash vary wildly, ranging from a low of 2 percent to a high of 87 percent of all survivors. The range is so wide because most epidemiological reporting focuses on car deaths rather than injuries, and most tracking systems lose touch with people once they have left the hospital, leaving long-term consequences of their injuries undocumented.[11] While the National Highway Traffic Safety Administration (NHTSA) collects highly detailed data on crashes, it has, according to Judy Stone, president of the Advocates for Highway and Auto Safety, "never funded the project of looking at the long term effects of crashes" on individuals and their families. Because people who have been involved in car crashes fall outside NHTSA's view if they do not die within thirty days of a car crash, even many car crash deaths are not counted.

In addition, America's emergency rooms and the rest of the health system in which car crash victims receive care are increasingly under great financial stress. Dr. Robert Galli, head of emergency medicine at the major trauma center in Mississippi, noted that funds for trauma services were boosted after the state's governor and lieutenant governor were each in severe crashes within a short time of each other. "But then 9/11 happened, and since then all the money has gone into medical equipment to sit in warehouses waiting for a terror attack. It's been a boondoggle. The state just got three separate six-tent field hospitals costing millions. The combined monies for all such homeland security grants have been in the billions. That same amount should have been put into a nationwide trauma system. There are people dying because the system doesn't reach everyone in 'the golden hour' that's critical for care after a crash."

THE THIRD IMPACT

After "the second impact" of the human body against the car interior, which follows the crash of the automobile, there is a vast and still unrecognized "third impact" of the crash. Tens of millions of American families have been torn apart by car crashes: they have had to cope with the loss of a father, mother, or child, or they have had a loved one returned to them with massive injuries that leave them physical, cognitive, or emotional shells of their former selves.[12] Looking at just the last twenty-five years of crashes—and their toll of over 1.1 million dead and 4.1 million disabled—and assuming that an average of 10 family members and friends are most closely affected, that is 52 million people who have lived and continue to live through the third impact. Some are endless mourners for the dead and others are ongoing caregivers. No small part of the impact is borne by the tens of thousands of emergency workers who go to the highway battlefield every week and themselves experience the trauma and anxiety of tending to crash victims.

What are those impacts? For those dealing with death or permanent disability, a bottomless well of grief, of course. But then also divorce, depression, suicide, substance abuse, and bankruptcy often follow a serious car crash. While some families try to repair the hole in their lives by having or adopting new children, for example, or throwing themselves into car safety advocacy efforts, others simply cannot cope. As one man described an old friend whose teenage daughter died in a crash: "It never goes away. The news story goes away, but the family tragedy never goes away. This was a family with two teenage daughters and a teenage son. The husband and wife within a year of the death were divorced. The younger teenage daughter became involved with drugs and alcohol. The son went off to Iraq and was injured. The chain of events was set in place when the daughter lost her life, and they will never be the same."

Our awareness of the nature of the third impact or even of the size of the community of the car-bereaved is limited. Those left behind have often done psychological work to bury their loss, hiding it from themselves and others. In one interview, for example, a small-business owner named Will spoke for nearly half an hour about his attitudes toward the car before it came to light that he had lost both of his parents in a car crash just a few years earlier. This tragic association, which might be expected to dominate his thoughts surrounding the automobile, did not come up until he was directly asked whether he knew anyone who had died in a crash. While some people more readily share the fact of losing a loved one, they can still remain closemouthed about some of the more painful aftereffects such as the social losses that occur when the dead person is an important link between families or groups of friends, or the unspoken anger or survivor guilt they may feel.

By contrast, when others share sharp and ready memories, seeing in the telling a means of honoring the dead, they illuminate for the rest of us what is often kept in the shadows. Janet Echelman, a successful artist, lost her older brother, David, when he was killed in a crash in 2002. A doctor on his way to work, David was killed when a woman in an SUV front-ended him in his Volvo. Jane remembered being texted by her mother to call home; she remembered that it was the Wednesday before Thanksgiving; she remembered the way the winter ground resisted the shovels at his burial; she remembered what she said at that morning's funeral service about her and her other two surviving siblings' loss. "My metaphor was that I had grown up with my life as a table with four legs . . . the four of us. We had faced the world together. We had a very difficult father, and we hung tight and supported each other. Yeah, I miss him a lot." And like the most re-silient car crash survivors, she found a way to make it onward: "Sometimes I will think I'm living something extra for him. I'll be driving someplace beautiful and think I should enjoy this twice over, for him. I shouldn't lose opportunities because life is so short." She paused to let some tears fall, then went on to explain that not all in the family have been so able to move for-ward: "My third brother has never married or had children, and said it should have been him . . . which is a very sad thing to feel."

Added to the families and friends of crash victims are the recruits in an enormous army across the country whose efforts make them veterans of the highway wars. Battalions of people work every day in what can be called the car crash health industry: EMTs, firefighters, and police; emer-gency room doctors, nurses, and assistants who conduct triage, stabilize and treat the victims; chaplains and social workers who manage and advise the often angry, distraught reactions of the loved ones who converge on the ER; and the doctors, home health aides, prosthetic device fitters, rehab therapists, and psychologists who deal with the physical and psychological aftermath of the crash. There are literally hundreds of thousands of people whose jobs include managing the car crash dead: rescue workers, ambu-lance drivers, morgue workers, funeral directors, and grave diggers who process the corpses. Imagine the whole annual highway toll taken care of in one place, and you get a clearer idea of the scope of the tragedy and the scale of the effort. Add the routinization of the process to the chaos in-volved, and a vast, surreal picture emerges.

Car crash emergency workers tend to be a particular lot—tough and caring aficionados of black humor, in perennial risk of burnout. Like sol-diers, they commonly do not discuss the mental health issues related to their jobs, although they know they are real. Also like soldiers, these workers, who are mostly men, don't like to admit that they need help, but acknowledge that others do. As one EMT explained, "We do have a service, a Critical Incident Stress Debriefing Team . . . they come to your facility, sit down, and talk about the call. Most of the time, people think they didn't do enough for the patient . . . it's really not that, it's just it upsets them that it's a kid or someone they know. They just have to talk it out and figure out it's not your fault, you didn't cause the accident, you did all you can. Not me, but [other] people use the resource."

These emergency workers see with their eyes what is shielded from the rest of us: the graphic images of destruction and death that disappear behind the statistics. Willard, a 56-year-old New Jersey father of two who now supervises his fire department's EMTs, was a paramedic when he was dispatched to the scene of a crash on the interstate: "It was nighttime, and it was one of those nights where you could see your breath. We got there, and it was a tractor trailer that had stopped on the roadway and a car, who hadn't seen the trailer stop, ran into it from behind. It took the top of the car off. The eerie part was you could see steam coming off the car seat itself, and when we got on location it was obvious that the person had been decapitated. The steam we saw was the blood, the warm blood, coming up into the cold air. His head was in the back seat. Obviously that was traumatic, and we could not do anything for the patient, he was obviously dead. . . . Most of them are not that severe, but accidents happen all the time. Every day you can bank on being dispatched to one or two . . . it's just the nature of the road, there's so many cars on the road."

Even the youngest and newest have experienced "the worst," as described by Kyle, a 23-year-old EMT, engaged but not yet married: "The worst one I think I was on was an individual who was running away from the police, lost control of his car going about 110 mph, got T-boned from someone coming home from work. The individual running from the police was killed instantly, his neck was snapped. The man who hit him was unconscious, he didn't know what was going on, he broke his femur, and we had to actually cut him out of the car. We had to get on top of the car and slide him onto the board because his blood pressure was extremely low. The medics pumped him full of saline, the man ended up dying a couple hours later due to a torn aorta. He was on his way to the O.R. I think that was the worst one. That was a double-fatal." In a subtle way of making plain that these experiences have an impact on the personal lives of these road warriors, Kyle closed his story: "It was two days before Thanksgiving."

Funeral directors have the special challenge of dealing with the body of a crash victim, and of communicating to families when, as often happens, it is impossible to reconstitute the body for viewing. Like other crash industry workers, one director, now in his late sixties, retains indelible images of his first car crash funeral—from almost 45 years earlier. He related, "That was a young woman, a beautiful girl. That was a time in my life when I thought all girls were beautiful anyhow. And, it was just such a waste. What a waste. Yeah, she was gorgeous, and the body was all . . . *yech*, just awful. I suppose I thought it could have been me. You know, I don't remember it all, I just still have that vision, even if the thoughts around it are long gone."

Whether you are an emergency worker or a loved one, when cars crash, they can also batter your basic trust in the world. One grief counselor who had helped many people through such calamitous events said: "When someone you love very much has died doing something that we all do pretty much every day—just get in a car and go somewhere, sort of accepting the quality of that car—I think there's a real shaking of the foundation of what is to be relied upon. Maybe gravity doesn't work either. Maybe chairs really aren't meant to be sat on. Maybe milk is all polluted. Nothing is reliable." In comparison with those who deal with the loss of a loved one as a result of illness, people who lose someone in a crash are more likely to have nightmares and to question the fundamentals. "If you die of cancer, people often think that everything medical science has to offer was inadequate in the face of it," she explained, "but it's different if you were doing something completely normal. There was someone whose brother was killed in a *poof!* instant when somebody ran a red light by accident. And the man sat here for week after week saying *he just went to get milk.*"

SAFER CARS AND SAFETY STALLED

The car death toll failed to significantly decline over the past decade, at least until the number of miles driven by Americans dipped in 2008. Individual cars, in general, are in fact safer today than ever before. People regularly crash and walk away from the wreck with nothing worse than a sore neck and the headache of body shop visits and insurance company calls. The use of seat belts is up, and medical technology used in emergency responses has also improved. There have also been demographic changes—including a decline in the birth rate, producing fewer of the young people who have the highest crash rates—that have helped make our roads safer. In some cases, advocacy and policy changes have had a significant impact. There has been a reduction, thanks largely to MADD and SADD, in the number of people who drive drunk. (Mothers Against Drunk Driving is widely known; SADD, Students Against Destructive Decisions, was founded as Students Against Driving Drunk, but now covers all sorts of safety-related behaviors.) Graduated licensing systems instituted since the mid-1990s in many states have reduced deaths among the youngest drivers. These licenses require longer initial periods of supervised driving, nighttime curfews, limits on the number of unrelated passengers who can be in the car, and a rise in the age before drivers qualify for an unrestricted license.[13] The outcome of all of these changes has been a decline in the number of deaths per vehicle miles traveled (VMT), down to 1.42 people per 100 million VMT, the lowest rate ever, as the U.S. secretary of transportation, Mary Peters, proudly announced in 2007.[14] Overall traffic fatalities dropped by 1,649 between 2006 and 2007, and still further the following year as Americans drove fewer miles.[15]

Frustratingly, though, the longer-term trend of steadily high death rates on the highway has persisted for a number of reasons. One is the repeal of the 55 mile-per-hour national speed limit in 1996; another is, paradoxically, that the focus on safer cars and highways has encouraged riskier driver behavior, the result of what is called "risk compensation." Risk compensation means that people drive less safely when they feel safer in their cars. So having air bags and antilock brakes persuades people to drive faster, follow other cars more closely, and change lanes more often (with or without turn signals). A smoother ride gives people less feedback from the road, encouraging more risky maneuvers and driving in poor weather conditions. More confident and thus more dangerous driving widens the safety gap that new safety equipment has narrowed.[16]

In fact, the larger and safer a driver perceives his or her car to be, the more likely he or she is to have an inflated sense of safety or, to use a more appropriate term, impunity. Drivers mistakenly confuse being higher up, having what they consider better visibility, and possessing stronger frames on their cars with being safer. Several studies have shown that SUV drivers overestimate the capabilities of their cars, are more likely to speed and otherwise drive aggressively, and are less likely to wear seat belts or have their children properly secured.[17]

Moreover, the many improvements to highways themselves, such as wider shoulders, straighter stretches of roadway, and better lighting have allowed drivers to feel it is more reasonable to talk on a cell phone while driving or to drive when they are tired.[18] One study estimated that such infrastructure improvements as these wider, straighter roads, with longer sight lines, have produced 1,700 additional deaths.[19]

And then, as noted, there are more distractions: cell phones, GPS systems, panels of comfort control buttons. A *British Medical Journal* study found that cell phones made crashes four times more likely, and that it mattered relatively little if the caller had both hands on the wheel at the time.[20] NHTSA found in 2003 that 955 people had been killed the year before by cell phone users driving distractedly (although it suppressed those findings).[21] While people no longer drive drunk as frequently as they did in the past, they now drive cell phone–impaired much more often. The head of the Fatal Accident Unit for the New Jersey State Police, Eric Heitmann, who has investigated by his estimate over 2,000 fatal or near-fatal crashes, agrees with experts that driver distraction is the main cause. Heitmann feels that the underlying problem is driver attitudes: "The thing that really needs to be taken into consideration is the seriousness of your responsibility as a driver of a car, and the possibilities that exist for not doing it correctly. Overall people need to take a lot more responsibility to care for each other on the highways. Everybody's in a rush but the necessity for you to get where you're going doesn't outweigh your responsibility to other people on the highway."

Safety experts now refer to the four "E's" of enforcement, education, engineering, and emergency response. In the first half of the twentieth century, however, Americans tended to hold individuals wholly responsible for any crashes that occurred. Car safety focused on the accident-prone or miscreant driver—with women, immigrants, or other outsiders often scapegoated as the worst. Cars were originally introduced without seat belts, and even when they became available as options in the 1950s, they were widely suspect: back then, one older woman told us, her mother became very wary of a young man she was dating because he had seat belts installed in his coupe: "'Why,' she asked, 'does he need them? Is he a crazy driver?'"

Influential research done in the 1960s by Detroit doctor Clair Straith and engineer Hugh DeHaven shifted the focus by pointing out that vehicle reengineering—softening rigid dashboards, eliminating sharp buttons, and adding restraining belts—would save lives. Ralph Nader's *Unsafe at Any Speed* (1965), the consumer rights movement more generally, and what one historian calls "the smoldering dissatisfaction with Detroit's marketing and design policies," including rampant dealer fraud, "banded into a 'perfect storm' of regulatory reform in the early 1960s."[22] Americans thereafter would come to rely on car engineers to keep them safe; they expected scientists to make it, as crazy as it sounds, "safe to crash." Today, crash avoidance has become as much of a concern as crash survival, but in the public's mind safety remains an engineering problem that is well on its way to being solved.

But the car companies and the federal government responsible for regulating them have an immense distance to go. Over the years, car companies have fiercely resisted every meaningful safety innovation from seat belts to air bags and continue to do so, although each new generation or type of vehicle brings with it new safety issues. The Ford Explorer/Firestone debacle, in which defective Firestone tires exacerbated a dangerous propensity of Explorers to roll over, was the subject of a flurry of news coverage beginning in 2000. The finger-pointing between Ford and Firestone generated much publicity, but numerous other safety problems with individual models received less notice. For example, many Americans are unaware that 1 in 7,500 GM pickups has been enveloped in a fireball as a result of a crash.[23] Throughout automotive history, the U.S. government has been less than vigorous in promoting safety when it conflicts with car industry needs. In the wake of the Ford/Firestone deaths,

Congress found that NHTSA had received information about 20 of the Ford/Firestone crashes but withheld it. The TREAD Act (Transportation Recall Enhancement, Accountability and Documentation) was passed in 2000 to protect the public's right to know such facts. The Bush administration, however, decided to allow the car companies to designate as "trade secrets" the information they have about safety problems with particular models, known as "early warning" information, including feedback from customer complaints about such things as brake or tire failure and information from their dealerships on equipment malfunction.

Congress currently spends about as much money for research on dental and other oral health (important, but rarely a life-threatening matter), as for research by our car safety agency, NHTSA.[24] Yet, this lack of research funding is less critical than the lack of political will to institute and enforce regulations when data support them. For example, activists continue to lobby the government to mandate greater car roof strength to prevent head and neck injuries in rollovers. A mere inch less roof crush in a crash can prevent a broken neck or death; making such a small change can be crucial in cutting the death rate. By regulating the fleet rather than individual models, the government has failed to limit the weight or aggressive car design of vehicles that put all others on the highway at risk.

Enforcement is part of the safety mix, although mainly this has consisted of enforcement of drunk driving laws. Much less has been done to control speeding, which NHTSA has identified as a factor in almost one-third of all traffic deaths. As mentioned earlier, engineering, in this case road engineering, gets in the way of safety: conventional wisdom is that wider, straighter, and less congested roads will be safer. But while research shows that less congested roads may have fewer crashes, the crashes that do occur are more severe because of the faster speeds at which traffic is flowing.[25] And crashes create congestion, of course: one estimate is 40 to 50 percent of all nonrecurring traffic jams are the result of a crash.[26] Traffic law enforcement in most states has not kept up with the increased number of cars on the road, and what many long-term traffic cops see as increasing lawlessness on the road. "I've had people tell me," one state police sergeant told us, "that they are allowed to drive 10 miles over the speed limit, or that the posted speeds are suggested minimums." And yet no one raises the very simple idea, seemingly a no-brainer, that cars be manufactured with speed governors preventing them from reaching over 70 or 75 miles per hour, speeds at which crashes become less avoidable and less survivable, no matter what safety equipment is aboard.[27]

Enforcement raises awareness, which, in conjunction with education, can bring about a revolution in driver attitudes. Drunk driving was redefined as a national problem largely through the efforts of a social movement, spearheaded by Mothers Against Drunk Driving (MADD). Ensuing enforcement efforts by police have even more firmly established the social unacceptability of driving under the influence. And after activists pushed unrelentingly for laws requiring seat belt use, this practice, once considered burdensome and uncool, has also become a cultural norm and thus an unnoticed habit of the driving public. Nonetheless, Americans on the whole still believe our cars and roads are safe and that it is individual drivers who are responsible for automotive injuries and deaths. News reports of any crash rarely treat it as a tragedy whose repercussions can last for decades. They invariably treat it as a stroke of really bad luck, or as inevitable due to poor driving conditions or bad driving behavior, rather than as part of a pattern that can be broken by driving less, using safer modes of transit, regulating car companies, and enforcing behavior on the road.

And thus, Americans on the whole, like the car companies we buy from and the government we elect, have resisted regulation and enforcement. By looking at the microcosm of our nation that is the American family, we can start to understand why. One man who recently gained insight into family dynamics around the car is Larry Selditz. Mr. Selditz sells car safety devices, including a small black box that monitors driver behavior by cataloging excessive speeds, aggressive acceleration, abrupt braking, and high-speed turns. When the governor of Ohio provided state money for schools to reduce the high number of adolescent crashes, one district decided to use the funds to buy Selditz's boxes. Selditz explained that the district offered the device without charge, along with some other incentives to any parents who requested it; when their teenager graduated they would simply return it so it could be made available to other parents. Parents might have been expected to snap up this opportunity, but only 35 in the whole district did so. "Parents just wouldn't take them—free! You can see that price is not the only barrier to entry here. Does society need to pay you to protect your child? Twenty-five of the systems are sitting there in a box and nobody will step up!"

Selditz now understands that "parents don't have the courage to take strong action to protect their child's safety" because they are "afraid of offending their kid." He no longer markets his product directly to parents, not because of the cost—the $295 price tag is similar to that on the cell phones, iPods, and Xbox systems that many parents shell out for—but because they don't have the "intestinal fortitude" to put it in their kids' cars. Just how would a safety device offend a child? The same way safety laws offend many adults: by making them feel that their privacy has been invaded and their autonomy threatened. As a nation, we ask the government, "What? You don't trust us?" Even more influentially, as teens break away from parents to become more independent, the car symbolizes their newfound liberation. Adult citizens, too, see regulation of their use of their cars as an encroachment on that paramount American value, freedom.

Plenty of adults may not be willing to cross their teens on car safety, but inspirationally, the young are confronting and challenging each other. Thousands of chapters of SADD have been established around the country since 1981. They bring crash-mangled cars to the front lawns of their schools to show what drink and speed can do, and some hold a "Grim Reaper Day" each year before prom. In one Long Island high school, for example, SADD members dress as the Reaper and walk around school sounding a gong every 20 minutes, representing another teenage car casualty. The Reapers paint a black teardrop on the cheeks of each of their chosen "victims," and hang cards around the victims' necks that tell the stories of how they were "killed"—stories culled from actual cases. The "victims" remain silent until all members of the student body assemble at the end of the day to hear the stories, mourn the dead, and resolve to drive as safely as possible.

THE HIGHWAY ARMS RACE:
HOW THINKING BIGGER IS BETTER HAS COST US

Most cars in the United States once weighed roughly the same and had their bumpers at the same height. But then in the 1980s and 1990s, vehicles of vastly different sizes, weights, and bumper heights flooded out of dealerships to all share the same roads. Behind this change is a complicated story of government capitulation to lobbying, which allowed SUVs to be categorized with trucks rather than cars. This made the SUVs eligible for huge tax write-offs (real estate brokers and doctors, for example, took advantage of this allowance to write off up to $100,000 of their Hummer H1s by claiming them as business tools), lower fuel economy standards, and more lax safety requirements, such as those for roof strength.[28] One of the reasons that car companies lobbied for this policy is that they make extraordinary profits from trucks and SUVs—$10,000 to $17,000 per unit (Ford made about $15,000 on each Excursion it sold).[29]

The outcome is that some vehicles are now more deadly to others, vastly outweighing them as well as creating a state of crash incompatibility. A large SUV's bumper, for example, is sometimes so much higher than the bumper of a regular passenger car that it does not serve the intended function of cushioning the blow, but rides up onto the car and slices into it at its much more vulnerable window level. Paradoxically, even with their additional safety features, SUVs can be less safe than other vehicles when they crash if they encounter highway elements, such as guardrails, designed for cars of lower height.[30] The top of guardrails are generally 27 inches from the ground, barely catching many SUV bumpers or grills. This makes SUVs much more likely than passenger cars to barrel straight through or over guardrails or to be caught in such a way as to "trip" and flip over.

SUV marketing initially sold the vehicle as overtly masculine and aggressive, sending the message that as the most powerful cars on the road they were less vulnerable or even invulnerable in a showdown with others. One car marketing guru who had great influence on the sales strategies for these vehicles drew on focus group responses to the most menacing-looking models to argue that their appeal is to "the reptilian part of the brain," which takes pleasure in dominating others on the road.[31] And plenty of SUV car advertising appeals to just this notion: one ad shows tanks emerging from a line of suburban garages, ready to do battle on the morning commute. The SUV owner can imagine himself an asphalt jungle warrior at the wheel, or alternately as a more defensive, masculine protector, a man who provides a ton of extra protection for his wife or child. Women more often than men say they own an SUV because they feel safer in it, while others might, in a frank moment, express it the way one young man from California did: "My SUV is definitely cooler. I feel more important, I guess, being higher up."

It is no surprise, then, that the SUV has become a trophy in the culture wars. For the left, it symbolizes the need for more government regulation to ensure car safety for all. For the right, it represents family first and a car market left free to let consumers choose. Addressing cultural attitudes like these is crucial for dealing effectively with safety issues, because neither the car companies nor consumers are operating as if the objective data on what makes the car system as a whole safer is relevant. If everyone is simply trying to get the *feeling* of safety or the *feeling* of stature, no one will be safe inside the U.S. highway system kill zone.

COMFORTABLE WITH THE NUMBERS: HOW SOMETHING THAT KILLS CAN SEEM SAFE

When death by car is so common—when our chances of crashing are 1 in 5, and of then being permanently disabled are 1 in 83—it is a wonder why we persist in believing that our cars are safe and that they won't kill us or our loved ones. Are crashes viewed as the price of progress, as drivers behaving badly, as inevitable given the limits of human skill and engineering, or as car companies' putting profit first?

The most important reason for the illusion of safety is the decades of effort and dollars the car companies have put into convincing us that our cars are safe. Their advertising tells us that cars are anything but dangerous: the relentless pitching of car safety in fact has helped convince most Americans that their vehicles will keep them from harm, with their air bags and side-impact panels and ferociously deterrent front grills.

In the newspaper, we occasionally see grainy small images of mangled post-crash metal, and on television and in the movie theater we witness the fictional fireballs of car crashes. But in Hollywood, it is usually the villains who drive off the edges of cliffs, while the wild-driving heroes walk away with only light flesh wounds. Pedestrians are rarely mowed down but usually manage to jump out of the way, something especially remarkable given how often those heroes are careening between fruit carts and baby carriages. Mostly, though, we are exposed, day after day, to advertising's glossy images of beautiful, safe, intact cars. The sense of invincibility the ads give us as drivers could not be more important in sending us out to our driveway each morning with confidence.

The illusion of car safety persists as well for the simple reason that people do not want to believe that something so necessary to our way of life is so dangerous. Those who have studied how humans respond to risk know that people often have a quite distorted view of what to fear: our fears depend less on the objective numbers (a one-in-a-hundred chance versus a one-in-a-million chance) than on other things. We feel less at risk when the activity is voluntary (such as driving or skiing) than when imposed on us (the air we breathe), when we are in control (like at the wheel of a car) rather than not (in the passenger seat or in a plane), when those activities are familiar (as when driving or working with heavy machinery at our jobs) than when novel (terror attacks or swine flu), or when we see the danger source as benevolent (like the Ford Motor Company or a surgeon) rather than neutral (a hurricane), or evil (a criminal).[32]

Car salespeople encounter a great deal of indifference to car dangers in their day-to-day work. As one very experienced salesperson said in exasperation, "This has always shocked me, because some people just don't care! You start to go through safety stuff, and they don't care! I'm like, 'Wake up! You're going 65 miles per hour in a tin can, driving down a road.' About half the consumers go 'Oh, safety seems to be a concern that everybody's talking about, so I should talk about it too.' And the other half have been in an accident, and really realized that it's—you get one chance, why not get the safer car and options?"

Another reason why cars seem safe to us is the profound pleasure we take in them, though for some, the speed and danger of cars is itself part of the pleasure. A college pastoral counselor—who could point out many trees on campus planted as memorials to students who had died in cars—observed of people's responses to the risk of auto death: "There's this terrible juxtaposition of how could something that is so ordinary, and often a source of real delight, kill. 'Look at my beautiful new car,' right? 'Look at all the cool things my car can do.' There was a student who died in a single-car accident at thirty-five miles an hour in broad daylight a few years ago, and I can still hear his family: 'He was just trying to find a cell phone that had gone under a seat, and he just took his eyes off the road.' It was an old, vintage car, and he and the father had tried to really fix it up, and for his father it was so difficult to cope with the fact that this thing that had been so much fun turned into some sort of a monster and ate the person you loved instead of protecting them or taking care of them."

The answer to the illusion of safety may also, oddly, have more to do with the automotive design engineers than the safety engineers. The car industry has produced an object of great beauty, and, as critic Elaine Scarry has argued, "Beauty restores your trust in the world."[33] Designers craft cars to please the eye, seeing their work as artistry and themselves as artists. That shiny, sleek piece of art in our driveway beguiles but could not betray us. Really, how could something that beautiful be deadly?

In addition, as we've seen, most people think they are good drivers and will not be involved in a crash—as if they could not be killed by someone who is a bad driver and as if most drivers who do kill don't also consider themselves good drivers. Most drivers overestimate their skill and underestimate the risk they take and the risk they pose to others.

Then there is the value placed on the idea of progress: cars are continually driving us into a future that must be better than the past. Moreover, we have learned to speak of "the price of progress." That is the idea, heavily peddled by industries, including those that pollute, that a little destructiveness goes hand in hand with becoming modern, that nothing good comes without a price tag, and that the health and life of a few must be sacrificed for the benefit of the many. Car crash death and disability is to our mobility what occasional toxic chemical spills are to the continued production of plastic toys and washing machines. We make a distinction between illegitimate and legitimate violence all the time, and some forms of car violence have become delegitimized, like deaths in cars driven by people who are drunk. But more generally car deaths are accepted as the sad but necessary and inevitable price to pay for our access to modern, individual mobility. What else explains that our justice system metes out serious charges to only 1 in 5 drivers who hit and kill pedestrians?

The idea that a certain number of car deaths is inevitable is swiftly de-bunked by a quick look overseas. Pedestrians in the United States, per trip, are three times more likely to be killed by cars than pedestrians in Ger-many and over six times more likely to be killed than those in the Nether-lands.[34] In the period from 1979 to 2002, during which wearing seat belts became mandatory and air bags and other improvements in vehicle crash-worthiness were installed, U.S. crash deaths declined by just 16 percent, while those in Great Britain declined by 46 percent, in Canada by 50 per-cent, and in Australia by 51 percent.[35] The greater declines in these coun-tries are accounted for in good part by their having, compared to the United States, fewer trucks and SUVs on the road and stronger govern-ment regulation of vehicle safety. These nations also reduced the number of vehicles traveling their roadways by imposing higher gas prices, new car taxes, and parking fees, while providing superior public transit systems. Fewer cars mean fewer crashes.

Bolstering the illusion of safety is the power of car marketing as well as the potency of two American ideals: individualism and progress through engineering. Individualism suggests that we can make our families safe through our own individual efforts, buying a tanklike car or one with a high safety rating. And so we fail to see that there is a difference between the feeling of safety and real safety, or that each individual family's efforts to make itself safer might be making other families or society as a whole less safe. The other root of the illusion is the American value and idea of progress as something that can be physically engineered and purchased as a consumer good. We have seen that all the road straightening and air bags have not reduced the highway carnage, as people drive more miles in riskier ways.

And the auto and oil companies are more than happy to sell us a shiny new or used SUV that feels safe, but is as likely as its predecessors to be a fatality or maiming waiting to happen. However, there are alternatives—available today and en route to our future—which we turn to next.

Chapter Ten

CONCLUSION

A CALL TO ACTION

The River Rouge Plant in Dearborn, Michigan, one of the largest and most modern automotive factories in the world, can churn out Ford F–150 trucks—the company's most profitable model—at an astounding rate. Six thousand workers can complete 432 pickups per eight-hour shift, using computerized flexible production methods to choreograph the movement of parts to the people on the line just as needed. In June 2008, after taking in the nearby Henry Ford Museum's upbeat displays of one hundred years of American automotive ingenuity, we joined a small group of tourists and boarded a bus that would carry us to the plant. The bus driver read a small, well-thumbed book of Psalms as she waited for the last of her charges to purchase the $14 ticket and file onto her vehicle for the ten-minute trip across Ford's River Rouge complex.

At the entrance to the plant, a ticket taker tore stubs, and a former union auto worker—now, like the ticket taker, working at minimum wage—directed visitors toward the screening of a documentary on the history of the factory. One floor up in a glass-walled observation room overlooking the vast compound, a docent gestured expansively across the factory grounds, highlighting sites of the company's environmental efforts. Spearheaded by Henry Ford's great grandson, Bill, the efforts include a football field's worth of factory roof covered in sedum to hold rainwater and help cool the building. Looking on among the crowd were a group of men of various ages in mechanic shirts brightly decorated with embroidered Ford, AAA, Hertz, NAPA, and BP sponsor patches. They were Master Technicians from Ford dealerships and top high school shop students who had won regional contests and were in Detroit for the finals of the Ford/AAA Student Auto Skills Competition. These and the dozen or so other visitors then filed onto the broad catwalk encircling the factory where they gazed out upon the Escher-like gridwork of conveyor belts and chains that carry door parts, seats, and dashboards down to the floor. Along the line, trucks stood in various states of assembly, from hollow cabs at the beginning to elaborately outfitted glossy vehicles at the end that looked ready to drive off toward the horizon.

But the plant floor was graveyard quiet that day. The only workers appeared as apparitions on TV monitors, giving the ambling catwalk visitors a friendly but spectral introduction to the stations where headlamps and doors are usually added onto truck bodies. The day shift had been canceled, as had many others over the previous several weeks, to reduce inventory. May 2008 was the month in which the Ford F–150 truck was ingloriously shoved from its pedestal as the best-selling vehicle in America—which it had been for a full 17 years—down to fifth place behind smaller gas-sippers like the Honda Civic and Toyota Camry. The scene at Rouge seemed foreboding, an image of an American auto industry transformed from vibrant hive to sleepy history museum. The mood in Detroit was bleak as the media sounded the death knell for the truck, the SUV, and the large car— the big three that had been keeping the Big Three afloat. While sympathetic toward the thousands who stood to lose their jobs in a transitioning industry, environmentalists rejoiced: change had finally come.

Rumors of the imminent death of the oversized vehicle, however, had once again, perhaps, been exaggerated. By December 2008, gas prices had plunged more than 50 percent and, although a deep recession prompted American consumers to buy fewer vehicles overall than they had a year earlier, truck and SUV sales increased enough to eclipse car sales for the first time in nine months.[1] Conspiracy theories abounded. Saudi officials were chastised by Leslie Stahl on *60 Minutes* for attempting to keep us gas junkies hooked on the liquid narcotic by dropping prices. If swayed by gas prices and little else, it appeared that Americans would be ready and willing to resume a lifestyle of buying big and driving long.

But a study published in the midst of the Chrysler and GM bankruptcy news suggests that the 2008–2009 dip in driving is the result of a broader phenomenon not solely attributable to higher gas prices and the recession.[2] Americans, by this analysis, drove eight percent less in early 2009 than would have been expected based on previous years with gas price spikes and high unemployment. Similarly, despite drastic dealership and short-term government incentives, car buying is predicted to remain low: The loss of home equity and retirement accounts has left people with a potentially long-lasting understanding of the senselessness of overspending on cars. Significantly, the cities with the largest drops in housing values (such as Las Vegas, down 37 percent) have been the most car-dependent, and the few cities with housing price gains (such as Portland, up 19 percent, and Seattle, up 18 percent) have good transit alternatives. Americans are beginning to move to places where their lives can be less ruled by the car.

YES WE CAN

So can we make lasting change, or can we make enough change to really cut into the major problems car dependency causes? Faced with pervasive attitudes toward the car, entrenched lifestyles, and powerful car and oil industries with too much government influence, real change is difficult to imagine. Our very landscape, economy, and politics have been shaped by the car in ways that promote its overuse and our reliance on gasoline-based technology. As we work to mitigate the car's impact, these obstacles may seem insurmountable. Even if we agree that our car dependency threatens the values we cherish, we don't want to give up our vehicles. That is an option that most Americans find repugnant and unrealistic.

However, recent developments provide hope that America can move forward toward a society not without cars but with a more balanced transportation system. Nationally, the car and oil companies are under keener scrutiny, with citizens now expecting them to better serve the public interest. The Obama administration's push for new emissions and mileage standards by 2016 is a promising step toward a saner national car fleet. A significant gas tax is under discussion, and, in any case, gas prices will inevitably rise again as the economy recovers and supplies dwindle. Moreover, the American Recovery and Reinvestment Act, better known as the stimulus plan, allocated $18 billion to develop a much more extensive and convenient public transit system.[3] At the local level, a number of cities are showing the rest of the country the way. Portland, Oregon, is demonstrating how a single metropolis can transform land use policies by investing in streetcar and light rail systems that lead to less driving. The Obama administration seems inspired by Portland's model, fostering hopes that federal funds might be forthcoming for localities that are proactive in pursuing transportation solutions.[4] And the political culture around energy and transportation issues has become more "yes we can" than "yes, they should" or "too bad they won't."

Change is both feasible and appealing, achievable through a twofold approach: reducing our individual dependency while increasing our collective alternatives.

To begin, we *can* alter the ways in which we view, purchase, and use our cars in some meaningful and even painless ways. There are many specific, immediate actions that individuals and families can take to reduce their reliance on the automobile and lower the price they, and all of us, are paying for the car. Most of us can easily drop hundreds if not thousands of miles from our annual driving, reaping a number of financial, emotional, and safety rewards. We can be healthier and wealthier, with more leisure and family time, and be better environmental citizens.

At the same time, we must become wiser about the ways of our national car system and demand alternatives. Because the system we have now impoverishes families, kills or maims millions of people a year, and is imperiling the planet, nothing less than a complete overhaul is necessary. The current system is dominated by the most powerful corporations on the planet—the oil and car companies (a power they retain—witness the bailouts). A national transit policy based on much more ambitious goals than the ones advocated by those groups could produce a system that shifts tax policy and subsidy support away from cars and toward convenient, eco-friendly public transit—not just for city and suburb but for country and exurb—and fosters government regulation of the auto companies to make cars cheaper, safer, and cleaner.

Here's how we reach both the modest goal of reducing car use, and the more ambitious goals of remaking our transit system so that we can allow more people to live car-free, slash transit's contribution to global warming, and create more jobs in a sustainable economy. As you'll see, our prescription does not require us to give up the real freedom that cars can provide. It does, however, point us toward a healthier, more balanced car culture that minimizes the manifold prices we pay for this freedom.

TAKE A FAMILY SNAPSHOT IN FRONT OF THE CAR

The first thing to do is sit down and figure out how much you use and pay for your cars, and begin to look at why. Here's how to start.

Keep a car diary to check in on how often you use your cars and what you use them for. It might seem nigh impossible to drive your car less than you do now or to live with fewer cars than you currently own. A dual-income family or one with children might be especially challenged to imagine getting by with one less car or with fewer miles driven. But the possibilities are illuminated when you examine your patterns of use. One way to do this is to keep in each car a simple log in which you record when you took the vehicle out, for how many miles, for what purpose, with what cargo or other passengers, and how long it took you, door to door. You might keep this car diary for several weeks or a full month. You may be quite astonished to realize how many trips you take that could be combined in a trip chain, for example. A car diary will also likely surprise you with how long it takes to reach some destinations. For example, a two-mile trip to the gym could easily take 10 minutes with traffic and the search for parking, putting your "real speed" of travel at 12 miles per hour, a speed readily reached on a bike. You may also find your pattern mirrors that of the average American driver, for whom more than one-quarter of all car trips are a walkable mile or less.

Compute your household car costs and decide whether you really want to be spending that much. If you do not know how much your car is costing you financially, you have less incentive to reduce these costs. The average American family is spending $14,000 a year without realizing it because most consider only a portion of the total when making important decisions about what car to buy or whether to drive somewhere. In addition, as we have seen, we have been encouraged to be payment shoppers, narrowly figuring our costs on a monthly, rather than longer-term basis. Use the calculator available at www.bikesatwork.com/carfree/cost-of-car-ownership.html to arrive at your current total car budget; in addition, calculate the total as a percentage of your annual gross pay and take-home pay. Most financial advisers would recommend that you spend 8 percent or less of your gross income on your vehicles. Using an online calculator enables you to anticipate what your savings would be if you sold a car, downsized to a cheaper or more gas-efficient model, or drove fewer miles.

DOWNSIZE IT!

Once you have seen how you use your cars and trucks and calculated their cost, you may well decide you can and should downsize your fleet or your individual vehicle. There are a variety of options for downsizing.

Sell your second or third car and use the proceeds and ongoing savings in other ways. Your second or third car may be expendable and replaceable with flexible and much less expensive solutions such as rentals, carpooling, or public transit. The thousands you save can be used to achieve the same mobility goals, with plenty left over for paying off debt, saving for college, or taking a vacation. If the car sold was a means by which one of you was commuting to work or school, carpooling could now make the drive valuable time spent with family members or friends. If you resist the idea of carpooling because it seems like a hassle, know that sharing the task of driving, having companionship, and being able to use HOV (high occupancy vehicle) lanes actually make carpooling a stress-reducer. Many communities sponsor services that match up interested carpool partners, like a dating service for commuters. If the car sold was only used occasionally, then take public transportation or rent a car from a traditional firm such as Hertz or Dollar or from a new hourly rental firm like Zipcar when one is needed. At $8 an hour or $60 a day, including insurance, gas, and parking, you could use Zipcar one out of every four days and still come out well ahead of owning. In mild climates, a bike or electric scooter could serve most of the functions of an extra car, particularly for a teenager who has been using the car to go short distances.

Donate your second or third car.   Many charities accept used cars to help fund their work. Think about donating to a charity that is working to mitigate the negative impact of the car, such as the American Lung Association, or donate to a charity that is helping poor or unemployed people obtain the cars they need to get and retain decent-paying jobs, such as Charity Cars for Military Families in Need or one of the many local groups such as Free to Be! in Anoka County, Minnesota. Come April, you can take a rewarding tax deduction on this contribution, while helping solve some of the social and health problems identified in this book.

Downsize your car or truck.   If you cannot get by with fewer cars, consider getting by with less car. Many Americans have downsized in response to gas price spikes, but others have resisted doing so. In part that is because we have been convinced to buy vehicles that fit peak, not usual, needs. Evaluate how much you really need that truck, minivan, or SUV by using the trip diary to see how many passengers it *usually* carries and how much and what kind of cargo it *usually* carries. You may realize that you are paying more for a larger car and its lower gas mileage and emitting a lot of toxins for the sake of a few ski weekends each winter or a few trips to Home Depot each summer. Downsize to the car or light truck you need for everyday and borrow, carpool, or rent a bigger vehicle when you need one for special trips. Many families buy larger vehicles to be able to drive groups of children from one activity to another, but renting a van for sports trips is more economical (the rentals could be organized ahead for the season). Unless it is used for daily business purposes, it is always much cheaper to rent than own an oversize vehicle. Some rental companies will even deliver the car to your door.

Postpone your trade-in.   Americans replace their cars for new ones far more often than is economical, as the greatest depreciation occurs in the first few years of a car's life. Putting off a trade-in for just one or two years can save you thousands. For example, a typical American sedan costing $25,000 will lose more than a third of its value in its first two years, or an average of $4,500 in annual depreciation, at which point it could be sold for perhaps $16,000. Holding on to it for three more years reduces the average annual depreciation to $3,000, so that after five years it could be sold for about $10,000.[5] The average amount saved, if invested in a college fund each year over 18 years, would leave you with $50,000 for your child's tuition.[6] Even trading in your SUV for a new car that gets better mileage could be postponed, as the amount you spend on gas may be no more than the amount you lose in instant depreciation by driving off the new car lot. An excellent car cost calculator at the Webwinder site (www.webwinder.com/wwhtmbin/jcarcost.html) will let you compare the true total cost of holding on to your current car versus buying a new or used vehicle of various models and vintages. Calculate your savings and consider how these savings could be put toward advanced safety features in your next car.

Use a car-sharing system.   Car-sharing companies have grown exponentially in the last few years, primarily in urban areas where they allow people to avoid the headache of car ownership. An industry launched in 1998 in Boston by Zipcar, there are now more than 15 car-sharing organizations in over 66 cities. These companies make it incredibly easy to get a car, even on a moment's notice. After you've registered online, you can make a reservation, a minute or a year in advance, walk to the car you reserved (often at a nearby parking lot), access it with your member's electronic card, and drive off. The company, not you, maintains the car, fills the tank, and pays for insurance.

BUY SMART

When you do buy a car, here are some ways to go about it that are environmentally, financially, and socially sound.

Create a priority list for car purchases.   *Before* beginning the process of buying a new or used car, develop a list of priorities and conduct meaningful research so that you can make sure you are buying a vehicle that meets your real needs. Avoid being swayed by car advertising, which as we have seen often appeals to emotions, including fear, that can limit the factors that we should consider when buying—in fact, turning the channel or page on car ads is a healthy idea. Read the critics critically: many automotive writers prioritize horsepower, newness, and glamour above other concerns. These may not be your priorities. Use unbiased expert advice to identify and narrow your choices, such as *Consumer Reports,* which accepts no advertising and is not beholden to the auto industry, and Greenercars.com to find the most eco-friendly choices. The key of course is that once at the dealership, you must stick to your list. Bring a frugal, level-headed friend or family member with you to make sure you aren't swept away by sexy car displays. Research has shown that it is not until we actually see something we don't need that we begin to desire it.[7] If you have a short and serious priority list before you start looking at cars, you have a better chance of buying only what you really need.

Buy a used car.   For the same reason—depreciation—that later trade-ins make sense, buying a car that is just a year or two old can save you thousands of dollars. Many used cars come with warranties as good as those on new cars, and state lemon laws protect you from dealers (and sometimes from private sellers, too).[8] Numerous makes and models have proven themselves to be highly reliable used car purchases; check *Consumer Reports* for a list of these. Buying used not only saves you money but is environmentally friendly. Well-meaning people sometimes reason that they should buy a new, more energy-efficient car in order to have a lighter carbon footprint. However, about a fifth of a car's lifetime carbon emissions are produced in the manufacturing process.[9] Even if the new car you are considering is much more fuel-efficient, it is usually greener to keep your old car, which would continue to be driven by someone else in any case. For financial or other reasons, however, you may still decide to buy a new, more fuel-efficient car.

Buy a car that makes financial sense.   Make sure you are buying a car you can really afford. Common mistakes are looking only at the monthly loan payments and not including the cost of other items, such as insurance, maintenance, and repairs. Those three items alone average $262 per month for the typical American sedan.[10] Also figure in the possibility that gas could well reach $6 or $7 a gallon at some point during the life of the car. Even without accounting for these future increases, a good rule of thumb is to double the monthly car payment to figure the total cost of owning and using your car.

Although one car may have a lower sticker price than another, it may not be the best choice, based on its depreciation rates and what it will cost to fuel and maintain it. To compare the cost of owning different cars you are interested in, use an online calculator such as Edmunds.com's True Cost to Own[SM]. Reliability scores, which help estimate the cost of repairs over the life of the car as well as its resale value, are critical. J. D. Power and Associates' resale data show that vehicles from brands with above-average scores tend to hold $1,000 more of their value than brands with below-average dependability.[11] Finally, you should factor in the possibility that you will be socked with a deductible charge for as much as $1,000 for even a fully insured car that is hit or stolen.

Save to buy or finance carefully.   Ideally, you would save up before buying a car and pay cash. You would then shoulder only the actual price of the vehicle, not hefty additional financing costs. As we have seen, under the worst circumstances, a $17,000 car can end up costing $34,000. And of course, unlike home mortgages, car loans are not tax-deductible. The reality is that, unfortunately, paying cash is not always possible. If you must borrow, read the cautionary tales and advice on the web site Stop-AutoFraud.com. It is also usually best to make a purchase with a sane car loan rather than leasing a vehicle, because although leasing can make for lower monthly payments, doing so can lead you to lease a more expensive car rather than pocket the monthly differential. Be aware that leasing is a much better deal for the dealer than for you, since you are paying for the most expensive years of a car's life, those when it is depreciating most quickly. And of course, at the end of the lease, you do not own the car, but have paid for the decline in the car's value and interest.

Buy a hybrid vehicle.   At this point in time, hybrids may not appear to be the most budget-conscious option. The higher sticker price of a hybrid model means that even with better gas mileage and any tax breaks offered, it can take several years for hybrid owners to "break even." However, if gas prices increase in the next several years, this "break-even" period is likely to shorten. If you must buy a new car, a hybrid presents an option that is kinder to the environment than most. The Prius and Highlander SUV each produce 55 percent fewer CO_2 emissions than other vehicles in their respective classes.[12] In addition to the psychic and material rewards of polluting less, hybrid owners get the immediate and ongoing perk of fewer trips to the gas station. If you buy a hybrid, be prepared to be happy. *Consumer Reports* notes that hybrid owners report very high purchase satisfaction; in fact, 95 percent of owners of the Toyota Prius said they would buy or lease it again.

Buy an electric car.   While we wait for the big automakers to finally produce an electric car for the mass market, some electric vehicles are already here. So-called neighborhood electric vehicles or NEVs are available from several vendors, including Zenn, for example, which sources its three-door hatchback car from a European maker.[13] The Zenn charges in an ordinary outlet in a matter of hours, has minimal maintenance costs, and fuels up at a fraction of the cost of a gas or even hybrid vehicle.[14] Resistance to the idea of electric cars comes mostly from a fear that you will not be able to drive very far in them. While the Zenn and similar vehicles already available aren't for everyone, with a range of 30 to 50 miles per charge and a low maximum speed compared to an ordinary car, they make great sense for a large number of city dwellers, commuters who drive to the train station, or drivers who make a lot of trips within their own neighborhood.

Most drivers also say they prefer the electric car's acceleration, which is smoother and faster at lower speeds.[15]

You could also get on the wait list for the Chevy Volt at GM's web site as a way of demonstrating to the big automakers that there is consumer demand for electric vehicles. According to GM, the four-seat Volt will have a minimum battery range of 40 miles before its gas engine kicks in, eliminating the anxiety that an electric vehicle will run out of power and leave you stranded somewhere.

Buy an unconventional conventional vehicle. Even people who are not comfortable being at the forefront of automotive technology can buy a car today with emissions quite below average and with outstanding gas mileage. Honda, Toyota, and MINI are producing most of the high-mpg small cars out there. Check out www.fueleconomy.gov to see a list of cars with the best mile-per-gallon performance for the kind of driving you tend to do and to see how your current car rates in terms of its carbon footprint and contribution to air pollution. Use Greenercars.org to comparison-shop for an environmentally friendlier car that meets your other needs.

Invest in safety, both for yourself and for your neighbors on the road. Over the past few decades, car manufacturers have been continually adding new safety features to their cars, but not all come standard. When you buy a new or used car, choose one with options that make it easier to avoid collisions or help protect you during one, such as antilock brakes, front and rear side impact air bags, head-protection curtain air bags, and electronic stability control (ESC), which helps a driver gain control of a vehicle that is skidding or sliding in a turn by automatically braking individual wheels. Many consumers undervalue safety features, perhaps because they do not know just how important they are in enabling drivers to avoid and survive deadly crashes. In just one example, a National Highway Traffic Safety Administration study showed that cars with ESC were involved in 30 percent fewer fatal single-vehicle crashes than cars without it. For SUVs, the numbers were doubly impressive: SUVs equipped with ESC had 63 percent fewer fatal single-vehicle crashes than those without it. You can also enhance the safety of both new and older cars by adding accessories, including quite inexpensive ones such as electronic deer alerts.

Thoroughly research crash and rollover test data before making a purchasing decision. Do not assume, as some consumers do, that a vehicle is safer simply because it is bigger or more expensive. If at all possible, to avoid putting yourself or a loved one in the position of killing someone else in a crash, do not buy outsize cars and trucks; as we have seen, crash compatibility allows for more survivors overall.

STEP BACK FROM THE CAR, SIR

Whether or not you downsize your family car(s), you can lower the number of miles you drive and car trips you take each week.

Be an efficient gopher.   Most of us already combine errands to some extent to save time, for example, when stopping at the grocery store on the way home from work. However, you may still find yourself running one errand, heading home, and then going out again the same day for several days in a row. Plan ahead for the rest of your day, week, and even further in advance. If you have an appointment at the dentist at the end of the week, postpone any trips to nearby shops until then. You can also avoid unnecessary trips by calling ahead to make sure stores have what you need, to comparison price, for directions, or for store hours before you get in the car to go there. Shop at stores and restaurants that deliver so you can eliminate some errands altogether.

If you find a regular pattern of separate trips to the grocery store by your family's fleet over the course of a week, you could decide to condense or eliminate those trips by, for example, using an Internet recipe search engine that allows you to make something with what you have on hand in your pantry. You could also decide to make it a goal to stock up on more at the supermarket at each visit, eliminating some of the incentive for additional shopping trips.

Shop on the Internet.   Many of the things we buy are repeat purchases that don't require us to actually see or feel the product before deciding to buy. Try an Internet grocery delivery service (such as Peapod, Netgrocer, or FreshDirect), which will store your shopping list and deliver to your door. In addition to the time and travel savings, shopping at home can also save you money by reducing impulse-buying. You can also feel good because taking out the middleman, the retail store, means that fewer acres of land will need to be paved for new stores and parking lots. Finally, if each American family replaced just three car shopping trips with internet trips, by Oak Ridge National Laboratory's estimate, that would eliminate half a million metric tons of CO_2 emissions.[16]

Walk or bike.   For short trips you would normally take in your car, especially during good weather and good air quality days, walk, jog, or bike instead of driving. Just an hour of walking at a moderate pace burns 207 calories off the average woman and 244 calories off the average man. An hour of biking with moderate effort can burn 518 calories for women and 609 calories for men. Use a Walking Calories Calculator like the one at CalorieLab.com to calculate how many calories you could burn on typical short errands. Examine the irony of *driving* to your gym to work out and consider canceling your gym membership, at least during temperate months. Walk, run, or cycle for exercise instead. You could find you are reintroducing yourself to old friends and neighbors and improving your social life simply by walking more often through the neighborhood.

Buy your children bicycles and have them bike or walk.   Teach your children the importance of exercise, responsibility, independence, and/or ecological citizenship—take your pick—by walking or biking to activities. To have your child walk safely to school, you can go with them, or organize a group of parents and children from the neighborhood to walk together. Get the neighbors together to work with your municipality to help build safe roads and lower speeds on the routes into school. Walktoschool-usa.org can help you make these plans. Moving to more independent mobility for your children will require becoming more realistic as a parent about what the crime risks to your child are. Watching less local news could help you avoid the exaggerated sense of danger and crime prevalence that heavy consumers of TV news often acquire.[17]

Delay your teen's driving.   Join other parents who are part of an increasing trend: they are putting off their child's first trip to the DMV. Given the very high crash rates among 16- to 17-year-olds, many states are starting to push back the age at which adolescents can get their full licenses. In the meantime, some parents are way ahead of the states and are willing to suffer their child's displeasure in order to keep them safe. More parents are also putting off their child's first car purchase. They find that the aggravation of being their child's chauffeur for another year or two, or, better yet, convincing them to bike or use public transit, is more than outweighed by the safety benefits and greater knowledge of when and where their children are coming and going. Parents who encourage their teens to carpool and use public transportation are also helping them avoid falling into the early debt patterns that car ownership often sets.

Consider installing a safety monitor in the car when your teenager does start driving. The Safe Driving Monitor™ device is available for about $100; it gives a teen instant feedback when he or she drives too fast or brakes too hard and provides a record that can be reviewed by a parent afterward (www.rootfour.com). Other companies sell a variety of kinds of monitoring devices that allow parents to download driving data (e.g., www.roadsafety.com). As an owner of one of those companies who has measured in-car teen driving notes, "Trust me when I say that you would be shocked to see how fast and how aggressively teenagers drive when you are not in the car with them." These are crash-prevention tools, far superior to any car safety feature, a reliance on trust, or the assumption that somehow your teenager is the exception to the rule.

Pursue telecommuting.   Talk to your employer about the possibilities of working at home one or two days a week. Many who now telecommute simply approached their employer and were able to quickly prove the idea a good one by remaining as or more productive, given the time and stress they saved by staying off the roads. While certain careers and jobs lend themselves better to "telework," the *Wall Street Journal* estimated that 100 million Americans were likely to have worked from home at least eight hours a week in 2008.[18] If you are an employer, get help starting a telecommuting program at your company with *The Telecommuting Resource Guide* available at www.cleanair.org.

Check out public transit.   Research your public transportation choices. Ask at work about Commuter Choice, a government-funded program that enables employers to provide tax benefits and services to employees who use transit or commute in vanpools. (The web site Commuterchoice.com has information on this program.) There may be trains, subways, trolleys, buses, or vans available to take you to work, school, or shopping of which you are unaware. The biggest resistance to using public transit is in people who have never tried it or have not used it recently.

While some public transportation systems may be unreliable, or have historically been unreliable, there has been much improvement and one can now find very punctual service on most heavily used lines. Public transit, especially rail and buses along routes with HOV lanes, can be much more reliable and faster during rush hour than car travel given the regular eruption of traffic jams. Experiment by taking public transit for a week and track your costs and time spent. To compare costs, people often contrast the cost of a ticket on the bus or train with the price of gas per mile traveled, thinking that a 40-mile round-trip, say, from a suburb of Boston to the city costs $18 for train and subway tickets, and $10 for gas for a car ride. But the true cost would be more like $26 for the car trip, when all costs are taken into account, not even counting the cost of parking. Even if travel times turn out to be greater on public transit, remember that the time on public transit can be used to read, work, nap, catch up with friends on the cell phone, or just relax without the stresses of driving. The image of public transit as a relatively unsafe alternative is also generally false—nothing can compare with the dangers of driving your own car. Getting past this anxiety might require the same local news diet mentioned earlier in relation to rethinking your children's safety risks.

CHANGE YOUR PERSONAL CULTURE OF DRIVING

Many of the problems and risks of driving can be mitigated by driving differently. Take a deep breath before you get in your car and try the following.

Set your cruise control at the speed limit. Using cruise control to steady your speed has been shown to improve gas mileage an average of 7 percent. Lowering speeds is also important. Driving at 65 versus 75 mph can save 12 percent of the gas you would otherwise use. Most importantly, avoid aggressive driving: one test showed a remarkable 31 percent average gas savings when drivers accelerated and braked more gently.[19] And of course, all of these techniques could save your life, that of your passengers, other drivers, their passengers, pedestrians, wildlife, and pets. When the federal government mandated 55 mph on its highways in response to the 1973 gas crisis, it was estimated that somewhere between 3,000 and 5,000 American lives were saved each year as a result. You can help by making clear that speeding is as unacceptable as drunk driving because it is just as deadly—and even more voluntary. Argue for saner speed limits and pressure local and state police to enforce existing laws against speeding.

Practice safe driving. In addition to driving at lower speeds, there are dozens of things that you can do as a driver to make you and your family safer. Just a few safety precautions all too often ignored:

- always use your seat belt
- know your route, check your tires and mirrors, and adjust your seat before you start your car
- follow the "two-second rule," staying two seconds behind any vehicle directly in front of you
- make fewer lane changes
- use defensive driving techniques
- never drive tired
- have a designated driver if you plan on drinking
- don't use a handheld phone and avoid using a hands-free phone

- don't eat or drink while driving
- observe traffic rules, especially with respect to signaling and passing

Remember that all driving is dangerous. Many Americans feel irrationally safe on the road, especially in larger vehicles. But the number of car deaths remains high year after year, and the surest way to keep your family safe is to drive less. The fewer miles you and your family drive, the safer you are.

Help your loved ones to drive more safely.　　Help drivers be safe by reducing the number of distractions they face. First and foremost, do not call someone you know is driving, and if they call you, tell them to pull over to talk or call you when they reach their destination. As a passenger, you can play a role in safety by keeping conversations light: emotional topics can distract a driver, so shelve any heavy personal discussions or political arguments until you get home. You can also help with navigation and take charge of the radio, the GPS, or the comfort controls that cause drivers to take their eyes off the road.

Buy insurance that rewards you for driving less.　　There are some recent innovative car "use-based" insurance programs from a number of companies that reward customers for driving and polluting less, being less risk-exposed, and saving money. In several states, Progressive offers a policy called MyRate that charges the customer based on how much and how safely he or she drives. Insurance costs are reduced an average of 25 percent, and studies have shown that the enticement of these savings reduces customers' driving by 10 to 15 percent.[20]

FIND THE SWEET SPOT

Make your moves count.

Factor the commute into big life decisions.　　We often fail to seriously evaluate the new commute when we are choosing a school, considering taking a new job, or buying a home. Do the math on the commute you will be required to make each day: a 15-mile commute from work to one potential house purchase versus an 18-mile commute to another may not seem like much—just three miles, for goodness' sake—but it would add up to 1,440 additional miles each year, or more than $1,000 a year. Depending on traffic, that could mean an additional 58 hours of time away from home, 58 additional hours of highway crash risk, and a bigger carbon footprint. Ask your potential employer about public transportation to their site. If public transit is not an option, test drive the route you would have to take during the morning and evening rush hours. Factor the cost in terms of time, health, and finances into your decision. A job paying a lower salary that is easier to get to may well leave you with more spending money. If a new job opportunity will require you to buy a new car, even if you think you can carpool to work, complete the car calculation sheet at www.webwinder.com before accepting an offer.

When considering a move to a new community or home, ask your broker to show you homes that are convenient to public transportation routes to work, school, and friends. Check out the web site www.walkscore.com, which has ranked 2,508 neighborhoods in the largest 40 U.S. cities by their "walkability." The site can also calculate a "walk score" for any address across the country, enabling house hunters to compare how dependent they would be on their car to run most errands and enjoy local amenities if they moved to different homes. If you can get by without a car or with fewer cars, you will be able to afford a wider range of homes.

GET POLITICAL: DEMAND A NEW TRANSIT SYSTEM

Stay informed and make demands on our politicians.   Pay attention to local, regional, and national news related to cars, transportation, and energy. Stay abreast of proposed legislation related to sidewalks, roads, highways, parking, open space and development, and public transportation in your area, and write to or call your elected officials to let them know your position. Identify political candidates and government officials who are beholden to oil and gas companies, automotive interests, and real estate developers; web sites such as the Center for Responsive Politics (for the national scene) and the National Institute for Money in State Politics (for your individual state) are a good resource.

As this book has argued, the car is deeply intertwined with issues of environmental health, social justice, and quality of life. The onset, in 2008, of the most significant economic crisis in modern U.S. history can also be connected to a failure to remake our car- and oil-dependent way of life. Transit policy changes can be the centerpiece of economic recovery and a new environmental stewardship. Investing in public transit could create more jobs per dollar than focusing on road building and repair and could make mobility more affordable for everyone.[21] Regulation of the auto and oil industry would help reduce dependence on foreign and domestic oil, as well as mitigate global warming. The public transit system we already have supports 2 million jobs, saves 4.2 billion gallons of gasoline, and prevented 37 million metric tons of carbon emissions in 2008 alone. Since one-third of those who live near rail transit regularly use it, it is an investment that would have an immediate and broad benefit. If the amount invested in public transportation increased enough to create just 10 percent more annual ridership, those benefits would rise: by 2020, public transport could support 8.9 million jobs and we could nearly eliminate our oil imports from the Persian Gulf and drastically cut carbon emissions.[22]

Specifically, tell elected officials you want them to do the following:

1. *Reallocate significant amounts of public funding away from building and operating roads for private cars to building and operating public transit.* The huge sums that go into building new traffic lanes and maintaining and policing them could easily be transferred to the capital and operating costs of public transit. Right now, the government requires much public transit to "pay its own way" in operating costs but does not ask the same of private car transit. A "pavement moratorium" would provide the funds to get more people and freight moving more safely and cheaply on public transit. Detroit in late 2008 dropped to its knees, not just because of a few faulty decisions about building SUVs versus smaller cars, but because the entire car-and-oil system has reached the limit of sustainability. Now is the ripest moment in the history of the car system to retool the auto industry into a transit industry. The government can and should institute a national public transit–building

program on the scale of Eisenhower's interstate highway system in the 1950s. While the nation's road and bridge system is in massive decay, repairs should be prioritized, fixing only those roads that are needed to fill in the gaps of the excellent, world-class transit system that will be under construction. Demand that state departments of transportation cease asking for highway money rather than public transit money; the Missouri DOT's 2008 transit wish list, for example, was $800 million worth of projects, 95 percent of which were for roads.[23] Demand to see and comment on that list in your state.

2. *Institute land-use planning policies and regulations that are transit-oriented, and encourage development in areas that are within one-quarter mile of public transit, so that most people can do most of what they need to do each day without a private car.* Most world-class cities, including New York, Paris, and London, already have such policies. Transit-oriented planning would include such things as zoning smaller lot sizes, creating incentives for high-density building, requiring employers to provide incentives for public transit use as much as or more than for parking, putting parking in the back of rather than around stores (so that entrances face sidewalks instead of parking lots), removing parking requirements for builders of commercial spaces, and instituting other anti-sprawl and walkability measures.

3. *Follow through on enforcement of the Obama administration's new, much higher emission standards for cars, and set new, higher safety and crash compatibility standards. Enforce 2007's truth-in-testing law that requires manufacturers to list mile-per-gallon performance figures that are accurate, not 20 percent higher than the mileage drivers actually achieve. Fund research on, and provide incentives for production of, electric cars and plug-in infrastructure, particularly as a condition of any future financial help to the auto industry.* If electric cars are powered by dirty, coal-burning power plants (coal combustion accounted for 49 percent of all U.S. electricity generated in 2006), however, that is not much of an improvement; alternative energy sources would need to be brought online by more federal research monies, and tax policy and subsidies would be needed to encourage

these nonpolluting electricity alternatives. It is no alternative to use coal-to-liquid fuel—so-called clean coal—since it requires burning more coal to produce it and so releases more CO_2 than burning coal straight out.[24] Avoid the distracting focus on hydrogen fuel cell technology: more efficient fuel technologies already exist but have not yet been implemented.[25] We must pursue and enforce the 35.5-mpg CAFE standards required for 2016. Aggressive government promotion of electric cars running on solar, wind, and other alternative fuels would radically reduce the incentive for oil resource wars and for environmentally dangerous offshore drilling. In an ideal world, the federal government would simply ban automakers from producing the gasoline-based internal combustion engine, the National Highway Traffic Safety Administration's budget would be doubled from its current paltry levels so that the true extent of car-related death and disability could be monitored and the positive effect of changes measured, and new standards would require crash compatibility, more robust roof strength and rollover avoidance, and weight limits on vehicles. Many safety experts agree that heavier cars are often deadlier to other drivers and that lighter materials can be used in designing safer cars.

4. *Apply revenue-generating measures that encourage a large public movement to rail and public transit,* such as road user charges, congestion pricing, and truck weight and distance fees.

5. *Amend regulations to encourage more equity and ecology from car insurance.* Insurance companies should be required to offer only pay-by-the-mile coverage and to charge higher rates for SUVs and other massively destructive vehicles, which would help reduce driving and cut purchases of vehicles that pollute more. Outlaw charging poor urbanites more for their coverage. Require car insurance to cover all crash injuries and funeral expenses for crash victims—in other words, the true cost of crashing.

Support advocacy groups. You can help make these changes happen by joining forces with other citizens already at work on the issues. Make a contribution to or volunteer with environmental groups, medical and health associations, victims' advocates, consumer groups, anti-poverty and environmental justice groups, groups promoting public transportation, and other interested charities, lobbyists, and support groups. Some national groups that are working hard and making progress on important automotive-related issues that affect you include Public Citizen's auto safety section, Mothers Against Drunk Driving, the Center for Auto Safety, the Surface Transportation Policy Project, the Ecology Center's Clean Car Campaign, Sierra Club, U.S. Climate Action Network, the National Resources Defense Council, the Smart Growth Network, and the League of American Bicyclists.

Support media democracy efforts to encourage our airwaves to report news on the car system—without muffling by the auto and oil corporations. Some examples include Free Press, Fairness and Accuracy in Media, and Chicago Media Action, and local alternative media or indymedia (Independent Media Center) groups.

Finally, it would only require a few small actions by each household to have a powerful positive effect. We have already seen, with the help of gas prices, that reducing car use is possible. When gas prices peaked above $4 in the summer of 2008, Americans drove 12.2 billion miles less in just one month than they had in the same month a year earlier, a nearly 5 percent decline.[26] This gives just a glimpse of how much control we really do have over our driving and what we can accomplish as consumers acting together. As we also know, much more than a temporary reduction is necessary and we should not wait for rising gas prices to force our hand again. If every driver in America drove just 1,000 fewer miles per year, as a nation we could save more than 10 billion gallons of gasoline annually. If every family in America that owns multiple cars owned one less, as a nation we could reduce household debt by $1.4 trillion. If both of these actions were taken, there would likely be thousands of lives saved and tens of thousands of fewer injuries from car crashes. The lowered emissions from our passenger vehicles would result in a perceptible increase in air quality and fewer deaths from pollution. We can reverse a trend that has seemed irreversible.

The social mobilization that emerged around various candidates during the 2008 campaigns should provide encouragement for the idea that as a people we have the power to make change. We can have a better transportation system, one not beholden to the car and oil companies. Mass-scale change in our everyday landscape is possible when people organize to demand it. Take the model of equal opportunity access that the Americans with Disabilities Act of 1990 mandated. We entirely remade aspects of our built environment in a generation, making virtually every public building accessible to, and every sidewalk navigable by, people in wheelchairs. We've also already upended some seemingly entrenched cultural attitudes about the car. In just a few years, we changed the widespread mindset that drinking and driving is acceptable. And citizen pressure forced the government to demand seat belts and air bags from car companies.

Higher standards are entirely possible and absolutely necessary, both to halt—not just slow—global warming, and to reduce our car culture's harmful consequences. No one, much less 40,000 people per year, needs to die on the highway, and no one, much less thousands of American soldiers and Middle East civilians, needs to die in the effort to secure access to oil. No one, much less millions of Americans, should be shut out of the job market by lack of transportation, and no one should be at risk of being stranded in a natural disaster by the same. No one should be left unprotected from usurious car loans and dealer scams, or have to spend large chunks of their paycheck just to get to work. If the car system is not just the car and oil companies, but us, then its future is one that we can build by taking one easy, healthful, and socially just step at a time.

$\mathscr{Endnotes}$

PREFACE

1. Unless otherwise indicated, all quotations in this book are taken verbatim from our interviews.
2. Critics of the car have existed alongside its fans from the very beginning, and while their querying voices have been heard throughout the century, they are usually lost as history is written by the winners within the car system (Brian Ladd, *Autophobia: Love and Hate in the Automotive Age* [Chicago: University of Chicago Press, 2008]). The fact that so many more people now lose in that system means that a critique of car dependence can begin to have more of an impact.

CHAPTER 1

1. U.S. Department of Transportation, *Highway Statistics 2005* (Washington, DC: Federal Highway Administration, 2006.) The average is 2.3 vehicles per household. The global total has ballooned as well, reaching 1 billion vehicles in 2008, and is projected to total 2 billion within just a few decades. Daniel Sperling and Deborah Gordon, *Two Billion Cars: Driving Toward Sustainability* (New York: Oxford University Press, 2009).
2. Experian Automotive, "New Study Shows Multiple Cars Are King in American Households," February 12, 2008. http://press.experian.com/documents/showdoc.cfm.
3. In fact, just over one-third of households own three or more vehicles. Ibid.
4. Horsepower increased by an average of 86 percent from 1987 to 2006, and acceleration by 26 percent. U.S. Environmental Protection Agency, *Light-Duty Automotive Technology and Fuel Economy Trends: 1975 through 2006* (Washington, DC: EPA, 2006).
5. U.S. Department of Transportation, *Automotive Fuel Economy Program: Annual Update Calendar Year 2004* (Washington, DC: National Highway Traffic Safety Administration, 2005).
6. U.S. Department of Transportation, *Highway Statistics 2006.*
7. Juliet B. Schor, *The Overspent American: Upscaling, Downshifting, and the New Consumer* (New York: Basic Books, 1998).
8. Most of these vehicles (58 percent) are buses. "Transportation of the United States, Scope of the American Transportation System," *National Atlas,* www.nationalatlas.gov/transportation.html.
9. Jane Holtz Kay, *Asphalt Nation: How the Automobile Took Over America and How We Can Take It Back* (Berkeley: University of California Press, 1998).
10. 61 *million* cars were bought and sold in 2007, 16 million of them new cars and trucks. 14 million junkers were sent to the scrap yard. Scotia Economics, *Global Auto Report,* July 2007. The recession of 2008 caused an even steeper decline in new car sales, with 13.2 million new and

36.5 million used cars sold. Even with a plunge in new car sales in 2009, there were still approximately 125,000 new and used cars sold daily that year.

11. Terry Tamminen, *Lives Per Gallon: The True Cost of Our Oil Addiction* (Washington, DC: Island Press, 2006).

12. "Transportation of the United States." 13. This includes freight and passenger lines; Ibid.

14. Oasis Design, "Factsheet: What does driving really cost?" www.oasisdesign.net/transport/cars/cost.htm.

15. R. D. Watts et al, "Roadless Space of the Conterminous United States," *Science,* 2007, 316: 736–38.

16. U.S. Department of Transportation, *Traffic Volume Trends* (Washington, DC: Federal Highway Administration, April 2008).

17. Diane Williams, "The Arbitron National In-Car Study: 2009 Edition" (New York: Arbitron, 2009).

18. According to the NASCAR web site, "more Fortune 500 companies participate in NASCAR than any other sport," www.nascar.com/guides/about/nascar/.

19. Martin Buckley, *Cars in Film* (Somerset, UK: Haynes, 2002). See also "Road Movies," a list by Richard F. Weingroff "celebrating the 50th Anniversary of the Eisenhower Interstate Highway System," at U.S. Department of Transportation, Federal Highway Administration web site: www.fhwa.dot.gov/interstate/roadmovies.htm/.

20. *Reality Bites,* Ben Stiller, dir., with Winona Ryder and Ethan Hawke. Jersey Films, 1994.

21. Institute of Labor and Industrial Relations, University of Michigan and the Center for Automotive Research, *Contribution of the U.S. Motor Vehicle Industry to the Economies of the United States, California, New York and New Jersey in 2003* (Ann Arbor: University of Michigan, May 2004).

22. There are 2.2 million employees in the auto parts and supplies sector and 3.2 million in the used car industry.

23. Keith Bradsher, *High and Mighty: The Dangerous Rise of the SUV* (New York: PublicAffairs, 2004), p. 81. (Published in hardcover as *High and Mighty: SUVs—The World's Most Dangerous Vehicles and How They Got That Way* [New York: PublicAffairs, 2002].)

24. Stan Luger, *Corporate Power, American Democracy, and the Automobile Industry* (New York: Cambridge University Press, 2000).

25. Center for Responsive Politics, analysis of FEC data; Ken Dilanian, "Carmakers Funnel More Funds to Democrats," *USA Today,* June 14, 2007.

26. Andrew Ross Sorkin, "As Political Winds Shift, Detroit Charts New Course," *New York Times,* May 20, 2009.

27. By 1969, 600,000 people were working in local, state, and federal governments exclusively on the planning, maintaining, and repairing of roads.

28. James Howard Kunstler, *The Geography of Nowhere: The Rise and Decline of America's Man-Made Landscape* (New York: Free Press, 1993).

29. Naomi Klein, *The Shock Doctrine: The Rise of Disaster Capitalism* (New York: Metropolitan Books, 2007).

30. Surface Transportation Policy Project, "The $300 Billion Question: Are We Buying a Better Transportation System?" January 2003. www.transact.org/report.asp?id=223.

CHAPTER 2

1. While the Mercedes sponsorship should lead us to take this claim with a grain of salt, 36 percent of a random sample of Americans with cars who were surveyed said they loved their cars. That percentage was even higher for certain groups: 42 percent of women said they did, as did 46 percent of luxury car owners, and 44 percent of those who live in the West. "Mercedes-Benz Explores 'Wheels of Attraction,'" *Motor Trend,* October 7, 2004.

2. *Rain Man,* Barry Levinson, dir., with Dustin Hoffman and Tom Cruise. United Artists, 1988.

3. In some ways, of course, the car's ubiquity means that there is nothing about the last century of American history, culture, and power to which it does *not* relate. But because it has been at

the economic, practical, and cultural center of everyone's lives for over a century, the car has been especially shaped by and influential in the shaping of these values and ideas.

4. These are just the vehicles currently in production. Model names that have come and gone include the Aztek, Bronco, Cougar, Thunderbird, Voyager, Comanche, Road Runner, Trailduster, Conquest, Eldorado, Tracker, Venture, Ranchero, and Excursion.

5. These speeds are not the maximum capacity of the cars, but the limit set by engineers by means of what is called a speed governor. Lisa Lewis, *It's No Accident: The Real Story Behind Senseless Death and Injury on Our Roads,* Lulu.com, 2006.

6. Amy L. Best, "Freedom, Constraint, and Family Responsibility: Teens and Parents Collaboratively Negotiate around the Car, Class, Gender, and Culture," *Journal of Family Issues,* 2006, 27 (1): 55–84.

7. Keith Bradsher, *High and Mighty: The Dangerous Rise of the SUV* (New York: PublicAffairs, 2004), p. 105.

8. Men now drive more miles, and women make more trips, but their patterns are becoming more similar. In 2001, men drove 65 percent more miles than women, but women have been catching up to men, as their mileage has gone up 160 percent since 1975, and men's has risen "just" 60 percent. Susan A. Ferguson and Keli A. Braitman, *Women's Issues in Highway Safety, Research on Women's Issues in Transportation, Report of a Conference* (Washington, DC: Transportation Research Board, 2006), p. 43.

9. In 1999, just 8 percent of car salespeople were female. Helene M. Lawson, *Ladies on the Lot: Women, Car Sales, and the Pursuit of the American Dream* (Lanham, MD: Rowman and Littlefield, 2000).

10. Best, "Freedom, Constraint, and Family Responsibility." See also Virginia Scharff *Taking the Wheel: Women and the Coming of the Motor Age* (Albuquerque: University of New Mexico Press, 1992).

11. Those are drivers aged 15 to 20. NHTSA, "Traffic Safety Facts: Young Drivers, 2005 Data." Young men are in more fatal crashes, even when controlling for the fact that they drive somewhat more miles than young women: Dawn L. Massie, Paul E. Green, and Kenneth L. Campbell, "Crash Involvement Rates by Driver Gender and the Role of Average Annual Mileage," *Accident Analysis and Prevention,* 1997, 29 (5): 675–85.

12. Throughout the history of the American automobile, a host of other groups, including African Americans, working-class truckers and bikers, and young "hot-rodders" have been singled out as dangers on the road (Jeremy Packer, *Mobility without Mayhem: Safety, Cars, and Citizenship* [Durham, NC: Duke University Press, 2008]). In part, this is a result of the fact that the car provided those same groups the opportunity to make a claim on the freedom and public space of the roads (Cotton Seiler, *Republic of Drivers: A Cultural History of Automobility in America* [Chicago: University of Chicago Press, 2008]).

13. Bill Vlasic, "Interest Fades in the Once-Mighty V–8," *New York Times,* January 16, 2008.

14. American politicians have parsed and pursued the world of voters in car-gendered ways. The soccer mom and NASCAR dad have become demographic voter types favored by pundits and political strategists trying to understand gender-specific political choices and feelings. Sociologist Arlie Hochschild argued, for example, that white, blue-collar NASCAR fans strongly supported George W. Bush in the 2004 election, not because his policies benefited them economically—which they distinctly did not—but because Bush offered to "let them eat war." This toughness resonated with the race car–loving man and, along with other emotional assurances, in Hochschild's view, it told the downwardly mobile white male that he would successfully push back the women and immigrants rising up behind him. Interview with Arlie Hochschild, "Leave No NASCAR Dad Behind," BuzzFlash.com, January 15, 2004.

15. This is primarily true of women with children, in comparison with men with children. See Ferguson and Braitman, *Women's Issues in Highway Safety,* p. 16.

16. James J. Flink, *The Automobile Age* (Cambridge, MA: MIT Press, 1988).

17. "Mercedes-Benz Explores," *Motor Trend.*

18. Russell W. Belk, "Possessions and the Extended Self," *Journal of Consumer Research,* 1988, 15: 139–68.

19. David E. Davis Jr., "American Driver: Cars as Self-expression," *Automobile,* June 8, 2005.

20. Terence S. Turner, "The Social Skin," in Jeremy Cherfast and Roger Lewin, eds., *Not by Work Alone* (Beverly Hills, CA: Temple Smith, 1980).

21. Lizabeth Cohen, *A Consumers' Republic: The Politics of Mass Consumption in Postwar America* (New York: Alfred A. Knopf, 2003), pp. 292–344.

22. Richard Heinberg, *Powerdown: Options and Actions for a Post-Carbon World* (Gabriola Island, BC: New Society, 2004), p. 110.

23. Robert Nisbet, *History of the Idea of Progress,* 2nd ed. (Piscataway, NJ: Transaction, 1994).

24. That culture shapes the supposedly purely technical nature of a car's life expectancy is demonstrated by wide variations across Europe including, in the 1970s, 15.4 years in Denmark as compared with 10.7 years in Germany. Wolfgang Sachs, *For Love of the Automobile: Looking Back into the History of Our Desires* (Berkeley: University of California Press, 1992), p. 138.

25. U.S. automakers for many years successfully argued that the problem of car crashes should be seen as one of driver error or incompetence: educating drivers was the solution. Consumer protection advocate Ralph Nader's breakthrough was to challenge this corporate thinking, and to call for *their* reeducation and for progress through improved car design.

26. Lemelson-MIT Program, "The 2009 Lemelson-MIT Invention Index," http://web.mit.edu/invent/n-pressreleases/n-press–09index.html

27. "The Problem with Biofuels," *Washington Post,* February 27, 2008.

CHAPTER 3

1. John B. Rae, *The American Automobile Industry* (Boston: Twayne, 1984).

2. Martin Fackler, "To Gain Market Share, Nissan Vows a New-Model Blitz," *New York Times,* April 26, 2006.

3. Claritas, www.MyBestSegments.com.

4. James B. Twitchell, *Living It Up: America's Love Affair with Luxury* (New York: Simon & Schuster, 2003), p. 76.

5. Nielsen, "Nielsen Monitor-Plus Reports on Ad Spending for the Automotive Industry," April 26, 2007.

6. Nielsen, "U.S. Ad Spending Fell 2.6% in 2008," March 13, 2009.

7. Nielsen, "Nielsen Monitor-Plus Reports."

8. Bradley Johnson, "Toyota Gets the Best Return on Ad Dollars," *Automotive News,* April 10, 2006.

9. 2006 Passat Creative, "VW of America Official Online Newsroom," May 12, 2008.

10. "North America's largest auto show generates $181 million for New York City's economy," *Motor Trend,* March 19, 2007. The Los Angeles show attracts similar numbers.

11. Twitchell, *Living It Up,* p. 154.

12. Russell W. Belk, Kenneth D. Bahn, and Robert N. Mayer, "Developmental Recognition of Consumption Symbolism," *The Journal of Consumer Research,* 1982, 9 (1): 4–17.

13. "Nickelodeon Secures Multi-million Advertising Deal with Chevrolet," *PR Newswire,* May 9, 2005.

14. John Consoli, "GM Comes to Play with Nick," *Mediaweek,* May 9, 2005.

15. Twitchell, *Living It Up,* pp. 94–95.

16. Jim Mateja, "Survey: Teens Favor VWs, Hondas to Dodges, Subaru," *Ward's Dealer Business,* December 18, 2004.

17. Tom Van Riper, "Brand Me," *Forbes,* February 10, 2006.

18. Georg W. Alpers and B. M. Gerdes Antie, "Another Look at 'Look-Alikes': Can Judges Match Belongings with Their Owners?" *Journal of Individual Differences,* 2006, 27 (1): 38–41.

19. Jennifer Aaker, "The Malleable Self: The Role of Self-Expression in Persuasion," *Journal of Marketing Research,* 1999, 36 (1): 45–57.

20. Ibid.

21. Juliet B. Schor, *The Overspent American: Upscaling, Downshifting, and the New Consumer* (New York: Basic Books, 1998), p. 3.

22. Ibid., p. 10.
23. Thorstein Veblen, *The Theory of the Leisure Class: An Economic Study of Institutions* (New York: Penguin Classics, 1994 [1912]), p. 64.
24. Income figures are from Emmanuel Saez, "Striking It Richer: The Evolution of Top Incomes in the United States (Update with 2007 Estimates)," August 5, 2009. http://elsa.berkeley.edu/~saez/TabFig2007.xls. Wealth figures are from The American Affluence Research Center, "Highlights of the Fall 2008 Affluent Market Tracking Study," Number14, October 2008.

CHAPTER 4

1. Micheline Maynard, "Car Buyers Who Pay Cash May See Unhappy Dealers," *New York Times*, July 27, 2007.
2. Ibid.
3. BIGresearch, "Consumers One Step Ahead of Fed," March 23, 2005, www.bigresearch.com.
4. James J. Flink, *The Automobile Age* (Cambridge, MA: MIT Press, 1988), p. 234.
5. Walter S. McManus, "The State of the U.S. Automotive Industry," The University of Michigan Transportation Research Institute, January 24, 2006.
6. "Best and Worst: The Highs and Lows from Our Testing Owner Surveys," *Consumer Reports*, April 2008.
7. Stop Auto Fraud, www.stopautofraud.com.
8. Pamela M. Danziger, *Let Them Eat Cake: Marketing Luxury to the Masses—As Well as the Classes* (Chicago: Dearborn Trade, 2005), pp. xi, xiii.
9. Cliff Banks, "Luxury Market Has Stronger Presence on Ward's Dealer Ranking," *Ward's Dealer Business*, June 15, 2006.
10. "Best and Worst," *Consumer Reports*. J.D. Power and Associates, "Report: Entertainment- and Connectivity-Related Technologies Garner High Levels of Interest Among Consumers Planning to Buy a New Vehicle Soon," June 3, 2009. http://www.jdpower.com/corporate/news/releases/pressrelease.aspx?ID=2009098.
11. J. D. Power and Associates. "Report: The Vehicle and Dependability Gap between Luxury and Higher-Volume Brands Narrows Significantly," August 9, 2006. More generally, though, the U.S. carmakers continue to lag, manufacturing all 13 of the least reliable cars on *Consumer Reports*' 2008 list.

CHAPTER 5

1. Nineteen cents of each dollar goes for shelter, 18 cents for transportation, and 14 cents for food. *Driven to Spend: Pumping Dollars out of Our Households and Communities*. New York: Center for Neighborhood Technology and Surface Transportation Policy Project, 2005. This study is based on U.S. Department of Labor figures, and transportation spending totals exclude air travel costs.
2. Bureau of Transportation Statistics, *National Transportation Statistics*, U.S. Department of Transportation (Washington, DC: RITA, 2008), Table 1–17: New and Used Passenger Car Sales and Leases.
3. Stacy Davis and Susan Diegel, *Transportation Energy Data Book: Edition 26* (Oak Ridge, TN: Oak Ridge National Laboratory, 2007), p. 8.
4. The AAA estimate at 54 cents a mile for a mid-size sedan (68 cents for an SUV) is lower and less accurate than the government estimate because AAA spreads the fixed costs of car ownership over 15,000 miles of driving, a higher yearly mileage use than the average for all cars; AAA, "Your Driving Costs," 2009 Edition. www.AAA.com/Public Affairs. (Note that in the typical two-car family, one car is usually driven more miles than the other, and one may be newer, with higher depreciation costs, but the average of the two—say 15,000 miles on one and 7,000 on the other—is 22,000 miles, and the average cost, based on that Department of Energy census, is $14,000 per household.)

Figure 5.1. AAA Estimate of Annual Costs to Drive 15,000 Miles in a New Mid-Size Car, 2009.

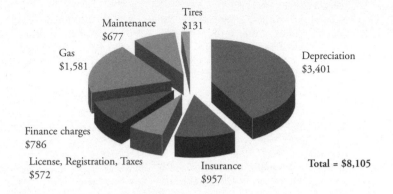

Tires
$131

Maintenance
$677

Gas
$1,581

Depreciation
$3,401

Finance charges
$786

License, Registration, Taxes
$572

Insurance
$957

Total = $8,105

5. One smaller car, for example, could set a family back an average of $6,200 a year, an SUV $10,000. A moderately priced sedan like a Nissan Altima could cost $7,500 a year, a similarly sized Cadillac $12,300. These are the annual average costs figured over five years of ownership and 15,000 miles per year of driving for 2008 models at www.edmunds.com. See also Oasis Design, "Factsheet: What does driving really cost?" www.oasisdesign.net/transport/cars/cost.htm.

6. Kelly Blue Book values show an average American car selling for $1,750 less when driven 15,000 versus 5,000 miles over the course of five years.

7. Jason E. Bordoff and Pascal J. Noel, *Pay-as-You-Drive Auto Insurance: A Simple Way to Reduce Driving-Related Harms and Increase Equity* (Washington, DC: Brookings Institution, July 2008).

8. "In the one-third of these metro areas that were found to be most sprawling, households devote 20 percent more of their spending dollar to transportation than do the one-third of metro areas with the fewest sprawl characteristics," *Driven to Spend*.

9. Ibid.

10. 24 percent of the troubles were car-related. "We Try Hard. We Fall Short. Americans Assess Their Saving Habits," Pew Research Center Publications, January 24, 2007.

11. See Joseph Hacker, "The Privatization of Risk and the Growing Economic Insecurity of Americans," The Social Science Research Council, June 7, 2006.

12. The selling of credit became especially aggressive after the deregulation of banking and the advent of computers, which made it easier to do screening and demographic targeting of consumers.

13. Steven Greenhouse, "Borrowers We Be," *New York Times*, September 3, 2006. This average includes all households, regardless of whether they have a credit card or not. The average outstanding credit card debt for households that have such cards was $10,679 at the end of 2008; Nilson Report, Issue 924, April 2009.

14. James J. Flink, *The Automobile Age* (Cambridge, MA: MIT Press, 1988), p. 189.

15. Lizabeth Cohen, *A Consumers' Republic: The Politics of Mass Consumption in Postwar America* (New York: Alfred A. Knopf, 2003), p. 123. See also Brett Williams, *Debt for Sale: A Social History of the Credit Trap* (Philadelphia: University of Pennsylvania Press, 2004).

16. "Cash for Clunkers Boosted Economy, Prompted Lower Car Prices," Edmunds Auto Observer, Edmunds.Com, September 17, 2009; Bill Vlasic and Nick Bunkley, "With Credit Drying Up, Car Buyers Bring Cash," *New York Times*, October 7, 2008.

17. Families have been able to increase their income levels incrementally over the last 30 years, however, by putting more family members into the workforce, and working additional hours.

18. Bureau of Transportation Statistics, *National Transportation Statistics*.

19. Juliet B. Schor, *The Overspent American* (New York: HarperCollins, 1998).

20. James B. Twitchell, *Living It Up: America's Love Affair with Luxury* (New York: Simon & Schuster, 2003), p. 70.

21. Jason Stein, "Upside Down and Sinking Fast," *Automotive News,* February 16, 2004.
22. Associated Press, "Saving in 2005 Worst Since 1933," *New York Times,* January 31, 2006.
23. California Energy Commission, *California Gasoline Prices Adjusted for Inflation,* www.energy.ca.gov/gasoline/statistics/gasoline_cpi_adjusted.html. Most people do not know that a gallon of gas was often near $3 a gallon, in today's dollars, through the 1920s and 1930s.
24. Micheline Maynard, "Buying 3rd Car as Way to Save on Price of Gas," *New York Times,* May 26, 2007.
25. Michael Klare, "Barreling into Recession," *Tom Dispatch,* January 31, 2008, www.tomdispatch .com/post/174888.
26. National Safety Council, "Estimating the Costs of Unintentional Injuries, 2001," www.nsc.org/lrs/statinfo/estcost2001.htm.
27. Ian Parry, Margaret Walls, and Winston Harrington, "Automobile Externalities and Policies," *Journal of Economic Literature,* 2007, 45: 373–99; L. Blincoe et al, *The Economic Impact of Motor Vehicle Crashes,* 2000 (Washington, DC: NHTSA, 2002).
28. U.S Department of Transportation, *Budget Overview, FY 2006* (Washington, DC: National Highway Traffic Safety Administration, 2006); "Motor Vehicle Safety, Health Care, and Taxes," *Prehospital and Disaster Medicine,* 1994, 9 (1): 11–23. A study of Maryland hospitals, for example, found that the over 7,200 people treated there in 2004 because of car crashes were charged almost $127 million, with $23 million coming from Medicare and Medicaid. Those dollars constituted 7 percent of the total cost of the Medicare program and 21 percent of all Medicaid costs in the state. Cambridge Systematics and Michael Meyer, "Crashes vs. Congestion: What's the Cost to Society?" Prepared for AAA, March 5, 2008.
29. *Auto Choice: Relief for Businesses and Consumers,* Joint Economic Committee Study of the 105th Congress, July 1998, www.house.gov/jec/tort/relief/relief.htm. Compounding the problem is the existence of widespread fraud and abuse. According to the Insurance Research Council, between 13 and 18 percent of total payments for auto injuries were for fraudulent claims. www.insurancefraud.org/blog/?p=194.
30. David Schrank and Tim Lomax, *2007 Urban Mobility Report,* Texas Transportation Institute, September 2007.
31. This figure includes maintenance costs of about $4,500 over the course of 30 years. Operations add more to the price tag.
32. Schrank and Lomax, *2007 Urban Mobility Report.*
33. Micheline Maynard and David Sanger, "U.S. Expected to Own 70% of Restructured GM," *New York Times,"* May 26, 2009.
34. Under this program, buyers of new cars received tax credits of between $3,500 and $4,500 if they turned in a less gas-thrifty older model. The new car could be as little as four miles per gallon more efficient or even one that served mostly a driveway ornament. Nick Bunkley and Sarah Peters, "Rules May Limit Cash-for-Clunkers Program," *New York Times,* June 26, 2009.
35. This figure includes both the $2.6 billion in breaks given by the Energy Policy Act of 2005 and $1 billion in oil depletion allowance tax breaks. Mark Clayton, "U.S. House Takes on Big Oil," *Christian Science Monitor,* January 18, 2007.
36. Ibid.
37. The Federal Highway Administration's budget in 2007 was $39 billion, targeted at maintaining the National Highway System as well as addressing the car's environmental and safety issues. United States Department of Transportation, *2007 Budget in Brief,* September 9, 2007, www.dot.gov/bib2007/admins.html#fhwa.
38. Surface Transportation Policy Project, "Transportation and Economic Prosperity Factsheet," www.transact.org.
39. Todd Litman, *Transportation Cost Analysis: Techniques, Estimates and Implications* (Victoria, BC: Victoria Transport Policy Institute, 2002).
40. City of Sacramento, Section—24: Transportation, *Proposed Budget 2006–07,* 2005, pp. 248–49. www.cityofsacramento.org/finance/budget/documents/25-Transportation.pdf.
41. DUIs cost the state of California alone $700 million per year. www.marininstitute.org/site/images/stories/pdfs/coststudygraphicfinal.pdf.
42. Taxpayers for Common Sense. www.taxpayer.net.

43. Ben Arnoldy, "How to Pay for U.S. Bridge and Road Repair?" *Christian Science Monitor,* August 10, 2007.

44. David S. Cloud, "U.S. Set to Offer Huge Arms Deal to Saudi Arabia," *New York Times,* July 28, 2007.

45. Most industries pay for their own private security when operating domestically or overseas. The oil and gas industry has been able to pass those costs onto U.S. taxpayers. Occidental Oil Company, for example, pays 50 cents a barrel for security services, and the U.S. government an added $3.70 per barrel. International Center for Technology Assessment, "Gasoline Cost Externalities: Security and Protection Services: An Update to CTA's Real Price of Gasoline Report" (Washington, DC: CTA, January 25, 2005). Michael Klare, *Blood and Oil: The Dangers and Consequences of America's Growing Dependency on Imported Petroleum* (New York: Metropolitan Books, 2004). Klare has written extensively on the problem of oil and security; he originated the concept of the military as an "oil-protection service."

46. Joseph E. Stiglitz and Linda Bilmes, *The Three Trillion Dollar War: The True Cost of the Iraq Conflict* (New York: W.W. Norton, 2008).

47. This estimate does not include the costs for a long list of other items including health care costs for veterans that are absorbed by families or private insurance, the costs attendant on oil price volatility, and the costs of tighter monetary policy as a result of war-induced inflationary pressure.

48. Bob Herbert, "Oil and Blood," *New York Times,* July 28, 2005.

49. This total was calculated using Edmunds Cost to Own Calculator on Edmunds.com. The estimate is based on the following assumptions: ownership of two cars; a new car purchased every five years; purchase of the top-selling and typical cost-to-own car, the Toyota Camry; 2009 model year prices; over the course of fifty years. Total cost to own = $918,760.

50. Ian Parry, Margaret Walls, and Winston Harrington, "Automobile Externalities and Policies," Resources for the Future Discussion Paper No. 06–26, January 2007.

CHAPTER 6

1. Sarah Anderson et al., *Executive Excess: 14th Annual CEO Compensation Survey* (Washington, DC: Institute for Policy Studies, 2007); Thomas Piketty and Emmanuel Saez, "Income Inequality in the United States," 1913–2002 (updated to 2007 at http://elsa.berkeley.edu/~saez/). In A. B. Atkinson and T. Piketty, eds., *Top Incomes over the Twentieth Century* (New York: Oxford University Press, 2007).

2. Jane Collins, "America in the Age of Wal-Mart," in Hugh Gusterson and Catherine Besteman, eds., *The Insecure American: How We Got Here and What We Should Do About It* (Berkeley: University of California Press, 2009).

3. Gary Younge, "The U.S. Needs to Talk About Class, But Politicians Don't Have the Vocabulary," *The Guardian,* April 14, 2008.

4. Paul Taylor et al., *Inside the Middle Class: Bad Times Hit the Good Life* (Pew Research Center, 2008).

5. Ibid.

6. *Figure 6.1 Percentage of Earned Income Spent on Transportation by Income Groups, 2007.*

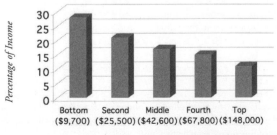

*Annual Income Distribution in the United States
(average income for each fifth)*

Source: US Department of Labor. Various transfer payments, including social security, disability, and food stamps, can raise the income figure given for the bottom fifth of the income distribution. These additional sources of income still often leave transportation as a big budget item for those families or leave them unable to afford a car.

7. Katherine Newman and Victor Chen, *The Missing Class: Portraits of the Near Poor in America* (Boston: Beacon Press, 2008).

8. Kerri Sullivan, "Transportation and Work: Exploring Car Usage and Employment Outcomes in the LSAL Data," National Center for the Study of Adult Learning and Literacy Occasional Paper, June 2003.

9. Gregg Krupa, "No Car, No Bus Means No Job," *Detroit News,* March 25, 2001.

10. Howard Karger, *Shortchanged: Life and Debt in the Fringe Economy* (San Francisco: Berrett-Koehler, 2005).

11. Ibid., pp. 158–62.

12. Paul Ong and Michael Stoll, "Redlining or Risk? A Spatial Analysis of Auto Insurance Rates in Los Angeles," *Journal of Policy Analysis and Management,* 2007, 26 (4): 811–30.

13. Linda Bailey, *Aging Americans: Stranded without Options* (New York: Surface Transportation Policy Project, 2004).

14. David Cole and John Lamberth. "The Fallacy of Racial Profiling," *New York Times,* May 13, 2001.

15. Despite the fear of driving that this common experience has created over the history of the car in the African American community (or perhaps in part because of it), there is, as one prominent observer notes, "an intense association between cars and freedom in black culture," celebrated especially in popular music. Paul Gilroy, "Driving While Black," in Daniel Miller, ed., *Car Cultures* (Oxford: Berg, 2001), p. 82.

16. In one survey of adults, self-reported rates of DUI were between 21 and 22 percent for white men, Native American men, and men of mixed race. Twelve-month arrest rates for DUI, however, were higher among Native American and mixed-race men; R. Caetano and C. McGrath, "Driving Under the Influence (DUI) Among U.S. Ethnic Groups," *Accident: Analysis and Prevention,* 2005, 37 (2): 217–24.

17. Allen Breed and Martha Mendoza, "Two Grieving Fathers Receive Different Forms of Justice in Two Hot-Car Deaths," Associated Press, July 30, 2007.

18. Meizhu Lui, Emma Dixon, and Betsy Leondar-Wright, *Stalling the Dream: Cars, Race and Hurricane Evacuation. State of the Dream 2006* (Boston: United for a Fair Economy, 2006).

19. 24 percent of black households and 17 percent of Latino households owned no car in 2000, while just 7 percent of white families were carless. One study showed that one in ten African Americans and one in five Latinos have missed getting medical care due to lack of transportation. That figure is just one in fifty among whites; Lui et al., *Stalling the Dream.*

20. Bailey, *Aging Americans,* p. 7.

21. Stephan Raphael and Michael Stoll, "Can Boosting Minority Car-Ownership Rates Narrow Inter-Racial Employment Gaps?," in William G. Gale and Janet Rothenberg Pack, eds., *The Brookings-Wharton Papers on Urban Economic Affairs,* vol. 2 (Washington, DC: Brookings Institution, 2001), pp. 99–145.

22. A 1999 survey showed that 94 percent of welfare recipients trying to enter or reenter the workforce used public transit to do so.

23. Paul M. Ong, "Car Ownership and Welfare-to-Work," *Journal of Policy Analysis and Management,* 2001, 21 (2): 239–52.

24. Larry Keating, *Atlanta: Race, Class, and Urban Expansion* (Philadelphia: Temple University Press, 2001).

25. African Americans, for example, are 13 percent of the population, but 19 percent of pedestrian deaths. Michelle Ernst, *Mean Streets 2004: How Far Have We Come?* (New York: Surface Transportation Policy Project), pp. 20–21.

26. This is due to a variety of factors, including less frequent seat belt and child safety seat use. Susan P. Baker, Elisa R. Braver, Li-Hui Chen, Janella F. Pantula, and Dawn L. Massie, "Motor Vehicle Occupant Deaths among Hispanic and Black Children and Teenagers," *Archives of Pediatrics and Adolescent Medicine,* 1998, 152: 1209–12.

27. Westchester Toyota advertising circular.

28. Michael Hudson, "Driven to Misery," *Southern Exposure,* Summer 2003. See also stopauto fraud.com.

29. Ibid.

30. ConsumerAffairs.com; Hudson, "Driven to Misery."

31. For a used car loan, 9.5 percent was the median rate for African Americans while whites paid just 7.5 percent; Mark Cohen, "Imperfect Competition in Auto Lending: Subjective Markup, Racial Disparity, and Class Action Litigation," *Vanderbilt Law and Economics Research Paper, No.07–01,* December 14, 2006.

32. Hudson, "Driven to Misery."

33. Department of Defense, "Report on Predatory Lending Practices Directed at Members of the Armed Forces and Their Dependents," Report to Congress, August 9, 2006, p. 16.

34. There were 931 locations that year (2004), and they repossessed seven percent of all the cars on which they made loans; Tennessee Department of Financial Institutions, "Report to the TN General Assembly, Pursuant to Public Chapter 440, Acts of 2005, Section 7(e)," Nashville, February 1, 2006.

35. Tom Feltner, "Debt Detour: Automobile Title Lending Industry in Illinois," A Report by the Woodstock Institute and Public Action Foundation, September 2007. See also Amanda Quester and Jean Ann Fox, "Car Title Lending, Driving Borrowers to Financial Ruin," Center for Responsible Lending and Consumer Federation of America, April 2005; Jean Ann Fox and Elizabeth Guy, "Driven into Debt: CFA Title Loan Store and Online Survey," Consumer Federation of America, November 2005.

36. Impact Lab, "Electronic Repo Device Stalls Cars of Late Payers," May 1, 2008, www.impactlab.com/2008/05/01/electronic-repo-device-stalls-cars-of-late-payers.

37. Karger, *Shortchanged,* p. 169.

38. U.S. Department of Transportation, *What Do Traffic Crashes Cost? Total Costs to Employers by State and Industry* (Washington, DC: National Highway Transportation Safety Administration, 1996).

39. Russell Gold, "Exxon's CEO Gets Raise," *Wall Street Journal,* April 14, 2009. Four of the top five highest paid CEOs in 2009 worked for oil companies; "Special Report: CEO Compensation," Forbes.com, April 22, 2009.

40. The story is the same in the car insurance, auto parts, and other car-related sectors. State Farm Insurance's chairman and CEO, Ed Rust Jr., for example, received a $5.3 million raise in 2006, earning a total of $12 million. "State Farm CEO Gets 82% Pay Raise," *Insurance Journal,* March 7, 2007.

41. Paul Krugman, "The Great Wealth Transfer," Rollingstone.com, November 30, 2006.

42. Truckers and Citizens of America United, www.theamericandriver.com.

43. Public Citizen, "The Best Energy Bill Corporations Could Buy: Summary of Industry Giveaways in the 2005 Energy Bill," www.citizen.org/cmep/energy_enviro_nuclear/electricity/energybill/2005/articles.cfm?ID=13980.

44. Tyson Slocum, "Hot Profits and Global Warming: Financial Firm and Oil Company Profits and Rising Diesel Fuel Costs in the Trucking Industry," Testimony before House of Representatives, Committee on Transportation and Infrastructure, May 6, 2008.

45. U.S. Government Accountability Office, "Mineral Revenues: A More Systematic Evaluation of the Royalty in Kind Pilots Is Needed," GAO–03–296, January 2003.

46. John Porretto, "Exxon Mobil CEO Gets $21.7 Million Pay Package after Record Year," Associated Press, April 10, 2008.

47. David Baker, "Chevron's Annual Profit Soars to Record," *San Francisco Chronicle,* January 31, 2009.

48. Arthur B. Kinnickell, *Currents and Undercurrents: Changes in the Distribution of Wealth, 1989–2004* (Washington, DC: Federal Reserve Board, 2006).

49. Cerberus invited other investors along for the ride in buying Chrysler, limiting its stake and ultimate loss. Andrew Ross Sorkin, "Running the Numbers on Cerberus' Chrysler Debacle," *New York Times,* May 4, 2009.

50. Evan Newmark, "Mean Street: Chrysler Crisis—You Lose, Taxpayers," *Wall Street Journal Blogs,* April 23, 2009.

51. Heidi N. Moore, "How the Ten Richest Hedge Fund Managers Got That Way," *Wall Street Journal,* April 16, 2008.
52. Marcia Vickers, "The Most Powerful Trader on Wall Street You've Never Heard Of," *Business Week,* July 21, 2003.
53. Meizhu Lui et al., "Stalling the Dream: Racial Gaps in the Car Culture," *The Black Commentator,* Issue 167, January 19, 2006.
54. Krugman, "Great Wealth Transfer."
55. Alliance for a New Transportation Charter. www.transact.org/ANTC/about.asp.

CHAPTER 7

1. U.S. PIRG Education Fund, "More Highways, More Pollution: Road Building and Air Pollution in America's Cities," March 2004. http://static.uspirg.org/usp.asp?id2=12484&id3= US-PIRG&.
2. Haya El Nasser and Paul Overberg, "A Comprehensive Look at Sprawl in America," *USA Today,* February 21, 2001.
3. Matt Woolsey, "America's Fastest-Growing Suburbs," *Forbes,* July 16, 2007.
4. Southern Environmental Law Center, "Nashville 840 Loop (TN): Agreement Brings Statewide Water Quality Consideration." http://southernenvironment.org/cases/nashville _840/index.htm.
5. Associated Press, "Survey Takes Americans' Traffic Temperature: Most Have Altered Driving Patterns, Would OK Higher Taxes," July 2, 2004.
6. David Schrank and Tim Lomax, *2007 Urban Mobility Report* (Texas Transportation Institute, September 2007).
7. Anthony Downs, *Still Stuck in Traffic: Coping with Peak-Hour Traffic Congestion* (Washington, DC: Brookings Institution, 2004).
8. Downs, *Still Stuck in Traffic,* p. 16; Schrank, *2007 Urban Mobility Report.*
9. The increase of 56 percent was reported between 1991 and 2003. "Americans and Their Cars: Is the Romance on the Skids?" Pew Research Center, August 2006, p. 2, http://pewresearch .org/assets/social/pdf/Cars.pdf.
10. Alan Pisarski, *Commuting in America III: The Third National Report on Commuting Patterns and Trends* (Washington, DC: Transportation Research Board), p. 16.
11. Ibid., p. 38.
12. Ibid., p. xiv.
13. Ibid., p. xiv.
14. P. O. Plaut, "The Intra-Household Choices Regarding Commuting and Housing," *Transportation Research Part A: Policy and Practice,* 2006, 40 (7): 561–71.
15. Pisarski, *Commuting in America III.*
16. Jenny Sullivan, "Housing Migrates Back to Cities," *Builder,* March 19, 2009.
17. Ariel Hart, "Survey: Shorter Commute is Main Reason for Moving," *The Atlanta Journal-Constitution,* August 24, 2007.
18. Jill P. Capuzo, "Where Walkable Encounters Affordable," *New York Times,* October 31, 2008.
19. Downs, *Still Stuck in Traffic,* p. 9.
20. Ibid., pp. 8–9.
21. Todd Litman, *London Congestion Pricing: Implications for Other Cities* (Victoria, BC: Victoria Transport Policy Institute, January 10, 2006).
22. Pisarski, *Commuting in America III.*
23. Marc Schlossberg, Page Paulsen Phillips, Bethany Johnson, and Bob Parker, "How Do They Get There? A Spatial Analysis of a 'Sprawl School' in Oregon," *Planning Practice & Research,* 2005, 20 (2): 147–62.
24. Tori D. Rhoulac, "Bus or Car? The Classic Choice in School Transportation," *Transportation Research Record,* 2005, 1922: 98–104.
25. Schlossberg et al., "How Do They Get There?"
26. Parents were not asked in this survey to define "convenient." When it comes to cars, "convenient" is an adjective that tends to be used by Americans in lieu of "habitual." When asked to

explain why driving is convenient, drivers will often state that they don't want to wait for the train or bus. When then pressed on how often they find themselves stuck in traffic or struggling to find parking, many will admit that driving some routes is often far less convenient than public transit.

27. Schlossberg et al., "How Do They Get There?"

28. National Highway Traffic Safety Administration, "Seat Belts on School Buses," May 2006.

29. Transportation Research Board, *The Relative Risks of School Travel: A National Perspective and Guidance for Local Community Risk Assessment* (Washington, D.C.: The National Academies Press, 2002).

30. In 2006, 14 percent of children age 2 to 5 were overweight, as were 19 percent of those age 6 to 11 and 17 percent of those age 12 to 19. Centers for Disease Control, "Childhood Obesity," www.cdc.gov/HealthyYouth/obesity.

31. Nancy McGuckin and Yukiko Nakamoto, "Differences in Trip Chaining by Men and Women," *Report Submitted to the Conference on Women's Travel Issues* (Chicago, November 18–20, 2004).

32. "Starbucks Fact Sheet," February 2008. www.Starbucks.com.

33. "Howard Schultz: The Star of Starbucks," *60 Minutes,* CBS, April 23, 2006.

34. Diane Williams, "The Arbitron National In-Car Study: 2009 Edition" (New York: Arbitron, 2009).

35. Pierre Bouvard et al., "The Arbitron National In-Car Study: 2003 Edition" (New York: Arbitron, 2003).

36. According to data from the 2001 National Household Travel Survey, the number of vehicle trips is higher on a Saturday at 1 P.M. than the peak hours in the morning or evening on a Wednesday, a typical weekday. Federal Highway Administration, *Our Nation's Travel: Current Issues.* See also Tom Vanderbilt, *Traffic: Why We Drive the Way We Do (and What It Says About Us)* (New York: Alfred A. Knopf, 2008).

37. Oregon Department of Transportation and Partners in the Drive Less Save More Campaign, "Drive Less Trip Diary," May 2008. www.tripdiary.drivelesssavemore.com.

38. Bureau of Transportation Statistics, *Pocket Guide to Transportation 2009* (Washington, D.C.: U.S. Department of Transportation, January 2009).

39. 27 percent of respondents in a 2006 survey reported driving purely for fun. Pew Research Center, "Americans and Their Cars."

40. To the point that more driving fosters additional nonautomotive spending, it is worth noting that all of the featured activities involve expenses and equipment beyond the car. The Schmidts' nature trip, for instance, would entail the cost of lift tickets, lunch on the mountain, and the purchase or rental of skis, boots, and clothes.

41. Pisarki, *Commuting in America III,* p. 3.

42. Expedia.com "Annual Expedia.com Survey Reveals 51.2 Million American Workers Are Vacation Deprived," April 25, 2007.

43. Williams, "Arbitron National In-Car Study."

44. Pisarski, *Commuting in America III,* p. xviii.

45. Ibid., p. xviii.

46. U.S. Census Bureau, "Most of Us Still Drive to Work—Alone: Public Transportation Users Concentrated in a Handful of Cities," June 13, 2007.

47. Associated Press, "Survey Takes Americans' Traffic Temperature."

48. Steven Mufson and David Cho, "Fuel Prices Challenge Cars' Reign," *The Washington Post,* June 10, 2008; Discover Financial Services, "Discover U.S. Spending Monitor Down Nearly a Point in June," July 9, 2009.

49. "Helping the Wallet and the Environment: GMA's Carpool Challenge," *Good Morning America,* ABC News, http://abcnews.go.com/GMA/story?id=5415258&page=1&page=1.

50. Lieven De Cauter, *The Capsular Civilization: On the City in the Age of Fear* (Rotterdam: NAi Publishers, 2004), p. 45.

51. Ibid., p. 81.

52. Car manufacturers responded to a similar loss of interest in autos among Japanese youth with a parallel strategy of marketing the car as a somewhat more immobile high-tech toy.

53. Pew Research Center's Project for Excellence in Journalism, "The State of the News Media 2009: An Annual Report on American Journalism," March 16, 2009. http://pewresearch.org/pubs/1151/state-of-the-news-media-2009.

54. Monster.com Blog, "Embrace Your Commute," February 28, 2005.

55. William G. Mayer, "Why Talk Radio Is Conservative," *The Public Interest,* 2004, 156: 86–103.

56. "The Top Talk Radio Audiences," *Talkers Magazine,* March 21, 2008.

57. David Barker and Kathleen Knight, "Political Talk Radio and Public Opinion," *The Public Opinion Quarterly,* 2000, 64 (2): 149–70.

58. Ibid.

59. C. Richard Hofstetter and David Barker, "Information, Misinformation, and Political Talk Radio," *Political Research Quarterly,* 1999, 52 (2): 353–69.

60. Barry Glassner, *The Culture of Fear: Why Americans Are Afraid of the Wrong Things* (New York: Basic Books, 1999), p. 6.

61. The AAA Foundation for Traffic Safety found that between 1990 and 1996, road rage contributed to 218 deaths and 12,610 injuries. Melissa Dittmann, "Anger on the Road," *APA Monitor on Psychology,* 2005, 36 (6): 26.

62. Dwight A. Hennessy and David L. Wiesenthal, "Traffic Congestion, Driver Stress, and Driver Aggression," *Aggressive Behavior,* 1999, 25: 409–23.

63. Greg Aragon, "After Angry Drivers Attack, Work Site Closes to Traffic," *Engineering News-Record,* June 20, 2007, www.enr.com.

64. Jack Katz, *How Emotions Work* (Chicago: University of Chicago Press, 1999).

65. Ibid., p. 33.

66. Ibid., pp. 34–35.

67. Joel M. Cooper, Ivana Vladisavljevic, David L. Strayer, and Peter T. Martin, "Drivers' Lane Changing Behavior While Conversing On a Cell Phone in a Variable Density Simulated Highway Environment," Prepared for the Transportation Research Board, January 2008. www.psych.utah.edu/AppliedCognitionLab/LC.pdf.

68. Richard Wener, Gary W. Evans, and Jerome Lutin, "Leave the Driving to Them: Comparing Stress of Car and Train Commuters," American Public Transportation Association, April 16, 2009; Birgitta Gatersleben and David Uzzell, "Affective Appraisals of the Daily Commute: Comparing Perceptions of Drivers, Cyclists, Walkers, and Users of Public Transport," *Environment and Behavior,* 2007, 39 (3): 416–31; Steven M. White and James Rotton, "Type of Commute, Behavioral Aftereffects, and Cardiovascular Activity: A Field Experiment," *Environment and Behavior,* 1998, 30 (6), p. 763.

69. Ibid.

70. Alois Stutzer and Bruno S. Frey, "Stress That Doesn't Pay: The Commuter Paradox," Discussion Paper, Institute for the Study of Labor, August 2004.

71. "One Lucky Commuter Gets a Morning Rush by Participating in Dodge 'Avenge Your Commute,'" *PR Newswire,* April 16, 2007.

72. Leon James and Diane Nahl, *Road Rage and Aggressive Driving: Steering Clear of Highway Warfare* (Amherst, NY: Prometheus, 2000), p. 39.

73. Ibid., pp. 176–77.

74. "Pontifical Council for the Pastoral Care of Migrants and Itinerant People," Guidelines for the Pastoral Care of the Road, August 2007, Holy See Press Office, www.vatican.va/phome_en.htm.

CHAPTER 8

1. Much of U.S. business runs on the delivery of goods by diesel trucks, which have enormous effects on public health. The exhaust from diesel engines contains 100 times more sooty particles than that from regular car engines. Diesel engines are responsible for 66 percent of the road-based particulate pollution and 26 percent of the road-based nitrous oxide; American Lung Association, "Diesel Exhaust and Air Pollution, 2008," www.lungusa.org/site/pp.asp?c=dvLUK9O0E&b=36089.

2. Surface Transportation Policy Project, "Transportation and Health," www.transact.org/library/factsheets/health.asp.

3. Sheldon H. Jacobson and Laura A. McLay, "The Economic Impact of Obesity on Automobile Fuel Consumption," *Engineering Economist,* 2006, 51 (4): 307–23.

4. John Pucher and Lewis Dijkstra, "Promoting Safe Walking and Cycling to Improve Public Health: Lessons from the Netherlands and Germany," *American Journal of Public Health,* 2004, 93 (9): 1509–16.

5. Ann Forsyth, *Reforming Suburbia* (Berkeley: University of California Press, 2005); Peter Katz, *The New Urbanism: Toward an Architecture of Community* (New York: McGraw-Hill Professional, 1994).

6. Jeff Gearhart, Hans Posselt, Claudette Juska, and Charles Griffith, *The Consumer Guide to Toxic Chemicals in Cars,* A Report by the Ecology Center, March 2007.

7. Ibid.

8. Douglas Houston, Jun Wu, Paul Ong, and Arthur Winer, "Structural Disparities of Urban Traffic in Southern California: Implications for Vehicle-Related Air Pollution Exposure in Minority and High-Poverty Neighborhoods," *Journal of Urban Affairs,* 2004, 26 (5): 565–92.

9. M. Wilhelm and B. Ritz, "Residential Proximity to Traffic and Adverse Birth Outcomes in Los Angeles County, California, 1994–1996," *Environmental Health Perspectives,* 2003, 111: 207–16.

10. D. A. Savitz and L. Feingold, "Association of Childhood Cancer with Residential Traffic Density," *Scandinavian Journal of Work and Environmental Health,* 1989, 15: 360–63; R. L. Pearson, H. Wachtel, and K. L. Ebi, "Distance-Weighted Traffic Density in Proximity to a Home is a Risk Factor for Leukemia and Other Childhood Cancers," *Journal of Air Waste Management Association,* 2000, 50: 175–80.

11. W. James Gauderman et al., "The Effect of Air Pollution on Lung Development from 10 to 18 Years of Age," *New England Journal of Medicine,* 2004, 351 (11): 1057–67.

12. University of Southern California. "Lungs Develop Better in Kids Who Move Away From Pollution," *Science Daily,* December 17, 2001.

13. Houston et al., "Structural Disparities."

14. Alan Lloyd, California Air Resources Board, *In-Car Air Pollution: The Hidden Threat to Automobile Drivers* (Washington, DC: International Center for Technology Assessment, 2000).

15. Thomas W. Kirchstetter et al., "Black Carbon Concentrations and Diesel Vehicle Emission Factors Derived from Coefficient of Haze Measurements in California: 1967–2003," *Atmospheric Environment,* 2008, 42 (3): 4123–24.

16. California Office of Environmental Health Hazard Assessment, "Health Effects of Diesel Exhaust," http://oehha.ca.gov/public_info/facts/dieselfacts.html.

17. Erika Brekke, "Diesel Exhaust Poses Health Threat to Port Truck Drivers: New Rules Needed to Cut Emissions in and around Ports," National Resources Defense Council, December 4, 2007.

18. Terry Tamminen, *Lives Per Gallon: The True Cost of Our Oil Addiction* (Washington, DC: Island Press, 2006), pp. 115–16.

19. A typical daily report looks like this: "National Outlook for June 10–11. Unhealthy AQI levels along the East Coast. In the East, an upper-level ridge of high pressure over the East Coast will yield mostly sunny skies, hot temperatures, and limited vertical mixing, enhancing ozone formation. In addition, high humidity will increase particle production. These conditions will result in widespread Unhealthy for Sensitive Groups AQI levels along the East Coast, with parts of New England and the Mid-Atlantic states reaching Unhealthy AQI levels. In the western United States, sunny skies and warm temperatures will aid ozone formation in the Southwest. As a result, AQI levels will be Moderate throughout portions of central and southern California, southern Nevada, and Arizona. In addition, AQI levels are expected to reach Unhealthy for Sensitive Groups in Las Vegas, NV and in parts of California's Central Valley."

20. Bernie Fischlowitz-Roberts, "Air Pollution Fatalities Now Exceed Traffic Fatalities by 3 to 1," Update 17: September 17, 2002. Earth Policy Institute.

21. A 2000 study in *The Lancet* estimated that of the 40,000 deaths annually in three European countries from air pollution, roughly half were the result of air pollution emitted by cars. N. Kunzli, MD et al., "Public-Health Impact of Outdoor and Traffic-Related Air Pollution: a European Assessment," *The Lancet,* 2000, 356 (9232): 795–801.

22. Fischlowitz-Roberts, "Air Pollution Fatalities."

23. Environmental Protection Agency, "EPA Fact Sheet: Final Revisions to the National Ambient Air Quality Standards for Ozone," 2008, pp. 4–5. www.epa.gov.

24. Rob McConnell et al., "Asthma in Exercising Children Exposed to Ozone: A Cohort Study," *Lancet,* 2002, 359 (9304): 386–91.

25. Neil MacFarquhar, "Refugees Join List of Climate-Change Issues," *New York Times,* May 28, 2009.

26. Peter A. Stott, D. A. Stone, and M. R. Allen, "Human Contribution to the European Heat-wave of 2003," *Nature,* 2004, 432: 610–14. See also Elizabeth Kolbert, *Field Notes from a Cat-astrophe: Man, Nature, and Climate Change* (New York: Bloomsbury, 2006).

27. Tamminen, *Lives Per Gallon,* p. 132.

28. Ibid., p. 134.

29. Matthew L. Wald, "Environmental Agency Tightens Smog Standards," *New York Times,* March 13, 2008.

CHAPTER 9

1. If the rates of walking had not plummeted with the rise of car culture, that number would be even larger. As with crashes more generally, men and boys are much more likely than females to die while walking: 70 percent of the pedestrian deaths in 2007 were male. Department of Transportation, "Pedestrians, Traffic Safety Facts, 2007," DOT HS 810 994, www.nhtsa.gov.

2. Carolyn Hirschman, "Take Control of the Wheel," *HR Magazine,* June 1999.

3. That number includes 5,154 motorcyclists, a number that has jumped in recent years, up 7 percent from 2006 as heavy motorcycle advertising and the rising price of gas put more peo-ple on the road on the aptly nicknamed choppers. Per vehicle mile traveled, motorcyclists are 35 times more likely to die and eight times more likely to be injured than car drivers; De-partment of Transportation, "Motorcycles: Traffic Safety Facts, 2007," DOT HS 810 990.

4. NHTSA, "Motor Vehicle Traffic Crashes as a Leading Cause of Death in the United States, 2005," *Traffic Safety Facts,* April 2008.

5. Injury figures are for 2000 in the United States: Leonard Evans, *Traffic Safety* (Bloomfield, MI: Science Serving Society, 2004).

6. An estimated 599,000 brain injuries occur each year involving motor vehicles, though only some of these will have permanent disabling effects; Joel Forkosch et al., "The Incidence of Traumatic Brain Injury in the United States," *Disability Statistics Abstract,* 1996, 14: 1–4.

7. P. C. Dischinger et al., "CIREN Report: Consequences and Costs of Lower-Extremity In-juries," DOT HS 809 871. Washington, DC: Department of Transportation, June 2005.

8. Edward B. Blanchard, Edward J. Hickling, Ann E. Taylor, Warren R. Loos, Catherine A. Forneris, and James Jaccard, "Who Develops PTSD from Motor Vehicle Accidents?" *Behav-iour Research and Therapy,* 1996, 34 (1):1–10.

9. Edward B. Blanchard and Edward J. Hickling, *After the Crash: Assessment and Treatment of Motor Vehicle Accident Survivors* (Washington, DC: American Psychological Association, 1997).

10. National Spinal Cord Injury Statistical Center, "Spinal Cord Injury," The University of Al-abama at Birmingham, May 2001.

11. Shanthi N. Ameratunga, Robyn N. Norton, Derrick A. Bennett, and Rod T. Jackson, "Risk of Disability Due to Car Crashes: A Review of the Literature and Methodological Issues," *Injury,* 2004, 35 (11): 1116–27.

12. Most of the severely disabled eventually are discharged from hospitals and rehabilitation cen-ters to live with their families. To take just the case of spinal cord injury, 11 percent go on to live in nursing homes, group living situations, or other institutional settings.

13. By the end of 2008, 13 states had instituted graduated licensing systems that NHTSA cate-gorized as "good." NHTSA recommends a three-stage licensing system; www.nhtsa.dot.gov/people/outreach/safesobr/13qp/facts/factgrad.html.

   Most of these changes do not involve classroom educational requirements, which makes sense, given research showing that driver education has not reduced the rate or severity of crashes for young people: J. S. Vernick et al., "Effects of High School Driver Education on Motor Vehicle Crashes, Violations, and Licensure," *American Journal of Preventive Medicine,* 1999, 16 (1): 40–46.

14. "Declining Traffic Deaths Lead to Lowest Highway Fatality Rate Ever Recorded, U.S. Transportation Secretary Mary E. Peters Announces," *Regulatory Intelligence Data,* July 23, 2007.

15. NHTSA, "2007 Traffic Safety Annual Assessment—Highlights, August 2008," www-nrd.nhtsa.dot.gov/Pubs/811017.PDF.

16. John Adams, *Risk* (London: University College London Press, 1995).

17. Jim Motavalli, "Driving; An SUV and Ice: A Recipe for a Rollover," *New York Times,* February 14, 2003.

18. The National Safe Driving Test & Initiative, "Poll: Drivers Admit to Frequent, Dangerous Behaviors on the Road," 2003; www.safedrivingtest.com/press_releases/poll_driversadmit.pdf.

19. Robert Noland, "Traffic Fatalities and Injuries: Are Reductions the Result of 'Improvements' in Highway Design Standards?," presented at the 80th Annual Meeting of the Transportation Research Board, 2001. Noland has concluded: "The effects of changes in infrastructure have resulted in about 1700 *more* fatalities in 1997 relative to 1985. Of this, about 900 of these fatalities are associated with changes in lane widths." Robert Noland, *Traffic Fatalities and Injuries: The Effect of Changes in Infrastructure and Other Trends* (London: Centre for Transport Studies, 2002).

20. Suzanne P. McEvoy et al., "Role of Mobile Phones in Motor Vehicle Crashes Resulting in Hospital Attendance: A Case-Crossover Study," *British Medical Journal,* 2005, 331: 428–30.

21. Matt Richtel, "U.S. Withheld Data on Risks of Distracted Driving," *New York Times,* July 20, 2009.

22. David Blanke, *Hell on Wheels: The Promise and Peril of America's Car Culture, 1900–1940* (Lawrence, KS: University Press of Kansas, 2007), p. 197. See also Flink, *The Automobile Age.*

23. In 2004, the Center for Auto Safety petitioned NHTSA to outlaw the dangerous "side saddle" gas tanks, which are located outside the frame and which GM installed in pickups from 1973 to 1987. Those tanks, the center said, have "resulted in over 2,000 fatalities in fire crashes, at least half of which deaths were due to fire, not trauma." Center for Auto Safety. Petition for Reconsideration- FMVSS 301, January 15, 2004.

24. The National Institute of Dental and Craniofacial Research received $390 million in 2006 to study cavities and gum disease; Edward Rossomando, "Is Federal Funding for Dental Research in Jeopardy?," *Compendium,* 2006, 27 (12): 486–87.

25. Cambridge Systematics with Meyer, "Crashes vs. Congestion," p. 2.3.

26. Ibid., p. 4.3.

27. Many people believe it is necessary to have the ability to go much faster than this for safety's sake. They believe you must often go over the speed limit to get onto the highway or get out of the way of trouble while on it. This is a fallacy, as the National Road Safety Foundation explains on their web site: www.nationalroadsafety.org.

28. Bradsher, *High and Mighty,* p. 428.

29. Friends of the Earth, "Gas Guzzler Loophole, 2000," www.foe.org/res/pubs/pdf/GG-Report.pdf.

30. Bradsher, *High and Mighty,* pp. 152–57.

31. Ibid.

32. John Tulloch and Deborah Lupton, *Risk and Everyday Life* (London: Sage Publications, 2003).

33. Elaine Scarry, *On Beauty and Being Just* (Princeton, NJ: Princeton University Press, 2001).

34. John Pucher and Lewis Dijkstra, "Promoting Safe Walking and Cycling to Improve Public Health: Lessons from the Netherlands and Germany," *American Journal of Public Health,* 2004, 93 (9): 1509–16.

35. Evans, *Traffic Safety.*

CHAPTER 10

1. "Edmunds.com Forecasts December Auto Sales: SUV and Truck Sales to Outpace Cars for First Time," December 19, 2008, www.edmunds.com

2. Nate Silver, "The End of Car Culture," *Esquire,* May 6, 2009.

3. "Recovery Accountability and Transparency Board. $8.4 Billion for Public Transit," March 5, 2009, www.recovery.gov.

4. Dylan Rivera, "U.S. Transportation Secretary Calls Portland's Streetcar, Light Rail a 'Model' for Nation," *The Oregonian,* April 14, 2009.

5. Use the Edmunds.com's True Cost to Own Calculator to see annual dollar depreciation on your current vehicle or a vehicle you are planning to buy in order to calculate exactly how much you would save by postponing trading it in or selling it to buy a new car.

6. This is based on a 6 percent annual growth rate, computed with the college savings calculator at www.finaid.org/calculators/scripts/savingsgrowth.cgi.

7. Juliet B. Schor, *The Overspent American: Upscaling, Downshifting, and the New Consumer* (New York: Basic Books, 1998).

8. See The American Bar Association's ABA Family Legal Guide, available at www.abanet.org; FindLaw, "Your Rights if Your Car is a Lemon," 2008, public.findlaw.com/lemon-law/lemon-law-basics/lemon-law-rights.html.

9. Piet Rietveld, "Transportation and the Environment," in Tom Tietenberg and Henk Folmer, eds., *The International Yearbook of Environmental and Resource Economics 2006/2007* (Cheltenham, England: Edward Elgar Publishing, 2007), p. 209.

10. www.edmunds.com.

11. J. D. Power and Associates, "The Automotive Industry Records Substantial Long-Term Vehicle Quality Improvements," June 29, 2005, www.jdpower.com.

12. Toyota Motor Corporation, "Prius Low Emissions and Highlander Hybrid Low Emissions," www.hybridsyncrgydrivc.com.

13. Todd Kaho, "Five Electric Cars You Can Buy Now," www.greencar.com.

14. www.zenncars.com.

15. Daniel Sperling and Deborah Gordon, *Two Billion Cars: Driving Toward Sustainability* (New York: Oxford University Press, 2009), p. 25.

16. Oak Ridge National Laboratory, "Shopping On-Line Reduces a Midnight Clear's Carbon Dioxide," December 21, 2007, www.ornl.gov.

17. Barry Glassner, *The Culture of Fear: Why Americans Are Afraid of the Wrong Things* (New York: Basic Books, 1999).

18. Christopher Rhoads and Sara Silver, "Working at Home Gets Easier," *Wall Street Journal,* December 29, 2005.

19. Philip Reed and Mike Hudson, "Fuel Economy: We Test the Tips," November 22, 2005, www.edmunds.com.

20. "Drive Less, Pay Less. 2008 Innovations Review," Environmental Defense Fund, November 19, 2008, www.edf.org.

21. National Resources Defense Council, "Transition to Green: Leading the Way to a Healthy Environment, a Green Economy, and a Sustainable Future," November 2008, p. 12–8.

22. "Changing the Way America Moves: Creating a More Robust Economy, a Smaller Carbon Footprint, and Energy Independence," American Public Transportation Association, Spring 2009, http://www.apta.com/resources/reportsandpublicatiosn/Documents/america_moves_09.pdf.

23. Deron Lovaas, "Stop the Secret Porkfest," Switchboard blog, Natural Resources Defense Council, December 12, 2008, switchboard.nrdc.org/blogs/dlovaas.

24. Michael B. McElroy, "Saving Money, Oil, and the Climate," *Harvard Magazine,* March-April, 2008, p. 35.

25. John DeCicco, "The Hydrogen Fuel Cell's Siren Song. Environmental Defense Fund," March 27, 2007, www.edf.org.

26. David Goldman, "Driving Declines for Eighth Straight Month," CNNMoney, August 13, 2008, money.cnn.com.

Acknowledgments

*T*his is the fun part: After all the toil of researching and authoring a book, writers get to call out the names of the people they have had the pleasure of learning from and enjoying life with while putting things together.

In our case, we have to begin with all of those whom we interviewed about the car—from the enthusiasts to the haters, from the aged to the coming of age, from the mechanics to the marketers. No one was indifferent to the subject of the automobile, and everyone had profound or quirky but often eloquently put ideas about how they live in the car and the car lives in them. We can only name some of them, and others we promised confidentiality, but all are owed a large thanks.

Our gratitude goes, too, to Jake Klisivitch, our Palgrave editor, and Ellen Levine, our agent at Trident Media Group. From our first encounters, they immediately cheered the project on and helped bring it to fruition. Many at Palgrave Macmillan worked hard on editing, production, and marketing, but we want to single out Alan Bradshaw for his unrelenting enthusiasm and careful critique.

An inspiration for this book, and counselor throughout, was our sister Karina Lutz, who has been an environmental reporter and activist for several decades. Her daily spadework for the peopled planet and her knowledge about how social and ecological systems work helped light the long path to finishing *Carjacked*. And, rich in family as we are, we have yet more sisters to thank—Mary Fox, Betsy Lutz, and Linda Lutz—for their loving support. At our foundation, of course, are two parents who inspired us to ask more of the world we live in—loving thanks to Carol and George. We know that you, Dad, would have been our first and most enthusiastic reader.

The research work itself was assisted by a smart and savvy group of students at Brown University, including Colleen Brogan, Inna Leykin, Lindsay Mollineaux, Rachel Starr, Julia Stein, Alexander Wamboldt, Posie Wilkinson, and Jenna Williams. Many thanks also to Chloe Frank for her marvelous work and spirit and to Doug Capra and the Nora Huvelle Group for their thoughtful input. Sasha Winkler provided eagle-eyed editing help.

A thank you is due to the Westport, Connecticut, community, where friends, students, parents, and colleagues provided interviews, contacts, insights, and moral support. "The Writing Guild" of Heather Colletti-Houde and Julia McNamee deserves special mention.

Brown University administrators Matilde Andrade and Deborah Healey helped keep the tires correctly inflated and the alignment straight. And we had fuel for the ride thanks to the generous funding of Brown and the Radcliffe Institute for Advanced Study, which provided a fruitful year for research and writing and fabulous fellows to work alongside.

Finally, and at the heart of everything, we want to thank Matthew Gutmann and Paul Fernandez-Carol, as well as Jonathan, Lianna, Liliana, and Marja who made life so very sweet while we wrote.

Index